D0944239

*The Covenant Idea in
New England Theology*

The Covenant Idea in New England Theology

1620 - 1847

by

PETER Y. DE JONG

WM. B. EERDMANS PUBLISHING COMPANY

Grand Rapids   1945   Michigan

THE COVENANT IDEA IN NEW ENGLAND THEOLOGY
1620 - 1847
by Peter Y. De Jong

Printed in the United States of America

TABLE OF CONTENTS

Preface 5
Table of Contents 7
Introduction 9

Part One — Foundations

1. The Covenant Idea in the Reformed Churches 15
2. The Covenant Idea among the Anabaptists 63

Part Two — Development

3. The Early Puritan Conception of the Covenant 77
4. The Beginnings of Change 94
5. The Synod of 1662: The Half-Way Covenant Adopted 110
6. Stoddardeanism: The Half-Way Covenant Modified 123
7. Jonathan Edwards: The Half-Way Covenant Attacked.... 136
8. The New Divinity: The Half-Way Covenant
   Overthrown 153
9. The Loss of the Covenant Conception 177

Part Three — Evaluation

10. The Influence of the Covenant Idea upon New England
    Religious Thought 195
11. The Weaknesses of the Covenant Idea in New England
    Theology 215
12. New England Calvinism in the Light of the Covenant
    Idea 220

Notes and References 227
Bibliography 251
Index 261

PREFACE

To many a book on the doctrine of the covenants may seem an anachronism. During the past century little has been written on this subject in American theology. Only lately has the thesis been advanced that during the early history of the churches in this country the covenant concept exerted a tremendous influence. In fact, it would be quite impossible to understand the doctrinal development of the American Congregationalists without a consideration of this theme.

The material which is presented here was submitted in somewhat another form and at greater length to the faculty of the Hartford Theological Seminary, Hartford, Conn., as partial fulfilment of the requirements for the degree of Doctor of Philosophy. It was my privilege to spend three years there, happy memories of which will always remain with me. Because of the kindly interest of many in this subject and the exceptional helpfulness of the publisher, this book now makes its appearance.

The study of this subject has brought me to the conviction that what American Protestantism needs desperately is a unified and unifying conception of the Christian life which such a concept as that of the covenant alone can give. Too much of our religious life, also in its practical expression, is at loose ends.

If the reading of this material leads anyone to a deeper reflection of the significance of the covenant idea not only for the history of the Congregational churches but also for the churches of our day the author will be amply rewarded.

PETER Y. DE JONG

INTRODUCTION

The earliest Congregationalists in New England were definitely Calvinistic in theology. From 1620 until the middle of the last century the historic doctrines, although modified in several directions, were quite consistently and conscientiously affirmed by the churches. However, at that time it became undeniably evident that historic Calvinism would be able to maintain itself no longer there. For more than a century various influences had been operative which created the change in the temper of the New England mind and rendered the virtual rejection of the old theology certain.

Thus the question has often been asked why New England lost its Calvinism. This cannot be answered by pointing out merely one change in its temperament and character. So radically did the temper of mind and the basic philsosphy of life change that the first settlers would hardly recognize the twentieth century Congregationalists as their spiritual descendants.

Herbert Wallace Schneider has pointed out in *The Puritan Mind*[1] that this change was accompanied by the rejection of the theocratic ideal which had inspired the first fathers. During the first two centuries after the colonization of those parts of America, culture and religion had drifted from those original ideals to the secular. Not only God's rule but even God Himself went quite definitely into eclipse.

In another study of the same type Joseph Haroutunian[2] has attempted to demonstrate that the loss of Calvinism of the American Puritans was co-incident with the gradual substitution of an external code of ethics for the intense spirituality of the forefathers. When genuine piety was again emphasized, it clothed itself with a type of religious and theological thought quite different from and even at variance with the old Calvinism.

This loss of Calvinism was attended by a shift of emphasis in a third direction also. As time went on the idea of the covenant relationship of the individual and his family to God in Christ was completely obscured. This was in large measure the fruit of the individualism and experientialism which rather radically differentiated the Congregational churches of New England from other Reformed communions the world over. At the beginning of their history there was an expressed appreciation of the organic view of man's religious relationship to God. However, this was virtually rejected, when the stress on conscious personal surrender to God as the essence of religion became dominant in the revivals during and after Jonathan Edwards. When a definite and thorough-going reaction to this one-sided view set in, natural law to a large degree was used to explain what was once attributed to the special, supernatural operation of the Holy Spirit. Thus there was no room left for historic Calvinism.

The full-fledged theory of God's covenant relationship to man is quite definitely peculiar to the Reformed churches. Although other groups have at times made use of similar terminology, this conception never dominated their theory of the religious relationship in which God and man stand to each other in creation and redemption. In the Calvinistic circles the idea has had an honorable history. However, the extremes to which the Federal School in the Netherlands[3] developed and applied the idea led to a strong reaction. For more than a century it was almost entirely neglected. Within recent years, however, largely under the leadership of Kuyper and Bavinck it has once more come into its own.

In America, too, there seems to be a renewed interest in this conception. The Presbyterians, as distinctively Calvinistic, took along with them from Scotland and Ireland the idea of the covenant and during their early history applied it in their theology. The influence of the revivals also in that communion obscured this teaching. There has been a recent contribution to American theological scholarship, however, which studied the significance of this teaching for the place which children occupy in the church and its life. We refer to Lewis Bevens Schenck's work on *The Presbyterian Doctrine of Children in the Covenant.*[4]

For all those, therefore, who have an interest in Calvinistic theology and its development this subject will have a measure of appeal. Before attempting to show that there was a definite connection between the rejection of the covenant idea and the loss of the Reformed heritage it will be necessary to outline the method here followed.

This aims at being a study in the history and development of some of the fundamental conceptions and theories current in the New England churches respecting the doctrine of the covenant. An attempt will be made to demonstrate in what way this doctrine was modified, especially in its application to the practices of the churches. Here indeed certain far-reaching changes were made which contributed not a little towards preparing for the final obscuring of this conception.

In order to evaluate and understand the loss of Calvinism in New England from this aspect, it will be necessary first of all to make a brief study of the doctrine of the covenant as developed in the Protestant circles in Europe, especially those of Calvinistic origin. Thereafter an attempt will be made to trace the manner in which this theory was taken over by the American Puritans and the development through which it passed during the first two centuries of Congregational history in New England (1620-1847). This includes the men and movements from the time of John Cotton to that of Horace Bushnell. Finally, an appraisal of the significance of the change is in order. In this criticism it will be necessary to demonstrate how this rejection of the covenant idea was accompanied by an entirely new conception of God and His gracious dealings with the sons of men.

Part One

FOUNDATIONS OF THE COVENANT
IDEA IN PROTESTANT THEOLOGY

Chapter 1.

The Covenant Idea in the Reformed Churches

NEW ENGLAND Congregationalism is a lineal descendant of the Protestant Reformation in more ways than one, not the least in the manner in which it used the covenant idea very early in its history. In order to show its relationship to other Reformed churches and the points wherein it differed from much of Calvinistic teaching, it will be necessary to trace its history within this group. This will be done by pointing out the teachings of leading Reformed theologians on this score, the development of the same idea in the creeds, and the basic pattern which it assumed in the religious life and theological thought of the entire group. Since the Congregational churches were not only influenced by Calvinistic positions but also took over much from the Anabaptists, it will be necessary in the next chapter to describe the influence of the latter on New England Puritanism. Much of the theological development among the Congregationalists can be explained in the light of a largely unconscious attempt on their part to fuse these two types of Protestantism.

In the welter of doctrines which were either discovered or uncovered during the Reformation the covenant idea gradually took form and loomed large. In fact, it was not until those days of zealous warfare for the truth that this conception received any significant attention at the hands of Christian theologians.

This statement should not be misconstrued, however, to imply that before the Reformation the Biblical idea of the covenant was unknown in the Christian church. Already some of the earliest writings made references to it. In the *Epistle of Barnabas* it is mentioned in connection with the distinction between the

15

Sinaitic and New Testament dispensations. The author concluded that the "covenant" belonged rightfully not to the Jews but to the Christians.[1]

Similarly IRENAEUS alluded to it. In his *Against the Heresies* he stressed the distinction between the dispensations of the Old and New Testaments but insisted that "there is but one author, and one end to both covenants." They found their unity in Christ, who was said to have fulfilled the old covenant and established the new.[2]

CLEMENT OF ALEXANDRIA had latent within his theories a philosophy of history controlled by the covenant conception. This is hinted at in his *Stromata,* the full title of which was, according to Eusebius and Photius, "Titus Flavius Clement's miscellaneous collections of speculative (gnostic) notes bearing upon the true philosophy." Clement spoke of seven dispensations of the covenant, thus seeking to honor the system of sevens which he found throughout the Scriptures. Speaking of the veil at the entrance into the Holy of Holies he wrote, "Four pillars there are, the sign of the sacred tetrad of the ancient covenants." The seven which he mentioned were 1—Paradise, 2—Adam after the Fall, 3—Noah, 4—Abraham, 5—Moses, 6—Christ, and 7—the Millenial period preceeding the Last Judgment and the Everlasting Kingdom.[3]

The last of the pre-Reformation writers to refer to the idea was AUGUSTINE. In his *De Baptismo contra Donatista*s he contrasted the old and the new dispensations. "To the carnal belongs the old covenant, to the spiritual the new." Each group had sacraments peculiar to the "dispensation under which they lived." The old covenant was that manifested by Moses and in it "was hidden the new covenant, because after a secret fashion it was typified." Under the old arrangement persons "were already spiritual, belonging secretly to the new covenant." So, too, in the "new covenant . . . many live who are natural."[4]

We might conceivably expect Augustine to touch on the covenant relationship in his discourse *De Peccatorum Meritis et Remissione, et de Baptismo Parvulorum.* This, however, he did not do. In it he insisted that all infants are guilty in Adam by virtue of natural descent from him. None are saved except through Christ. Infants he went on to describe as believers and penitents. Thus he added, "The whole of this (infant baptism) is done in hope, in the strength of the sacrament and of the divine grace which the Lord has bestowed upon the Church."[5] Out of such and similar ideas the Roman Catholic conception of the church and the efficacy of her sacraments was developed. On the basis of such a presentation of the mechanical operation of divine grace, the organic conception of the Covenant of Grace established by God with believers and their seed could not and did not flourish.

Not until the days of the Reformation did this idea receive any great degree of consideration. In opposition to the mechanical theories of the Roman Catholic church concerning the constitutional nature of man, the essence of saving grace, and the sacraments as vehicles of that grace, the reformers sought to emphasize the organic and spiritual relation in which man stood to God by virtue of creation. This bond, so Protestants affirmed, was not nullified by sin, even though it had been greatly disturbed and seriously impaired by it. Salvation by the grace of God in Christ they conceived of as re-creation, a restoration and perfection of the relationships rooted in creation. Man could therefore fellowship with the Living God by virtue of that saving grace apart from the mechanical mediation of sacraments functioning ex opere operato and an hierarchy of saints. With increasing clarity these men comprehended that the covenant bond was basic to man's relation to God.

Although LUTHER and MELANCHTHON both regarded the relation of the Christian to God as resting upon the covenantal basis sealed by the death of Christ, this idea does not seem to have been developed to any great degree in Lutheran theology.[6] Without a doubt the cause for this lies in the strong Christological emphasis which has always characterized the Lutheran churches. Because of this the problem of the relation between nature and grace, which lies at the root of the covenant conception, troubled these churches very little.

Two other streams of Protestant thought, however, gave considerable attention to this conception and made use of the terminology occasioned by various discussions. Both in Calvinistic and Anabaptist circles the idea became prominent. But from the outset their respective ideas were mutually antagonistic and exclusive. Two groups having such profound differences in emphasis and temper could not be expected to agree on the treatment of any one subject, least of all one which necessarily had such far-reaching implications for doctrine and life as that of the covenant. Because these two types of Protestant thought differed so radically on the subject of the relation between nature and grace, the manner in which they construed man's relation to God through Christ was necessarily affected.

The Covenant Idea According to the Reformed Theologians

The Calvinistic Reformation took its rise in Switzerland. Its two earliest centers of influence were Zurich and Geneva. Its two outstanding leaders were Zwingli and Calvin.

The most influential leader and great systematizer, though not the first advocate of the Reformed position, was JOHN CALVIN the reformer of Geneva. Although he never devoted his attention particularly to the subject of the covenant, he referred to it time and again in his writings, especially in his *Institutio Christianae Religionis.*[7] In developing his theology Calvin made the doctrine of the Triune God central, thus taking the most theocentric view possible. However, the covenant idea did receive its share of emphasis, especially in connection with the doctrine of the church and the sacraments. In studying the use to which Calvin put this idea, it must be remembered that neither he nor his successors utilized it in the development of their church polity as the Anabaptists did.

In the fourth book of the *Institutes* he discussed the doctrine of the church and the sacraments. When considering the nature of the church, he repudiated the "pure church" ideal of the Anabaptists, which he termed a "pestilential opinion." These people, he insisted, had revived the ancient heresy of the Novatians, "for they imagine that by baptism the people of God are regenerated to a pure and angelic life, which cannot be contaminated by any impurities of the flesh."[8] Calvin's view of church membership and the sacraments was entirely different from this. The sacrament of circumcision in the Old Testament and of baptism in the New were to be given in infancy and admitted the individual to the privileges of the covenant. This relationship was by no means broken by the offenses of the human members, but rather in and through it they were assured of divine forgiveness, if and when they sought it with confession and repentance.

Calvin defined the sacraments as "outward sign (s) , by which the Lord seals in our consciences the promises of his good-will towards us, to support the weakness of our faith; and we on our part testify our piety towards him, in his presence and that of angels, as well as before men."[9] Thus the basis for the covenant was found in the good-will of God alone, for "the Lord calls his promises *covenants* and the sacraments *seals of covenants.*"[10] Thus this idea is not borrowed from some human arrangement and used to symbolize in some way the gracious relationship between God and His people, but it is regarded as basic to all God's dealings with man.

Since the sacraments are to be viewed as signs and seals of grace already present, baptism becomes according to him "a sign of initiation, by which we are admitted into the society of the Church, in order that, being incorporated into Christ, we may be numbered among the children of God."[11] In answer to the question on what basis the incorporation into Christ rested, Calvin referred to the Covenant of Grace which God established with Abraham and his seed. Thus he found the "promise of eternal life" in the words of God to the patriarch recorded in Genesis 17:7. This is extended to his children, for the promise included them. "Whence it follows, that the children of believers are not baptized, that they may thereby be made the children of God, as if they had before been strangers to the Church;

but on the contrary, they are received into the Church by a solemn sign, because they already belonged to the body of Christ by virtue of the promise."[12] Upon this argument followed the sixteenth chapter of the fourth book, entitled "Paedobaptism Perfectly Consistent with the Institution of Christ and the Nature of the Sign." In it the author argued for the unity of the covenant in both dispensations. Throughout the discussion there is evident a profound conception of the sovereignty of God in the work of grace. Although the work of regeneration is not observed in its effects in the lives of little children, such is no proper ground for doubting its existence.[13]

The Lord's Supper is also a sacrament of the covenant. "For the covenant which he once ratified with his blood, he in some measure renews, or rather continues, as far as relates to the confirmation of our faith, whenever he presents us that sacred blood to drink."[14] Thus Calvin linked up the covenant also with the death of Christ.

That he believed that elect children who entered the visible church by virtue of the covenant promise were regenerated is apparent from his writings. "We ought, therefore, to consider, that just as in the case of Abraham, the father of the faithful, the righteousness of faith preceded circumcision, so today in the children of the faithful, the gift of adoption is prior to baptism."[15] "We conclude, therefore, that sacraments are truly called testimonies of the grace of God, and are, as it were, seals of the benevolence he bears to us, which, by confirming it to our minds, sustain, cherish, strengthen, and increase our faith."[16] Thus baptism is for old and young alike "a sign of our spiritual regeneration."[17]

Calvin would find "no small stimulus to our education of them (i.e. these covenant children) in the serious fear of God, and the observances of his law," when he reflects "that they are considered and acknowledged by him (God) as his children as soon as they are born."[18] A similar and even stronger passage is found elsewhere in his writings. "The offspring of believers are born holy, because their children while yet in the womb, before they breathe the vital air, have been adopted into the covenant of eternal life. Nor are they brought into the church by baptism on any other ground than because they belonged to the body of the Church before they were born."[19]

These blessings of baptism and its promises were, of course, only for the children of believers. Although all the inhabitants of Geneva were required to present their children for baptism, this was done upon the understanding that they had made a sincere profession of their faith in Christ. To admit aliens, that is such who had not received the promises of God, was to profane the sacrament. However, Calvin realized that not all who were baptized as members of God's covenant and church came into full possession of eternal life. This he ascribed to their unbelief. The presence of such unbelievers in the church in no way nullified the promise of God. It only enforced the need of careful watch on the part of the congregation through its officers that only those who could in the judgment of charity be considered Christians were admitted. This was to be done by receiving adults only on the basis of personal profession of faith in Christ, since this was the badge of their part in the covenant.

Calvin thus regarded the visible church as "the veritable church of saints," although he rejected the notions of those who "despised the society of all men in whom they could discover any remains of human infirmity."[20] He would therefore find the holiness of the church not in the purity of the lives of its members first of all but in the redemption effectuated for it by Christ who "works from day to day in smoothing its wrinkles and purging away its spots."[21] Thus he preferred to speak of the "true church" rather than of the "pure church."[22] In his conception of the church and the sacraments the covenant relationship in which the believer and his seed always stood to God because of the divine promises was plainly taught.

Another aspect of Calvin's teaching on the covenant which deserves mention concerns his idea of the Old and the New Testaments as covenants made by God with man. In presenting his views on this score in the second book of the *Institutes* he insisted that there is but one covenant with two distinct dispensations. The only difference between them is one of administration.[23] Thus he strongly stressed the spiritual benefits which accrued to the Israelites by virtue of their covenant relationship to God. The most significant element was the fact that they also possessed Christ as their Mediator. In this connection Calvin took up the objections raised by certain groups against his view of the spiritual unity of the Old and the New Testaments.

He was not blind to the difference between the two, however. A large section was devoted to this. He named the following: 1—In the Old Testament the spiritual benefits were revealed in the form of material benefits, whereas in the New God did not make use of such aids. 2—In the Old Testament Christ was revealed under the aspect of ceremonies, but in the New He appeared in the flesh. 3—In the Old Testament we find the dispensation of the letter of the law, but in the New that of the spirit. 4—In the Old Testament we find the dispensation of bondage, but in the New that of liberty. 5—The Old Testament was revealed only unto one people, but the New is shared by all peoples.[24]

This emphasis on the fundamental unity and harmony of the two dispensations had far reaching effects for Calvinistic theology. It served especially to maintain the place of infants in the church. Further the covenant idea, grounded in the work of Christ as the promised Messiah, was constantly emphasized. Because of this the outstanding characteristics ascribed to God in the Old Testament occupied a significant place in his presentation of God's relation to the world, especially to His people. This is further evident from the use which Calvin made of the decalogue in his theology.[25] All these: the unity of the two dispensations, the place of children in the church, the emphasis on the sovereignty and righteousness of God, and the importance of the decalogue for the Christian life, became integral elements of the Calvinistic faith.

From Geneva this teaching spread throughout much of Protestant Europe. While Calvin was busy enlarging his *Institutes,* many of the refugees who fled England and Scotland because of the bloody persecutions came in contact with these ideas. When after the accession of Queen Elizabeth they returned home, they took with them what they had imbibed of Calvin while in Geneva and in other centers of Calvinistic influence on the Continent.

Although the Reformed churches are more indebted to Calvin than to anyone else of the early period of the Reformation for their ideas, they did not really take over the covenant idea from him directly. This conception took its rise in the Reformed churches of Zurich under the combined influence of Zwingli and Bullinger.

The first father of the Reformed faith in point of time was ULRICH ZWINGLI. In the long and bitter controversy which he waged with the predecessors of the Anabaptists at Zurich he discussed among other subjects that of the nature and extent of the Covenant of Grace. The Biblical teaching on this score he conceived of as one of the outstanding arguments in favor of infant baptism, which the opposition had rejected and about which the struggle raged. According to Zwingli the children of believers were as much in the church of God as were the parents, because God's covenant extended to them no less than to adults. He first advocated his position publicly in his *Von dem touff, vom widertouff, und vom kindertouff*.[26] He asked the question, "But if they (such children) belong to God, who will refuse them baptism?" To him the divine institution of the sacrament of baptism to take the place of circumcision plainly included the children by virtue of their covenant relationship, and therefore it was a matter of holy obligation to administer the sign and seal of that relationship unto them.

Two years later he published his *In Catabaptistarum Strophas Elenchus*. The third part of the book dealt more specifically with the question of the covenant. In it he advocated the position that the children of believers who die in infancy have the sure promise of salvation because of the covenant relationship in which God has been pleased to enter with them.[27]

Although Zwingli left no treatise on the covenant, his teachings on that subject had a profound influence and soon bore fruit. Only a few years after his untimely death on the battlefield of Kappel, his disciple and successor HEINRICH BULLINGER wrote *De Testamento sive Foedere Dei unico et aeterno*. He was the first to formulate clearly the idea that all of religion consisted of the covenant relation in which man stood to God. The Biblical concept might not be reduced to a figure of speech borrowed from the realm of human relationships but expressed the essential nature of the bond between God and His people. Thus in his *Compendium religionis Christiana*e he wrote, "Quicunque ergo haec observant (scil. foederis conditiones), hi fideles Dei servi et foederati sunt ac vera religione utuntur. Religio enim non tam a relegendo quam a ligando dicta videtur. Deo vero obligamur et foedere iunginmur gratuita eius benignitate per fidem; quam ob rem idem sunt foedus Dei et religio vera. Religiosi autem sunt omnes hi, qui Deo foederati Huius verbo nituntur."[28] Of course, as Kuyper points out, it was still necessary to show that the covenant idea expressed the heart of man's religious relation to God better than any other Scriptural idea.

Bullinger only dealt with the subject of the Covenant of Grace. The relation in which the realm of saving grace stood to that of the created order had not yet received definite formulation. The position which he accorded the children of believers was identical with that of Zwingli and later of Calvin. In his sermons he asserted, "Since the young babes and infants of the faithful are in the number and reckoning of God's people, and partakers of the promise touching the purification through Christ; it followeth of necessity, that they are as well to be baptized, as they that be of perfect age which profess the Christian faith."[29]

Wherever the Reformed religion made its appearance, the idea of the covenant became prominent. Already there were discussions on various questions relative to its development. Those especially who stood in intimate relation to the theologians of Zurich made the idea of the covenant significant for practical Christian life. Both Olevianus and Ursinus had been in Zurich and were thus acquainted with the ideas of Zwingli and Bullinger. Very likely, therefore, their use of this concept is to be attributed to that fact.

ZACHARIAS URSINUS, in his Catechismus Major spoke of the Covenant of Works made by God with Adam as well as of the Covenant of Grace. In the much-disputed question of the time when the promises of God were realized in the lives of infants belonging to the covenant, he took the position that they were regenerated and united with Christ in earliest infancy. This argument he employed in his polemic against the Anabaptists.[30]

CASPAR OLEVIANUS, the other author of the Heidelberg Catechism, also taught the doctrine of the covenant. He spoke of the covenant of the law, the covenant of nature, the covenant of creation in contrast to the Covenant of Grace. It is true that he sometimes designated the Sinaitic arrangement in those various ways. However, he also taught that a covenant relationship should be sought between God and man before the Fall. However, in attempting this he did not always clearly discern the distinction between the relation in which man stood to God by virtue of creation and that by virtue of specific covenant.

Rather than trusting to the operation of divine grace supposedly localized in the means, the Reformer insisted that the promises of God to His people were the only sure basis of spiritual life. Thus in determining the boundary of the Covenant of Grace, Olevianus advocated the position that it was made by God with the elect in Christ. In this he was followed by such prominent men as MUSCULUS, POLANUS, and MARTINIUS of Bremen.[31] However this did not involve a rejection of the idea that the non-elect who are in the visible church sustain some relationship to the covenant and its promises.[32] Rather, they sought only to show that the essence of the covenant was realized in the lives of the elect alone. In his *De Substantia Foederis* Olevianus held that Christ was the Mediator and Surety of this Covenant of Grace. He had the double task of making satisfaction for the sins of those who were given unto Him and of effecting within their lives peace of conscience and a renewal after the image of God. In this way the work of Christ as Surety was not only regarded as the foundation of the covenant but also as the principle of its administration. All of salvation was considered the work of Christ, who not only merited eternal life for His people but applied all the graces necessary unto its enjoyment through the Holy Spirit.[33] In this way Olevianus and those who followed him maintained the unity of the work of salvation by presenting it as the establishment, administration, and consummation of the covenant relationship of God with His own.

Although several of the earlier writers had referred to the Covenant of Works made by God with Adam before the Fall, this teaching was first developed at length by FRANCISCUS JUNIUS.[34] He made obedience to God the essential element in man's calling. God dealt with Adam in Paradise as a free agent and came with the promise of eternal life and the threat of eternal death. By obedience man could be raised to a higher level of fellowship with his Creator than he enjoyed in Paradise. God was the original contracting party in the covenant, and His free desire formed its sole basis. The visible instruments to seal the covenant were the two trees, the Tree of Life as the seal of man's supernatural destiny and the Tree of the Knowledge of Good and Evil as the seal of man's obedience unto God.

By disobedience man lost his hope of that glory of supernatural fellowship. However, since God had determined to save some of the human race in spite of the entrance of sin, He forthwith proceeded to open up the way of grace in harmony with the demands of His own righteousness. This constituted the salvation of the believers through Christ, which became God's new method of dealing with man. Although there were different dispensations of this covenant, essentially they are one and the same. The fulfillment of all types and shadows, so characteristic of the various Old Testament dispensations, was Christ. God today also deals with His people "per modum foederis," according to Junius. He is the God of the pious and their seed. Their lives are characterized by obedience and devotion unto Him, and thus they are in spirit the true seed of Abraham.

The position of Junius was a thorough representation. The most conspicuous element is the way in which he made the transition from the Covenant of Works to the Covenant of Grace depend on the already established decree of predestination. There can be very little doubt that the Supralapsarianism of Junius prevented him from fully developing the reason why the Covenant of Works was necessary, when the salvation of the elect was already rendered certain by the decree of God from eternity.[35]

During the controversy between the Calvinists and the Arminians in the Netherlands both the Supralapsarians and Infralapsarians used the covenant idea in their disputations. GOMARUS in his *Oratio de foedere Dei* spoke of the Covenant of Works as the foedus naturale and the Covenant of Grace as the foedus supei naturale. MACCOVIUS, also a Supralapsarian, followed Junius and Gomarus in insisting on the two covenants.

The Infralapsarians, such as ALSTED, WOLLEB, WENDELIN, and others, attempted to work out the distinction between the Covenants of Works and Grace, in order to secure a place for the former in the history of redemption. This they did by affirming that in the mind of God the decree of election followed logically from the decree to permit the entrance of sin into the world.

Although from the very beginning the Reformed theologians, as we have seen, made constant and consistent use of the covenant idea, they were not altogether clear on two specific points. In the first place, such leaders as Bullinger and Olevianus did not clearly formulate the representative idea. Original guilt was considered transmitted to all men purely because of the natural relationship in which Adam stood to the race, thus in much the same manner as original pollution. It was not until some time later that the idea of his legal and representative relationship to the race was stressed as distinct from the physical. In the second place, these men were not always clear in distinguishing the covenant relationship in which Adam stood to God from his relation as creature.[36]

The Arminians were not one whit behind the Reformed in making use of covenant conception and terminology. ARMINIUS took over the idea of the Covenant of Works and insisted that God's law to man could rightly be considered a covenant, since it contained on the one hand the command to work and on the other hand promised a reward for obedience to this mandate and threatened punishment for disobedience or failure. In his teachings on the sacraments he dealt with the Covenant of Grace. This he linked up with Christ's priesthood, which rooted in His agreement with the Father from all eternity. In it the Father was said to desire that the Son give Himself as a hostage for the sins and transgressions of the whole human race. God the Father further promised Christ that He should see His seed, if He carried through this work and would thus become priest forever after the order of Melchizedek.[37]

CURCELLAEUS introduced the covenant idea into the Remonstrant confession. He found part of the new covenant in the revelation of God's decree of eternal salvation of the believers and the demands for a righteous manner of life as the means of attaining unto this. Because the Arminians denied the characteristically Reformed doctrines of double predestination, limited atonement, unconditional election, and the perseverance of the saints, their conceptions of the nature and place of the Covenant of Grace differed greatly from those of both Infralapsarians and Supralapsarians among the Calvinists.

By the time of CLOPPENBURG, in whom the covenant idea is wedded to the strictest form of Calvinism,[38] some of the points which had been indefinite in the earlier theologians were cleared up. He maintained that on the basis of man's creation in the image of God he received in Paradise the unchanging natural law. Because of the natural relation in which man stood to God in this state of rectitude, there was no need for a special covenant relation or agreement. The obedience which man owed to God was not first of all a covenant obligation but a natural duty. However, out of sovereign grace God added to this obedience the promise of eternal life, by which He made Himself a debtor unto man. On the other hand, God gave the arbitrary command not to eat of the fruit of the Tree of the Knowledge of Good and Evil. This was really a test of man's love for God and aimed at the perfection of man's spiritual obedience to his Creator.

Although after the Fall the Covenant of Works was abrogated as a means unto the attainment of eternal life and full communion with God, Cloppenburg insisted that God's eternal right and claim upon man was not obliterated. Thus in the Covenant of Grace the demand of complete obedience is maintained. The double aspect is found in the new covenant as well as in the old. However, now the promise of eternal life is rendered certain of fulfilment on the basis of Christ's work, who obeyed the law for His people. This gives the fullest reconciliation with God in the present and the sure expectation of everlasting glory for the future. These are the two aspects of the grace of adoption in Christ, who gives His Spirit as the seal of this relationship to God through Himself. It is of this grace that both sacraments are signs and seals.

It is evident from this brief summary that in Cloppenburg the Covenant of Grace is distinctly rooted in the Covenant of Redemption.[39] He rejected the Arminian distinction between Christ's work of meriting and applying salvation, and in his disputations against this position took his point of departure in his conception of the covenantal relation of believers to God through the Mediator Jesus.

After Cloppenburg came CocceIus, with whose name the covenant idea had been most definitely connected.[40] He derived his principium divisionis in theology from this idea. Thus he distinguished and treated successively the foedus naturae et operum and the foedus gratiae with its three subdivisions ante legem, sub lege, and post legem. This system is fully expounded in his *Summa Doctrinae de Foedere et Testamento Dei,* which appeared in 1648.[41]

The most famous pupil of Cocceius was CAMPEGIUS VITRINGA. Others of this period and later who discussed the subject were

HEIDANUS, BURMANNUS, and WITSIUS, the last of whom exerted a great influence in New England toward the close of the seventeenth century. However, because of his adoption of the Cocceian principles of interpretation, which were so vigorously attacked by Voetius and his disciples, and his emphasis on the place and methods of mysticism in Christianity, he can hardly be considered the defender of Reformed orthodoxy in the Dutch churches of that day. The champions of the stricter Calvinism at that time were TURRETIN and JOHANN HEINRICH HEIDEGGER.

A development of the covenant idea which was to exert a much more profound influence upon the churches of New England was that of the Scotch and English theological writers. It was formerly thought that the British followed the Dutch, when they spoke of the covenant and embodied the idea in their historic creeds. Now, however, it is definitely believed that the two groups developed independently of each other.[42] This would seem to prove that a type of Federal theology is a universal phenomenon wherever Reformed theology is seriously pursued. It is evident that also in these circles the whole message of salvation through Christ was thought of in terms of the covenant. Without a doubt the origins of this development in Scotland and England lay in the intimate relations between the Continental Reformers and those in the English State Church who sought to pattern their ecclesiastical life after that of Zurich, Geneva, and Strassburg. This is manifest in the correspondence of Bullinger and Peter Martyr with Hooper, Jewel, Cranmer, and others. The works of Calvin, Beza, and others were well known in England. For sometime Bullinger's *Decades* was used as a manual for the clergy, and Calvin's *Catechism* was ordered by statute to be used in the university. Thus during the first half of the seventeenth century the British theologians were busy discussing questions similar to those which demanded the attention of the Continental leaders.

The first who deserves mention is ROBERT ROLLOCK, first principal of the University of Edinburgh. In his *Shorter Catechism* he held that God revealed nothing to man outside of the covenant bond. The doctrine of the Covenant of Works was more clearly formulated by him than by Olevianus. In developing it he claimed that there was present a double righteousness, one upon which it rested and another which it demanded. The law of obedience remained in spite of the Fall, but as a rule of the covenant unto the attainment of eternal life it was abrogated. Christ fulfilled the Covenant of Works for His people by enduring the penalty and meriting their righteousness.[43]

One of the most detailed discussions of the many thorny questions which arose in this connection was the treatise of THOMAS BLAKE, *Vindiciae Foederis,* which first appeared in 1663. Others such as JOHN PRESTON, JOHN BALL, and JAMES USSHER gave considerable attention to these ideas and paved the way for the presentation of the material in the Westminster symbols, the doctrinal parts of which were adopted by the New England churches.

AMESIUS, by conviction an English Puritan and for years professor at Franeker, used the Reformed conception of the covenant as a weapon against the Arminians. In his view the Covenant of Redemption became the higher unity between Christ's objective work in meriting salvation and His subjective work of applying the same unto the hearts of His own by the Holy Spirit. This presentation was quite common among the British theologians.

All of this became to a greater or lesser degree the heritage of early American Congregationalism. During the great controversy between the Calvinists and the Arminians, the Separatists under the Rev. John Robinson were in the Netherlands. The relations between them and the Dutch Reformed churches were on the whole very amicable. Although it cannot be determined definitely what influence this struggle had on the English refugees because of the lack of writings referring to it among the Separatists, it is apparent from Robinson's *A Defense of the Doctrine Propounded by the Synod at Dort: against John Murton and his Associates* that in their theology they were strict Calvinists.[44]

The Covenant Idea as Developed in the Reformed Confessions

The second method by which we can arrive at some understanding of the place which the covenant idea occupied in the theology of the various Reformed churches is to trace it through some of the influential creeds which were written. More so than in Lutheran circles the Protestants of the Reformed group set forth their conceptions in a series of doctrinal pronouncements and symbols. In these the idea of the covenant appears from time to time.

Three things concerning this ought to be noted at the outset. First of all, whereas several other leading doctrines were almost fully developed and thus clearly expressed at the beginning of the creedal history in the Reformed churches, as for example the teaching concerning the Holy Trinity, this was not the case with the covenant idea. This is largely accounted for by the fact that whereas many other doctrines were developed and accepted by the church at large before the Reformation era, the covenant conception as an integral part of dogma was hardly recognized prior to that time.[45] Secondly, the development of that idea within the various creeds was gradual. At first it was applied almost exclusively to the doctrines of the church and the sacraments, especially in connection with infant baptism. Only as time passed did the idea receive wider application, so that it was explicitly used in connection with the formulation of the teachings on man's relation both to Adam and Christ, the second Adam. Finally, it should not be overlooked that the covenant concept was never developed into a very explicit and precisely circumscribed doctrine or dogma in any of the creeds. The majority do not even give it separate consideration. The Westminster symbols are the outstanding exceptions to this. It was generally used as a basic pattern underlying much of the theological structure. Thus although the idea gained in influence, it was not always definitely formulated in the creeds.

In tracing the development of this idea we will sketch briefly its place in the early Swiss confessions, the Magyar statements of doctrine, the early Calvinistic confessions which owed their stimulus to Geneva, and the later Calvinistic creeds.

The earliest confessional writings from the side of the Reformed were those of the Zwinglian group in German-speaking Switzerland. It was also within this group that the covenant idea first arose. That it was more clearly expressed and developed here was in large measure due to the struggle between Zwingli and the forerunners of the Anabaptists, who also made use of the idea but applied it in a way far different from that of Zwingli and his disciples. Although he was one of the first to speak of this idea, it has not found concrete expression in the symbols which owe their direct inspiration to him. There is evident however a strong tendency in that direction in the way in which he presented various articles of faith. Unless there had been some conception of the covenant in the back of his mind (which cannot be doubted by anyone reading his works), he could not have spoken the way he did on the place occupied by Christ and the relation of the believer to Him.

The first of these creedal writings is known as the *Sixty-Seven Articles or Conclusions of Ulrich Zwingli.*[46] Herein he taught several points which can hardly be construed otherwise than as a defense of the substitutionary theory of the atonement. Stating what he considered the heart of the gospel, he affirmed, "Summa des Evangelions ist, das unser herr Christus Jhesus warer gottes sun, uns den willen seins himmelischen vatter kundt gethon, und mit seiner unschuld vom tod erlosst, und gott versünt hat."[47] Further, there is evident a strong tendency to conceive of the relation of the Christian to Christ in some such way as leader and representative. "Dann Christus Jhesus ist der wegfürer und haubtman allem menschlichem geschlecht von gott verheissen, und auch geleystet. Das er ein ewig heyl und haubt sey, aller gläubigen die sein leichnam seind der aber tod ist und nut vermag on jn. Usz dem volgt, zu eim, dz alle so in dem haubt lebend glyder und kinder gottes seind, und das ist die kirch oder gemeynsame der heyligen, ein huszfraw Christi. Ecclesia catholica."[48]

On November 17, 1523, the preachers of Zurich, under the leadership of Zwingli and Leo Jud, prepared *Ein kurtze und Christenliche inleitung,* which consisted of the formulation of the Christian doctrine expounded in the second great public debate in that city during the month of October immediately previous. Herein there is an emphasis on experiential piety which was to characterize several of the outstanding Reformed creeds. After a brief introduction on the significance of the Word of God, the ministers dealt with the doctrine of sin and its origin. Concerning its beginnings they affirmed, "Von der geburt har sind wir alle sunder, denn wir alle von Adamen geborn. Nun ist Adam, ee er ie gebar, in die sund, presten und tod gvallen, also volgt ouch das alle die von im kumend solchen presten von imm erbend. Denn als wenig mag der gevallen sundig Adam einen unsuntlichen mentschen geberen."[49] This was followed by the doctrine of deliverance through Christ in a section entitled "Evangelium." Therein the riches of saving grace are described. So great are these benefits that "ob wir glych fromm wärind und one unsere geprästen unnd dientind got allen unseren lebtag nach sinem gevallen, noch ist des menschen lebtag der langen ungemensznen ewigkeit nit wirdig."[50] However, according to the Christian gospel Christ has bestowed these on the basis of His work. The main purpose of the treatise was to refute the Roman Catholic teachings on images and the mass. Thus in the last section there is a reference to the significance of Christ's work for His people, which was later on developed more consistently from the covental approach. Speaking of the institution of the Lord's Supper the authors held, "Denn Christus hatt uns, wie obstatt, mit sinem blut vergeissen widrumb mit sinem himelischen vatter gefridet, und ein ewigen pundt gemacht durch inn zu gott ze kumen."[51] Thus Christ restored what Adam lost for us, namely the friendship of the Lord and therefore the indwelling and Guiding Spirit of God. What was left was "zerbrochnen natur,"[52] which is transmitted to all. It is apparent that at this time the natural relation of the race to Adam was stressed rather than the representative relation.

The Basle Confession of 1534 spoke of the relation in a similar vein. Speaking of Adam and the relation of his first sin to his descendants, the writers maintained, "Er ist aber mutwillgklich gefallen in die sund durch welchen faal das gantz menschlich geschlecht verderbt, der verdamnusz underworffen worden, ouch unser natur geschwecht . . ."[53]

One of the earliest presentations of the doctrine of original sin in the creeds can be found in Zwingli's *Fidei Ratio* of 1530. He regarded this as the pollution and infirmity with which all mankind since Adam's fall has entered the world. He had already taught this quite clearly in his *Einleitung*, wherein he held, "Von der geburt har sind wir alle sunder, denn wir sind alle von Adam geborn."[54] In describing the tragic consequences now he said, "Also ist der erst tod Adams, das er die huld gottes verloren hat."[55] These ideas, then, received a more mature and developed formulation in his defense addressed to the German Emperor Charles. The origin of sin is said to lie not in creation itself but in human perversity. Quoting Romans Zwingli maintained, "Unus enim Adam ist, suius culpa mors cervicibus nostris imminet." [56] Death came as a result not only upon Adam but upon all mankind. This is transmitted "nam parens, ex quo nati sunt, sclere hoc commeruerat."[57] Furthermore, in this treatise we find the first careful parallel drawn between man's fall in the first Adam and his redemption and salvation in the second. "Et nos esse natura filios irae scio, sed gratia, quae persecundeum Adam, Christum, casum restituit, inter, filios Dei recipi non dubito."[58] In fact, Zwingli affirmed that we receive life through Christ "quemadmodum in primo Adam sumus morti traditi."[59] It is also on this basis that he insisted on the salvation of the infants of believers. "Videlicet quod Christianorum infantes, quotquot sunt, de ecclesia populi Dei sunt, eiusque ecclesiae partes et membra."[60] To prove this he adduced the case of God's dealings with the Jews in the days of the patriarchs. Thus he asserted, "Non enim soli qui credunt baptizandi sunt, sed qui fatentur, qui de ecclesia ex verbi Dei promissis sunt."[61] In this way the author stressed the organic and objective aspects of religion fully as much as the subjective and personal.

The Reformed movement soon spread from Zurich to the neighboring cities, especially to Berne. Realizing the need of a statement of doctrine, the two Reformed pastors of that place, Francis Kolb and Berthold Haller, drew up the *Ten Conclusions of Berne* in 1528. They were carefully revised by Zwingli and published for a large conference to be held in that city. All the leading Swiss reformers as well as several prominent men outside of Switzerland approved of this formulation. In it the headship of Christ over the church as well as His death in behalf of the sinful world was affirmed. It introduced the idea of the covenant in connection with a consideration of the Old Testament. The means used there were conceived of as types and shadows prophesying the coming of Christ. In these various signs therefore God preached His gospel, and thus, "Er ward ouch der bundnusz halb die Arch der zugnusz, der tempel unnd die statt Hierusalem, Gott der herr genannt, dann by disen worzeychen ward Gott verstanden."[62] Thus the covenant idea was used to designate the method by which God revealed His grace unto the children of Israel.

When during January 1532 the Synod of Berne met, at which two hundred and thirty pastors were present, the sacramental theory of the Swiss churches was discussed. They regarded the sacraments not as "blosse zeychen" but insisted that they were accompanied with the "heymlich krafft Gottes."[63] Against the Anabaptists they maintained strongly the place and purpose of infant baptism in the churches. "Aber wir touffen unsere kind also, das wir sy durch unser touffen zur gemein gots von ussen annemen, gutter hoffnung der herr werde nach siner ewigen gute hie nach syn ampt by jnen ouch uszrichten, und sy mit dem h, geyst warhafftig touffen, und haben solichen kinder touff für ein war sacrament . . ."[64] Furthermore the assembly declared "das by dem kind wol noch nit im werck (of faith) angelegt, aber by uns die zu gegen im handel syn, ist es angelegt."[65] Thus on the basis of the organic relation of the children of believers to the church infant baptism was upheld. The definition of the church or congregation was "das glöubig völclin."[66]

The *Confessio helvetica prior* (1536) was composed by the Swiss divines Bullinger, Grynaeus, Myconius, and others. In it there is very little material referring directly to the idea of the covenant, although like most confessions of that day this conception was basic to several articles. Christ was called the "mediator, intercessor, hostia, idemque et pontifex, dominusque, et rex noster."[67] In the Swiss edition prepared by Leo Jud and of equal authority with the Latin, although it was a free and somewhat enlarged rendering of the original draft, the great purpose of this work of redemption and reconciliation was the coming of that time when "er uns zu der bildnus, zu deren wir geschaffenn sind, reformieren und wyderbringe, und jnn die gemeinsame sins gottlichen lebens jnfur."[68] Although this confession spoke of Christ's work as "expiationem,"[69] yet the forensic element was overshadowed by the organic conception in which believers stood to Him. The significance of the sacraments is plainly taught as more than symbolical. "Desshalp wir bekennend, das die Sacrament nit allein ussere zeychen syend Christenlicher gsellschaft. Sonder wir bekennendts fur seichen gottlicher gnaden . . ."[70] The confession insisted on infant baptism based on the covenant relationship between God and the children of believers. "Quo quidem sancto lavacro infantes nostros idcirco tingimus, quoniam e nobis (qui populus Domini sumus) genitos populi Dei consortia rejicere nefas est, tantum non divine voce huc designatos, praesertim quum de eorum electione pie est praesumendum."[71]

In the *Confessio helvetica posterior*[72] Bullinger stressed the natural relation in which the race stood to Adam. "Peccatum autem intelligamus esse nativam illam hominis corruptionem, ex primis illis nostris parentibus, in nos omnes derivatam vel propagatam . . ."[73] In this consideration of the work of the Lord Jesus Christ the forensic aspect was strongly affirmed. "Etenim

Christus peccata mundi in se recepit et sustulit, divinaeque justitiae satisfecit. Deus ergo propter solum Christum passum et resuscitatum, propitius est peccatis nostris, nec illa nobis imputat, loquendo, Deus solus nos justificat, et duntaxat propter Christum justificat, non imputans nobis peccata, sed imputans ejus nobis justitiam."[74] In connection with baptism the covenant was again vigorously affirmed. Baptism was regarded as the perpetual sealing (obsignatio) of our adoption. Explaining its significance the writer held, "Etenim baptizari in nomine Christi est: inscribi, initiari, et recipi in foedus atque familiam adeoque in haereditatem filiorum Dei . . ."[75] By this token God separates unto Himself a peculiar people, distinct from all others. "Separat item Deus nos baptismi symbolo ab omnibus alienis religionibus et populis, et sibi consecrat ceu peculiam."[76] Because of this strong stress on organic relations, those who accepted its positions also strongly affirmed their rejection of Anabaptism. "Nam juxta doctrinam Evangelicam horum est regnum Dei, et sunt in foedere Dei, cur itaque non daretur eis signum foederis Dei?"[77]

As early as the year 1528 there appeared in an altogether different corner of Europe another expression of the Reformed faith which bore a rather striking resemblance to these early Swiss creeds. It was entitled *Summa ende bekenninghe Christliker leer der predicanten in Oostfrieslandt.* The first article affirmed that God loves and blesses only His own who are "in sinem enigen lieven soon Christo."[78] This love was hidden until Christ was manifest in the flesh, and the Holy Spirit bestowed it upon those who had come to believe. The emphasis on the active obedience of Christ, His fulfilment of the law on behalf of His own, is found in the fourth article. "In hem geft hi al wat hi van uns eyschet doer die wet . . ."[79] In harmony with the requirements of faith God has given to His church the sacraments. Both with and in baptism and the Lord's Supper God grants His Holy Spirit, though not necessarily at the time of the preaching of the Word or the administration of the Sacraments by using them as vehicles, for "Gods werck mach an ons werck niet gebunden sijn."[80] Only the initial operations of

God's Spirit are effective unto consolation and assurance of the conscience. Yet the external means do have significance. "De waterdoope dient tot avtellinge off inscrivunge tot dat getal van anderen Christen, als de mit Christo willen off solden sterven van horen sundigen leven ende weder opstaen tot eyn nyeu leven."[81] Although all these and the other ordinances are for the "utverkoren kinderen unde liefhebbers gods,"[82] they have no efficacy unless accompanied by that inward operation of the blessed Spirit which stirs up faith. This declaration gives evidence of having the spirit of experiential piety which later became so characteristic of the Anabaptists. The emphasis throughout is on the subjective rather than on the objective aspect of the Christian religion. Perhaps it constitutes the closest approach to the purely subjective in any Calvinistic creed.

The Reformed faith also spread eastward with the result that many of the Magyars accepted it. With them we find some explicit appreciation of the covenant idea in their earliest creeds. In fact, the first Reformed creed to devote a separate article to it was the *Erlauthaler Confession* of 1562. It gave a rather comprehensive definition of what was understood by the covenant in those days. Thus first of all the Old and the New Testaments were distinguished by describing the former as instituted through the revelation of God's law, in order that His justice might be vindicated and man rendered without excuse. It was definitely temporary in its administration. However, "Noevum foedus dicitur testamentum aeternum, dedicatum ex gratia ea misericordia Dei in sanguine aeterni sacrificij Christi, in Christo fundatum per omnes causas."[83] God the Father is recognized as "stipulator et promissor."[84] However, since in all covenants there are two parts, so too in the new covenant of God with man there are obligations which must be met. Recognizing and elaborating upon this the confession states, "In nove foedere Deus stipulator est, Christus autem factor, obligator nostro nomine."[85] Because this covenant has God both as foundation and goal, it is eternal. On the basis of the work of Christ His church is to be regarded as perfect. In the chapter on "De perfectione" the authors insist, "Duplex est perfectio: Capitis Christi, et membrorum."[86] The perfection of Christ is described as "absolutissima plenitudo et sufficientia ad omnia naturae et officij sui opera consumanda, etc. . . ."[87] That of the members of Christ is of a different kind. "Haec perfectio est imputativa, ex gratia Dei propet Christi iustam perfectionem, etc. . . ."[88]

Thus the position of the believers was said to rest upon a forensic act of God. This confession is not altogether clear as to the transmission of original sin to the human race, although it states definitely that all men without exception are sinners. The Covenant of Grace is viewed as the ground of the perseverance of the saints. "Ideo electi non amittunt Spiritus S. in lapsu, nec ad mortem peccant, quia sunt in foedere Dei, Dominus supponit manum, semen Dei est in illis."[89]

The next confession of the Hungarian churches dates from the same period. It was entitled *Compendium doctrinae christianae, quam omnes Pastores et Ministri Ecclesiarum Dei in tota Ungaria et Transylvania, quae incorruptum Iesu Christi Evangelium amplexiae sunt, docent ac profitentur*. It has been generally known as the *Torczal-Tordaensis Confession* in honor of the two synodical gatherings which accepted it. It is far more systematic than the previous symbol and follows as did the other the chief doctrines held by the Calvinists. It is clearer on the doctrine of original sin and its transmission. "Itaque peccatum originis est universalis quaedame labes ac corruptela totius humanae naturae, ad Adamo in omnes posteros propagata, quaeque in iis tria peccatorum genera quasi fructus profundit."[90] In the lengthy article on Infant Baptism it is agreed that the infants of believers can possess the "habitu fidei."[91] The parents have the promises of God which are to be appropriated by faith. The objection of those who maintain that not all who are born of Christian parents are saved is answered. The authors held, "Et in genere ex promissionis formula praesumimus sanctificatos esse, quicunque ex fidelibus parentibus . . ."[92] Thus they are to be enrolled and considered as members of the church, which is of comfort both to parents and children. This seal received at the hands of the church may comfort the parents that those children who die in infancy or early youth are saved. For the Lord seals unto these as well as unto the ones in whom the fruits of faith later become manifest the gifts of forgiveness and adoption.

The Summa Confessionis et Conclusionum Synodi Debrecinum (1567) postulated practically the same doctrines as those affirmed in the other Magyar confessions. The significance of these symbols lies not so much in their influence upon Reformed churches outside of their own natural and national group, for that was at best rather small. However, they are important because of the picture which they gave of the way in which the basic teachings of Calvinism were expressed and taught by the leaders in that country.

Soon after Calvin's return to Geneva, his influence became dominant. This is reflected in many of the confessional writings which owe their origin to those who accepted his teachings. Already in the first distinctively Calvinistic confession we find a stronger tendency to emphasize the absolute sovereignty of God and the holiness of the church than in some earlier Reformed creeds. This first confession is the *Confession de la Foy laquelle tous bourgeois et habitans de Geneve et subjectz du pays doyvent jurer de garder et tenir* (1536). It is said that the misery of man lies in his abandonment of God.[93] In Christ there is salvation, because by the shedding of His blood He satisfied the justice of God necessary unto forgiveness. The purpose of the sacraments is "pour la (our faith) fortifier et confermer aux promesses de Dieu."[94] Infants as well as adults are to receive baptism "comme membres de son Filz Jesus."[95] The objective basis of this is strongly affirmed in these words, "Or puisque noz enfans appartiennent a une telle alliance de nostre Seigneur, nous sommes certains que a bon droict le signe exterieur leur est communique."[96] The same is taught in the *Geneva Catechism* of 1545. The reason why the covenant was not emphasized more directly may be attributed to the fact that Calvin made the doctrine of the Triune God basic in his theology, as is evident from the *Institutes*. Hence the relationship between God and man was not as clearly defined as elsewhere.

The *Confessio rhaetica* of 1552 linked up the doctrine of Adam as representative with that of the restoration of our human nature through Christ in this way, ". . . per mortum ejus, qua Deo reconciliati fuimus: per resurrectionem ejus vivificam, qua peccato morte et inferis devictis vitam nobis reduxit."[97]

The *Confessio gallicana* of 1559 likewise followed this construction of man's relation to Adam. It insisted that all his posterity was in bondage to sin, which is "un vice hereditaire."[98] The question how this is transmitted from one generation to another is not answered. However, the tragic consequences are described in strong language, ". . . qui suffit a condamner tout le genre humain, iusques aux petis enfans des le ventre de la mere."[99] In fact, God is said to consider it such, with the result that all pardon necessarily proceeds only from sovereign grace. The sole ground of salvation is the obedience of the Lord Jesus, which is imputed with the result that sins are blotted out and favor in God's sight is received. The chief ground for the baptism of infants is not sought so much in the covenant relationship as in the command of Jesus.[100]

The *Confessio belgica* followed that of the French churches rather closely in the doctrine of original sin and the relation of all men to Adam as the natural head. Original sin is universally present as "quodque veluti radix."[101] The author insisted that it is never imputed to God's children unto condemnation. This would imply that it is imputed unto condemnation in the case of all the rest of the race. The word imputation, implying the recognition of a forensic relation of man to God, demonstrates that the reformers felt already early that the natural relationship of all men to Adam did not sufficiently explain the tragic consequences of original sin and the necessity of salvation through Christ.

Although plainly teaching a relation between Adam and his posterity resulting in the universality of sin, the *Scotch Confession* of 1560 did not elaborate on the subject in any way.

The *Irish Articles* of 1615, forerunner of the Westminster symbols, teach fundamentally the same with respect to man's relation to Adam by nature and to Christ by grace as the confessions referred to above. Thus it affirmed, "Original sinne standeth not in the imitation of Adam (as the Pelagians dreame) but is the fault and corruption of the nature of every person that naturally is ingendred and propagated from Adam: whereby it cometh to passe, that man is deprived of originall righteousness, and by nature is bent unto sin."[102] Christ is considered the "mediator of the second Covenant."[103] It is that of grace in contrast with "the covenant of the lawe." In the article on Justification and Faith the forensic relation to Christ is strongly affirmed, for "we are accounted righteous before God."[104] As in the *Confessio gallicana* infant baptism is not directly connected with the covenant promises.

The Thirty Nine Articles of the Church of England (1562) are in many ways similar to other early Calvinistic confessions. In the minds of the authors there seems to have been a close connection between baptism and regeneration. Furthermore, the baptism of infants is retained as "most agreable with the institution of Christe."[105] The idea of the covenant is not expressed in this symbol.

The last of the earlier Calvinistic creeds is the *Heidelberg Catechism* of 1563. Written by Ursinus and Olevianus, it is more in harmony with the spirit of Zwingli than that of Calvin. It speaks of the covenant in connection with the Lord's Supper. Question eighty-two asks whether the unbelieving and ungodly may be permitted to partake of the sacrament. The answer is given in the negative: "Nein, denn es wird also der Bundt Gottes geschmecht, und sein zorn uber die gantze gebein gereitzet."[106] According to the seventy-forth question and answer infants as well as adults are to be baptized, "denn deweil sie sowohl also die Alten in den Bund Gottes unnd seine gehoren, unnd jhnen in dem Blut Christi die erlosung von sunden, und der heilig Geist, . . . nit weniger denn den Alten zugesagt word: so sollen sie auch durch den Tauff, als des Bunds zeichen, der Christlichen kirchen eingeleibt, und von der unglaubigen kinder under-scheiden werden."[107] The Catechism teaches that Christ purchased the redemption for His own and covers their sinfulness with His innocence. The satisfaction theory of the atonement is taught in the sixteenth question and answer. The believer is said to receive Christ's merits by imputation. In dealing with the question of original sin corruption is emphasized, although the idea of guilt is not entirely lacking, since it is maintained that God will punish "inborn sins" as well as "actual sins"[108] both in time and eternity.

The high-water mark of the creedal development of Reformed theology is to be found in the symbols adopted by the synods of Dort and Westminster. The Synod of Dort (1618-1619) adopted the *Canones Synodi Dordrechtanae* as the true statement of the Reformed doctrine of predestination in opposition to certain theories held by the Arminians. In connection with the first sin of Adam the natural relationship sustained by the race to him is stressed. The pollution of that first sin is transmitted by heredity. After the fall all men are corrupt "per vitiosae naturae propagationem, justa Dei judicio, derivata."[109] The first error rejected under the Third and Fourth Heads of Doctrine dealt with the theory that original sin is not a sufficient ground for condemnation. This error the Synod vehemently denounced. Christ is viewed as man's surety (sponsor), having become a curse (maledictio) on our behalf.[110] The teaching on the value of His death is in harmony with the penal substitutionary theory.

A very strong statement concerning the significance of the covenant promise to the children of believers is found in the first head of doctrine. "Since we are to judge of the will of God from his Word, which testifies that the children of believers are holy, not by nature, but in virtue of the covenant of grace, in which they together with the parents are comprehended, godly parents ought not to doubt the election and salvation of their children whom it pleases God to call out of this life in infancy." Here the question of infant salvation is made to depend entirely upon the gracious covenant relation.

Of far more direct significance for the development of the doctrine of the covenant in New England are the *Westminster symbols*. Original sin as the transgression of Adam and Eve in Paradise is transmitted "to all their Posterity descended from them by Ordinary Generation."[111] In chapter seven the question of the covenant comes up directly. Herein is affirmed that men could never have "any Fruition of him (God) as their Blessedness and Reward but by some voluntary Condescension in God's Part, which he hath been pleased to express by way of Covenant."[112] The first was the Covenant of Works, which required of Adam perfect and personal obedience. Since man had made himself incapable of earning life by that covenant, God was pleased to reveal another. It is frequently set forth in the Holy Scriptures "by the Name of Testament" in reference to "the Death of Jesus Christ the Testator."[113] Thus the essence of the Covenant of Grace was found in the fact that herein "he (God) freely offereth unto sinners life and salvation by Jesus Christ, requiring of them faith in him that they may be saved, and promising to give unto all those that are ordained unto life his Holy Spirit, to make them willing and able to believe."[114] Westminster was also firm in rejecting any idea that the difference between the Old and New Testaments was sufficient to allow for the conception of "two covenants of grace differing in substance."[115] The twenty-seventh chapter dealt with the sacraments. The definition is given first. "Sacraments are holy signs and seals of the covenant of grace, immediately instituted by God, to represent Christ and his benefits, and to confirm our interest in him, as also to put a visible difference between those that belong unto the Church and the rest of the world; and solemnly to engage them to the service of God in Christ, according to his Word."[116] Regarding the possibility of receiving this grace which the sacraments signified and sealed, the Confession said, "The grace which is exhibited in or by the sacraments, rightly used, is not conferred by any power in them, neither doth the efficacy of a sacrament depend upon the piety or intention of him that doth administer it, but upon the work of the Spirit, and the word of institution, which contains together with a precept authorizing the use thereof, a promise of benefit to worthy receivers."[117] Concerning the significance and value of baptism this creed declared, "Baptism is a sacrament of the New Testament, ordained by Jesus Christ, not only for the solemn admission of the party baptized into the visible church, but also to be unto him a sign and seal of the covenant of grace, of his ingrafting into Christ, of regeneration, of remission of sins, and of his giving up unto God through Jesus Christ to walk in newness of life; which sacrament is by Christ's own appointment to be continued until the end of the world."[118] It was stated that neglect of this ordinance constituted a great sin, yet not so that without it one was excluded from heaven, nor yet so that having it guaranteed the possession of the grace of regeneration. This sacrament was "not only (for) those that do actually profess faith in, and obedience unto Christ," but should also be administered to infants of believing parents. Various texts were adduced to prove this.[119] Concerning the second sacrament a similar line of argument was pursued. It, too, was conceived of as a sacrament of the New Testament, thus a sign and seal of divine grace. With respect to the benefits received from participation it was held that "Worthy receivers, outwardly partaking of the visible elements in this sacrament, do then also inwardly by Faith, really and indeed, yet not carnally and corporally, but spiritually, receive and feed upon Christ crucified, and all benefits of His death; the Body and Blood of Christ being then not corporally or carnally in, with, or under the bread or wine; yet as really, but spiritually, present to the faith of believers in that ordinance, as the elements themselves are to their outward senses."[120]

The two catechisms, *Greater* and *Shorter,* were composed at the same time. The strongly dogmatical *Catechismus Major* was based rather largely on the *Compendium theologiae* of Wolleb, the theologian of Basle.[121] Adam is considered in it a "persona publica"[122] in whom the race has sinned. The state in which man now finds himself is described as "in corruptione naturae suae."[123] Original sin is transmitted "per generationem naturalem."[124] The Covenant of Grace was made by God with Christ the second Adam, and in Him with the elect as His seed. In this God's grace was manifest, by which He forgave man's sins and granted the gift of His Holy Spirit. Christ is spoken of as the Mediator of the Covenant of Grace. The visible church consists of all those professing the true religion in all places and at all times with their children. The sacraments are linked up with the Covenant of Grace as in the *Confession.* Such children are to be baptized whose parents, either one or both, are believing and obedient or in covenant with God through baptism.

The *Shorter Catechism* followed the other throughout, simplifying the questions and answers in many instances and reducing their number.

The last of the great Reformed symbols appeared in 1675 under the title *Formula Consensus, Ecclesiarum Helveticarum Reformatorum.* As the last of the Calvinistic confessions of this period it was also the one which postulated most definitely the double relation in which Adam stood to his posterity and the consequent results of this for the doctrine of original sin. Its guilt is imputed unto all who descend from him in the way of natural generation. "Censemus igitur, peccatum Adami omnibus ejus posteris, judicio Dei arcana et justo, imputari."[125] Pollution was said to be transmitted through heredity. Justification was promised by God either on the condition of perfect and personal obedience by man (Covenant of Works) or by "justitiam alienam Christi"[126] (Covenant of Grace). Although more than the elect are included in the temporal administration of this covenant, only the elect are saved in it. The double relationship in which men stood to Adam parallels the double relation of the elect to Christ. He is both Covenant Head and Representative of them, thus rightly called the second Adam.

From this brief consideration of the leading confessions of the several Reformed churches the following important facts for our study have become plain. First of all, every creed without exception emphasized the sovereignty of God in the work of salvation. There was no place for the free will of the individual man to work out his own reconciliation with God. Although some of the confessional writings did mention free will, it was always in the sense of a free will unto sin. Nowhere is man viewed as capable of making a choice unto holiness without the regenerating grace of God. In many of the standards the idea of election was very prominent, especially towards the close of the period. This was in large measure due to the controversies which raged at that time, but also to a deeper realization on the part of the churches that salvation in its entirety had to be traced back to God and His eternal plan. It is because of this strong insistence on election that the doctrine of the covenant assumed a radically different form among the Calvinists than among the Anabaptists, where the human response to the gospel call was always placed in the foreground.

Furthermore, in everyone of these symbols the human race was regarded not as an aggregate of individuals, each responsible solely for his own personal spiritual welfare. The organic relationship of all to Adam as well as the relation of children severally to their parents was maintained instead. Thus herein all the Reformed followed Augustine in his solution to the problem of the universality of sin. The Anabaptists on the contrary seemed to lose sight of these organic relations in their effort to stress the need of personal surrender to the will of God. Thus they never could carry out the covenant idea completely in their construction of Christian theology. Whereas the Reformed made it basic to their whole presentation of God's dealings with man in the state of rectitude as well as in the state of sin, these others preferred to speak of it as an oath of allegiance on the part of the individual to God.

Not only did the Calvinists in their endeavor to maintain the sovereignty of God insist on the objective and organic aspects of the work of salvation, but they also gave a significant place to the forensic aspect of the same. This was done especially in connection with the work of Christ. Thus in their interpretation of the teachings of St. Paul they spoke of imputation and representation. This aspect, however, was also applied to man's relation to Adam as the Representative of the race in the Covenant of Works. Already in the earliest creedal writings Christ was regarded as the second Adam. His work was to reveal the Father unto men, to deliver the race from the power of death, and to reconcile the elect unto God. Through the shedding of His blood the possibility of peace with God was rendered certain. Thus through the new covenant of Christ's blood man could come unto God. Although in the earlier Zwinglian confessions the emphasis fell on Christ as the Head of the human race, this was soon paralleled with the teaching that Christ was also representative and substitute for His own. Thus the *Confessio helvetica prior* spoke of Christ both as mediator and sacrifice, through Whom was effectuated the necessary expiation for sin.

Therefore there is by no means an antithesis between the covenant and the forensic representations of man's relationship to God. It is true that in Zurich, where the covenant idea first came up, the legal aspect of Christ's work was not as clearly seen and concisely formulated as in the more strictly Calvinistic confessions. However, the covenant idea easily embraced the forensic representation and was thus itself enriched. It did precisely this in the Westminster symbols, which have been quite generally regarded as the most complete and mature development of Reformed theology in creedal form.

The Covenant Idea as Applied to Specific Doctrines

From the above study it is apparent that the place occupied by the covenant idea in Reformed theology is by no means easy to define precisely and accurately. It has ramifications which control the whole structure of Christian doctrine. Rather than considering it a specific dogma or doctrine of the church, we should regard it as a basic motif or pattern controlling and modifying various doctrines in systematic theology. Hence any detailed discussion of it will inevitably lead to a consideration of many rather than few doctrines. Some of the fundamental teachings within the Calvinistic churches which have been developed in the light of the covenant conception include the following: 1—the nature and extent of sin, 2—the relationship between God the Creator and man the creature, 3—the bond between Christ and the race, 4—the doctrine of the church and the means of grace, 5—the doctrine of the Christian life, 6—the place of children in the church, and 7—the Christian philosophy of history. These will now be discussed briefly in the above-mentioned order.

Sin is an everywhere present phenomenon. Its influences have been experienced by men of all ages. Nearly every religion, therefore, has developed in some form or another both a definite conception of it and ways of escape from its tyranny. None, however, has such a profound conception of it as Christianity. In fact, the Christian religion is par excellence the religion of redemption from sin. Thus whatever the multitude of views concerning Jesus Christ, the most influential has been that of Jesus as the Savior of the world. In connection with this Christianity has grappled with the question of the nature and extent of sin.

In Reformed circles it has been customary to conceive of sin as rebellion against the lawful authority of God, Who has given His commands by revelation unto man. By breaking these man broke also the covenant bond which united him with his Creator and Sovereign and guaranteed happiness unto him in the way of fellowship with his Maker. The heinous character of sin is nowhere more clearly manifest than in man's refusal to submit to God. Thus sin attacks God as God. In wrestling with the problem of the universality of sin, Christianity on the basis of the Scriptural records has traced it back in some form or another to Adam. This is especially true of the Augustinian-Lutheran-Calvinistic tradition. And in the last named the covenant idea was definitely formulated as an explanation for sin's universality. All men are said to have descended from common parents, Adam and Eve. Adam as the first father of the race stood in a peculiar relationship to humanity as his offspring. He was both head and representative of all. The covenantal bond was first represented as resting upon the physical or natural connection between him and all others. The pollution of his transgression was thus transmitted unto all who descended from him in the way of natural generation. As the doctrine of the Covenant of Works was gradually developed, the idea of Adam as legal representative was definitely taught. Thus in him the whole race became guilty, the guilt of that primal sin being justly imputed to all by God. This double relation received its most careful formulation after the rise of the school of Saumur, which taught only a mediate imputation of the guilt of that sin. By means of the covenant idea, then, the Reformed insisted upon the universal depravity of the race and the guilt of all men before God. This, it was held, explained the justice of the Almighty in penalizing sin with physical, spiritual, and eternal death.

The question of the relation between God and the world is one of the most basic, if not the most basic, in any religious interpretation of the universe. Christianity regards God as the Creator and Sustainer of all. Thus it seeks to guard against pantheism on the one hand and deism on the other. Both too great a removal of God from the affairs of human life and too close an identification of Him with the same undermines the possibility of personal fellowship between God and man, which lies at the heart of religion. God being what He is, it has been quite consistently recognized in Christianity that revelation in some form or another is necessary unto knowledge of and fellowship with Him. The Reformed have applied the covenant idea when interpreting this relationship, not only to the communion which the believer has with God through Christ but also to that which he enjoyed in the state of innocence as man created in the image of God. As Creator God upholds his claim on all creatures. Man as the crown of His creative activity was entrusted with the entire universe for the purpose of having dominion over it and subduing it to the greater glory of God. In revealing this high goal God manifested Himself in covenantal form unto man.

That covenant included the test for the creature. By remaining faithful he would have experienced the strengthening of the bond which bound him to his Creator and the improvement of his fellowship. Thus seeking not only His own glory apart from man but also aiming at the happiness of His creature, God condescended to reveal Himself by coming down to the level of man. Berkhof explains this act on the part of God thus, "He entered into legal compact with man, which includes all the requirements and obligations implied in the creaturehood of man, but at the same time added some new elements. 1—Adam was constituted the representative head of the human race, so that he could act for all his descendants. 2—He was temporarily put on probation, in order to determine whether he would willingly subject his will to the will of God. 3—He was given the promise of eternal life in the way of obedience, and thus by the gracious disposition of God acquired certain conditional rights. This covenant enabled Adam to obtain eternal life for himself and for his descendants in the way of obedience."[127] By means of this formulation the Reformed could relate the whole creation to God as Creator and Sovereign. And since they contended that saving grace restored the realm of nature, they did not limit the significance of Christ's work to soteriology but spoke of its cosmic significance.

Since Adam fell into sin, and through his fall sin and death passed unto all men, for that all sinned, redemption became necessary. Although the sense of human need for reconciliation with God in some from or another is not limited to Christianity, it finds its triumphant solution there in the doctrine of the person and work of Jesus Christ. His life and death as atonement for sin have reconciled God and man. In formulating the connection between Christ and fallen humanity the Reformed again approached this from the aspect of the covenant. It is true that the doctrine of election, strongly emphasized in all historic Calvinistic churches, tended towards individualization. However, this was nearly always balanced by an appreciation of the way in which God was said to honor the natural relationships which He Himself had ordained at the beginning. This was consistent with the Calvinistic stress on the teaching that grace did not consist of a new and radically different creation but was the old restored and heightened.[128] Thus the elect were found largely in the generations of those who believed, by which token the decrees of God were said to have taken into account the relation in which children should stand to their parents. By this, however, was never meant that saving grace could be inherited. With the strong insistence on universal sinfulness and the absolute necessity of regeneration such a position could not be harmonized. The individual needed the personal renewal and indwelling of the Holy Spirit. Without being dependent in any way upon the education, example, and precepts of the parents, God worked out His plans in harmony with them by including the children of believers in His work of salvation. Not only family relationships but also the relation of the individual to the whole race was honored, for Christ was regarded as the second Adam, the head of the Covenant of Grace. In and by Him the salvation of the race was secured. Thus His death was viewed as a payment of the penalty due to sin and a victory over the tyranny of the devil. Since Christ's work as Mediator and Savior was not only sufficient but also efficient unto salvation, it was necessary to accept the theory of limited atonement. This harmonized with the theory of election. It was also applied to the covenant idea, since Christ became by virtue of His position, vocation, and honor the head of the renewed race. Although not all individuals received the gift of salvation, the race as an organic whole was saved through Him. In order to make the salvation rest upon an eternal foundation Christ as Mediator of the race and second Adam was viewed as being Himself in covenant with God. Salvation was never construed in Reformed circles as purely the work of the second person of Trinity become flesh. Rather, it was regarded as the work of the Triune God. To secure this construction they developed the idea of the eternal Covenant of Redemption, the parties to which were God the Father representing the Godhead and God the Son. Thus the whole work of redemption was grounded in the eternal and immutable divine counsel. It was further necessary to distinguish between the Covenant of Redemption and the decree of election which logically preceeded it. In the former the question of the manner in which electing grace was to be displayed had to be answered. Thus it was evident that the covenant motif could be carried through consistently. God, it was held, never revealed Himself and His purposes except in this covenant way. He was a God who approached individuals in their relationships to Him, the created order, and fellow-men. This especially was the approach taken by Westminster.

The covenant idea was also employed in connection with the doctrine of the church and the sacraments. The salvation merited by Christ for His people was viewed as applied to the hearts of His own by the special and irresistable operation of the Holy Spirit. In distinction from many of the sects, however, the Reformed regarded this application effected in connection with the use of the means of grace. This was not construed in any way which would impinge upon the sovereignty and omnipotence of God. The means were never regarded as effective per se. To bring about regeneration and renewal the direct and supernatural operation of the Spirit was necessary. But here again God, it was held, honored His creation ordinances by appealing to the human reason and conscience. In the Calvinistic theology the intimate relation between the covenant and the church was always maintained. The institutional church took its rise in the covenant which God had made with the believers and their children. These two classes alone constituted proper material for the church. All others, if they slipped in, had to be excluded by ecclesiastical censures and excommunication. Although the work of regeneration was not effected through the means, it was generally taught that it occurred in connection with the preaching of the gospel. The reason for this construction was that it alone secured the possibility of strengthening and developing spiritual life by the use of the administration of the

Word and Sacraments. The reason why the Reformed did not use the covenant idea in their church polity follows from their insistence on the monopleuric origin of the Covenant of Grace. Man has nothing to say about whether he is to be born within the covenant or not. Thus, although the covenant was basic to the idea of the instituted church and the intimate relation between the covenant and the church was expressed time and again by the theologians and in the creeds, it was never made the constitutive element of its polity.

Baptism as one of the means of grace was regarded as the sign and seal that the individual was in covenant with God and therefore had a right unto church fellowship. Both in the case of infants and adults the ground of baptism was not personal profession, as with the Anabaptists, but the covenant promises of God. This position was already taken by Calvin in the *Institutes*. Only in this way could the unity of infant and adult baptism be maintained. Otherwise the ground for baptism in the case of infants would differ from that in the case of adults. Thus Kramer says respecting Calvin's position, "Calvin finds occasion here in connection with infant baptism, now that he has taken the standpoint of the covenant, to draw the line farther. Up to this point he has not called attention to the fact that adults too are baptized according to the rule of the covenant. And therefore it might seem that there was a difference between the baptism of adults and that of children. The adults to be baptized on the ground of their faith, infants, on the ground of the covenant of God. No, the Reformer declares, the only rule according to which, and the legal ground on which, the Church may administer baptism, is the covenant. This is true in the case of adults as well as in the case of children. That the former must first make a confession of faith and conversion, is due to the fact that they are outside of the covenant. In order to be admitted into the communion of the covenant, they must first learn the requirements of the covenant, and then faith and conversion open the way to the covenant."[129]

The fifth use of the covenant idea in Reformed circles concerned the Christian life. The idea was here applied to the whole of the believer's life and experience. Thus although at the beginning it was somewhat restricted to the doctrine of the church and especially of the sacraments, soon the implications of the covenant conception for the whole of life became evident. The usual representation began with the eternal Covenant of Grace made by God with the elect sinner in Christ. This was once and for all established in and by the death of Christ on the cross as the climax of His redemptive work. Both active and passive obedience had their part, thus effecting for the elect a perfect and complete salvation. That work was subjectively applied by the indwelling of the Holy Spirit in the individual believer as a member of the true church. Since God in working out His plan of salvation in time chose to make use of the laws and relationships which were grounded in His own work of creation, the Holy Spirit worked in and through an institution and the means of grace entrusted to it. In this way the institution played a significant role in the life of the individual and received a large share of attention at the hands of Calvinistic theologians, quite in contrast to the sect type of Protestantism manifest among the Anabaptists.[130] Here the idea of the church as a society of experiential believers instead of as a divinely chosen group of believers and their children was dominant. In Calvinistic circles the life of the child began with the church. He received baptism as a sign and seal of the covenant relationship existing between God and himself at her hands. Although it was recognized that not all those who had received baptism in infancy would manifest saving grace in their adult life, it was believed that the baptized children before reaching maturity should be regarded in the judgment of charity as recipients of God's saving grace until the contrary became plainly evident. It is true that later on with the sad decline of spiritual and theological development in certain Reformed bodies throughout Europe this view underwent some modification and was even neglected if not denied. However, the above position was generally held. Those who did not go quite so far in applying the promises in the cases of the children individually nevertheless did maintain that God by and large took His people from and continued His church by bestowing saving grace to the covenant seed. Thus although numbers might fall away, the seed as a group was regarded as saved. All who received this sign and seal of grace were expected to acknowledge from their side their acceptance of this covenant relation when attaining maturity. This was done by a personal and public profession of their faith. When this was done, permission was given to attend upon the administration of the second sacrament, the Lord's Supper. By means of it especially Christ nourished the believers unto life everlasting, thus strengthening the bond of fellowship between Himself and them. Every celebration of that ordinance should serve to remind the believer of the eternal Covenant of Grace which God had been pleased to establish with him. The fact that believers and their children stood in a peculiar covenant relationship to God was taken to mean that they constituted His people in distinction from all others. In every way they were to regard themselves as separated unto His service. This had to be demonstrated in their lives by holy obedience unto the law which He had revealed unto them as the rule for their lives. Thus the doctrine of the covenant exerted a powerful influence in practical Christian life. It broadened the vision of those who accepted it, causing them to see that their entire life ought to be consecrated unto Christ and God. Thus the emphasis fell on covenant duty and responsibility. In these men, who stressed election, there was nevertheless a healthy disinclination towards passivity. However, instead of falling back into the Roman Catholic principle of righteousness through works, they stressed the fact that only the spiritual indwelling of Christ in the believer restored the image of God and thus led to good works. The covenant also became the ground of comfort and assurance of faith for the believers. Because they possessed the principle of grace which according to God's Word could not be lost, they felt that they rested upon an immutable and unshakeable foundation. This gave a spiritual stability to their lives which enabled them to face tremendous odds successfully. That they believed that God was on their side and would never fail them was not the fruit of spiritual pride but rather of humble acknowledgement of His saving grace through the covenant established with them in Christ.

Because of their basic principle that saving grace restored the creation of God, the Reformed could find a place for children in the church and strongly stressed religious education by the parents and officers of the church. In opposition to the Anabaptists the Reformed maintained that children had a place in God's plan of redemption, also as children. The difference between the two resolved itself quite largely into this, that whereas the latter made the objective aspect of Christ's saving work the more basic, the former stressed the subjective application of it. Among these then the personal response to the gospel of salvation was all-determinative. Since children as such could not join in this, there was no place for them in the instituted church. The others insisted that man's response to the offer of grace was preceded by God's plan and purpose. Thus the objective side was emphasized in such a way which allowed for the possibility of possessing grace in immaturity without being conscious of its presence. This was said to be the case with the children of believers as the seed of the promise. It was true that not all these children possessed or received grace. Some very evidently remained strangers to it. This brought up the question: How must the children of the church be regarded? Some held that in the judgment of charity all were to be considered heirs of the promise until the contrary became evident in their lives. In this group there were some who held that the elect among them were already regenerated before baptism, and that presumptive regeneration was to be held as the ground for baptism. Others however maintained that regeneration was not necessarily connected with baptism in this way. This gift could be bestowed either before, during, or after the administration of the sacrament. A milder answer to the original question was given by those who preferred to hold that out of the group of baptized children God was pleased to raise up a seed unto Himself.[131]

This widely-held Reformed position, that the children of believers were baptized on the basis of God's covenant promises, did not immediately secure for them all the privileges of church communion. They could neither take an active part in the government of the church nor partake of the second sacrament. These limitations, however, were not due in any way to a possible deficiency in the grace sealed unto them by baptism. Rather, here again God was said to honor the laws of natural development. Children were immature, and with this fact the church was bound to reckon. Faith, which was a gift of God in the moment of regeneration, had to become active before the child could appreciate the privileges of full communion. It could not be rightly expected that this faith-principle would be completely developed until a measure of natural maturity was attained. Since faith in God through Christ implied a sure knowledge of God and His promises as well as a hearty confidence that all personal sins, both original and actual, were forgiven for Christ's sake, it was necessary that the child learn to examine himself properly. Thus there was place for the subjective appropriation of the way of salvation also. In the doctrine of the Covenant of Grace both the objective and the subjective aspects of Christianity could come to their own. Thus before the child could become an active member of the church, enjoying all the privileges of membership, it was necessary that he make personal profession of his faith in the God of his baptism. This profession was then not to be regarded as a uniting with the church on his part, since this had already taken place before by virtue of the gracious act of God. Rather, it was a personal acknowledgment and recognition of this fact. The reason why the subjective element was not obscured is to be found in the fact that although the Reformed insisted that God was the sole author of the covenant, they also firmly believed that in its administration there were two aspects: first of all, that which

God promised and sealed to the believers, and secondly, that which the believer in turn owed to God. This latter was required only in accordance with the development of life. Thus much less was expected of the children in the way of assuming their responsibility of walking according to the demands of the covenant holiness than of the adults, although both were regarded as in full possession of the principle of saving grace. The reason why children were not allowed to partake of the Lord's Supper lay in the fact that they could not prove themselves and thus eat of the bread and drink of the wine in an acceptable manner according to the admonition of Paul in I Corinthians 11:28, 29. But as a child grew up within the covenant and the church, it was expected that he would grow spiritually too. Where this was not the case, sooner or later excommunication would be applied, since such an individual did not manifest the presence of divine grace. The implications of this theory for the religious education of children are very apparent. Although the child was considered prone to all manner of evil because of the presence of the principle of sin within him, he as a child of the covenant was also regarded as the recipient of divine grace. That principle of renewal would have to be developed, and this development consisted of nurture. This was done by a constant and consistent appeal to the reason and will of the child. Because of the principle of sin, there was a need for wholesome discipline and restraint. However, all his faculties having been inwardly renewed and quickened by the Holy Spirit in regeneration were to be developed and trained for the service of God, the Creator, Sovereign, and Savior of His people. Thus the doctrine of the Covenant of Grace in connection with the teaching on the place of children in the church was the basis upon which the Reformed believed in the continuity of the visible church. In this way they broke much more radically with the Roman Catholic position than did the Lutherans,[132] who based their faith on this score in the presence of grace in the means which had been entrusted to the church. To the Reformed God's promises were sufficient, and of these promises the sacraments were but signs and seals.

Upon the promise alone they based their hope that the children who had received the sacrament in accordance with the covenant demands of God would also enter into its fellowship consciously. Thus the church was not regarded as the institution in which the child has a place in order that he may be considered a hopeful candidate for receiving God's grace. Rather, he has a place in the institution because he possesses that grace either by virtue of promise or presence. In the church that principle of grace signified and sealed unto him by God in the sacrament receives a congenial atmosphere in which to develop.

The last way in which the Calvinists used the covenant motif was in their philosophy of history. Thus not only the life of the individual believer and the church was regarded as in this covenantal relationship but a much broader application was given to this conception. It was the basis for their view of the world and its history. They were convinced that God had created the universe for His own glory, and thus was maintaining it for the sake of the elect whom He had chosen as vessels of mercy. In and through them He was working out His eternal counsel of glorifying Himself in the revelation of His mercy and justice. In order that there might be a measure of continuity in that work of salvation God gave a place to the organic relationships of life, not only by comprehending the family in the covenant but also the larger group, the nation of Israel in the Old Testament dispensation especially. These Hebrews were viewed as the bearers of divine revelation. Through them God revealed His purposes unto the world. They constituted the covenant people in the national sense. This particular aspect was definitely temporal. The New Testament period is more glorious than the Old partly because in it the grace of God is extended far beyond national boundaries. However, all those whom God calls unto Himself out of every tribe and tongue and people and nation constitute His separate and peculiar people. They alone are in covenant with Him and possess His promises and assurances of grace. In them the principle of saving grace operates to realize the goal of a reborn and renewed human race. The highest goal of man is full fellowship with God. And this will not be realized until the final, eternal kingdom of glory becomes manifest at the end of the ages. That will constitute the most complete realization of the covenant bond between God and His own. In this way, then, the Reformed interpreted human history from Paradise lost to Paradise regained in the light of the covenant relationship.

Thus it was principally in connection with these seven major themes in theology that the covenant idea was applied. In the history of New England Congregationalism all of these questions were discussed at one time or another. And gradually as the emphasis was shifted, and some of these constructions were obscured or denied, the churches in that part of the new world lost their Calvinism.

Chapter 2.

The Covenant Idea Among the Anabaptists

ALTHOUGH the New England Congregationalists were directly indebted to the Calvinistic branch of the Reformation for their theology, they at the same time owed much of their unique emphasis to the Anabaptists. There was among the Puritans both in England and America far more intense individualism, a larger emphasis upon good works as the "signs" of election, and a more radical distinction between the sacred and the secular than was characteristic of those who followed Calvin more closely. Troeltsch in his description of Congregationalism states that the differences between it and the other branches of the Calvinistic Reformation were those of the sect-type contrasted with the church-type of Protestantism.[1] In another place he very definitely claims that they took over Baptist ideas especially in regard to the church covenant.[2]

In order to appreciate the dominant features of early Puritan religious life in America, it will be necessary to trace the debt which this group owed to the Anabaptists as the radical branch of the Reformation. This was especially twofold: first of all, the emphasis on the church covenant as the Scriptural mode of ecclesiastical organization, and secondly, the stress of voluntary membership in the covenant of those who measured up to the ideal of experiential Christianity.

Early Anabaptists

The second great movement in the Reformation to make use of the covenant idea and terminology was that of the Anabaptists. From the very earliest beginnings according to Champlin

63

Burrage these received a restricted usage among them. They seemed to be content with using the concept as a basis for their church polity. In the early years not one of them seems to have made a thorough study of the Scriptural use of the term as was done from time to time by the Calvinists. Because they felt the need of each other's help in their struggle against many adversaries they banded together in Christian brotherhoods. Burrage suggests that the use of the term covenant for such religious unions may even have preceded the days of the Protestant Reformation by a century or more.[3] Thus practical needs dictated the form of their organization more than anything else.

Among the Anabaptists the first to advocate the church covenant idea was Hans Locher, whose *Ein Tzeitlang geschwigner christlicher Bruder* appeared in 1523. It included the fundamental ideas of Anabaptist church polity. Those who belonged to the brotherhood had dedicated themselves in faith to the Lord's service, had pledged this visibly in baptism, and sought in consequence to avoid evil and do good.

By 1525 or 1526 the Anabaptists appeared as a more or less well-defined reformatory movement within the larger group. At a meeting held in Augsburg in 1526 they determined upon believers' baptism as the unique characteristic of their communion. Soon after Michael Sattler stressed the idea of the church as an organization of those only who had entered into voluntary covenant with each other. His book recorded the famous seven articles of Schlatt. Since they have been very significant for the development of the movement and have in the course of church history strongly influenced the Congregationalists in their church covenant idea they deserve mention here: 1—believers' baptism as the qualification for membership in the group; 2—local churches independent of each other; 3—all churches constituted only by baptized experiential believers; 4—unity of the members expressed by and in the Lord's Supper; 5—excommunication from the group as the sole weapon to enforce spiritual laws; 6—rejection of all "servitude of the flesh" as exemplified in Roman Catholic, Lutheran and Zwinglian church worship; 7—the state regarded as a necessary evil because of sin and therefore a sphere in which the believers have no place.[4] Throughout the emphasis fell on the Christian's call to absolute separation from the world.

The articles of Hans Hut show even more clearly the relationship in which the covenant idea stood to adult baptism and church membership according to Anabaptist ideals.[5] The personal pledge was also very strongly stressed by Balthasar Hubmaier in his *Von der briederlichen straff*, published at Nicolsburg in 1527.

Perhaps the most significant piece of evidence for the Anabaptist use of the church covenant idea is found in the confession of Jakob Kautzen and Wilhelm Reublin before the magistrates of Strassburg. After acknowledging the darkness in which they had formerly walked, these men affirmed, "But when God in His mercy and grace, through His Word, which He sent, called us from the Devil whose servants we were to himself, and from darkness, in which we sat, into his marvellous light, we were not unmindful of the heavenly message, but made a Covenant with God in our hearts, all the days by his strength to serve Him henceforth in holiness and to make known this our purpose to the covenant members. We have also by receiving water baptism had ourselves embodied into the body of which Christ is the head."[6] This statement is very important, because it emphasizes the act of the individual who by surrendering himself to Christ thereby becomes a member of the church. This radical insistence upon individualism and experientialism became very characteristic of the whole group.

The most violent antipaedobaptist of that time was the ill-fated Melchior Hoffman. He strongly stressed the covenant idea, especially in his *Die Ordonnantie Godts*. Hoffman insisted that all true disciples of Christ should break with Satan and the world and allow themselves to be joined to Christ by the "true covenant sign" which was believers' baptism.[7] The covenant relationship he conceived of was in terms of a marriage contract, the pledge of which was the Lord's Supper, which he compared with the wedding ring. Friedrich Otto zur Linden has made the claim that Hoffman was the first to teach "that the whole relation of man to God is consummated in the form of a covenant."[8] It should be noticed, however, that Zwingli made a similar statement at an early date, and that Bullinger not long afterward produced the first monograph on the subject. It seems more likely that Hoffman was indebted to the Strassburg Anabaptists for many of his ideas. There was in turn an intimate relation between this group, which Hoffman had joined in 1529, and the original group in Zurich with whom Zwingli had contended so heatedly. No doubt, both groups found the idea embedded in the Scriptures and made use of it, the Zwinglians to support their conception of the relation between the Old and New Testaments and the Anabaptists to reinforce the idea of a pure church of professing Christians united on a voluntary basis.

After the Munster tragedy of 1535 the Anabaptists went into temporary eclipse. Both Roman Catholics and Protestants were zealous in attempting to exterminate them. Those who escaped were widely scattered and because of an ineradicable tendency towards individualism became divided into several parties. Among these was the group of Mennonites which has preserved more of the characteristics of the original Anabaptists than any other.

Menno Simons, the leader, championed especially two doc-trines: 1—the need of regeneration, and 2—the gathering of a church which should be truly and completely the body of pro-fessing believers. By the beginning of the seventeenth century the idea of the church covenant was well defined and well formu-lated.[9] Burrage traces this to the connection of the Mennonites with previous Anabaptist principles and practices. Especially in Holland was this unique emphasis preserved. Both through the Dutch refugees who went to settle in England and the English refugees who sought a haven of safety in the Netherlands Ana-baptist ideas and ideals entered the stream of English Dissent.

Influence Upon English Dissent

Quite early the Dutch had begun to settle the low swampy land on England's east coast.[10] The section of Lincolnshire which they reclaimed from the sea they called Holland. Many of these early immigrants were weavers who settled in and around Norwich, which as a result soon became the second city in the kingdom. Here Wyclif had found his most numerous and powerful following. During the persecutions of the Protestants more than a century later a steady stream of refugees left the Netherlands. By 1560 it was estimated that more than ten thousand had come from Flanders alone since the accession of Philip II. Less than two years later this number was trebled. Various estimates as to the number present in England at the close of Alva's reign of terror have been made. Davies put the total at 100,000 heads of families. A much more conservative estimate is that of Green, who claims that at least 50,000 souls had made England their new home.[11] After the fall of Antwerp and the banishment of her sizeable Protestant population, one third of her merchants found a home in London. Among the English the Dutch soon gained a good reputation for honesty, industry, sobriety, and godliness. Although it would be impossible to demonstrate conclusively the impact which these groups made upon the religious life of their English neighbors, there can be no doubt but that their presence was one of the contributing factors towards making London and Norwich strongholds of English Puritanism and the lowlands about the Humber and the Wash hotbeds of non-conformity and separatism.[12] It must be remembered that the Protestantism of the Netherlands at that time was chiefly that of Menno Simons and his followers. When Menno died at Oldesloe in Holstein, he left behind "a band of men, which in 1561 had a mightier hold on the Lowlands than the Dutch Reformed Church."[13] Thus though Calvinistic principles were not unknown, the most pronounced type of Protestantism which the Dutch refugees took along with them was Anabaptism.

A much more direct source of influence upon the development of Puritanism and Separatism may be found in the migration of several English groups to the Netherlands. Although by this time many merchants had come over from the island, they did not profoundly affect the religious situation. The majority of these seem to have been in accord at least formally with the ecclesiastical order at home. However, there were others who fled persecution, and these were men of another stripe.

The first to aid in the new development of English Dissent in the direction of the Anabaptist emphasis on the church covenant was Robert Browne, generally referred to as the Father of Congregationalism.[14] He strongly opposed the parish system and hierarchy in the State Church and declared that "the kingdom off God Was not to be begun by whole parishes, but rather off the worthiest, Were they never so Fewe."[15] While at Middelburg in the Netherlands, whither he had fled in the fall of 1581, he penned three tracts by means of which he hoped to convert his countrymen to the Congregational polity.[16] These bore the titles *Booke which sheweth the Life and Manners of all true Christians, A Treatise upon the 23. of Matthewe,* and *A Treatise of Reformation without Tarying for Anie.* Although forbidden in England, they were widely disseminated especially among the poorer classes, and in 1583 John Coppin and Elias Thacker were hanged for their part in propagating these views.

In the first tract Browne made extensive use of the church covenant idea in developing his church polity.[17] It contains one hundred eighty five questions and answers. The doctrinal aspects present nothing new. In harmony with the usual Reformed teaching he treated the knowledge of God, his nature, attributes and providence, the fall of man and salvation through Christ. However, his view of the nature and government of the church was not at all like that of the Calvinistic Reformation. He insisted that the church is a voluntary association of those who have pledged themselves by covenant to lead a Christian life. The sacraments he regarded as seals of the conditions of the covenant. The covenant or condition on God's behalf, Browne claimed, included His promise to be our Savior, to be the God of our seed, and to bestow the gift of His spirit as an inward calling to the children of the church. The covenant or condition on man's behalf included a giving up of the children to God and a profession of allegiance to God and His laws.[18]

How much Browne owed to the Anabaptists is a much disputed question. Surely he did not reject infant baptism as they did. He plainly taught that God's covenant with man included the seed of the believers. However, his insistence upon the purity of the church, the necessity of strict discipline and the voluntary character of the covenant on our part were definitely in harmony with Anabaptist positions. In seeking an answer to this question Scheffer insists that Browne came closer to the Anabaptist position on the nature and government of the church than he was willing to admit, "lest he might, in addition to ever so many gibes be reproached with the appellation of 'Anabaptist.' "[19]

While sojourning in the Netherlands the Brownists made the acquaintance of the Mennonites. After the language barrier fell away, several of them united with Mennonite congregations in Amsterdam in spite of their difference on the validity of infant baptism. This difference was minimized by Ainsworth and his companions, who claimed that all baptism received at the hands of the English State Church was invalid. They insisted on their personal rebaptism not on the basis of their covenant relation but upon their personal profession of faith. That many of these men were in more sympathy with the position of the Mennonites than the Reformed is evident from the Matthew Slade incident.[20] When this man, who had been an elder in the Brownist congregation at Amsterdam, united himself with the Dutch Reformed Church, the members of the former congregation sent him a list of eleven articles stating why they disapproved of his transfer of membership. These were later published as *Articles against the French and Dutch by Francis Johnson.* The author claimed that the Reformed congregations were too large to be considered true churches, since the size prevented brotherly supervision of the members. Furthermore, the charge was made that the Dutch churches baptized children of non-members. Both of these practices conflicted with their pure church ideal, which was also upheld by the Mennonites.

Less than ten years later Henry Barrowe and John Greenwood published their *London Confession of* 1589. It dealt largely with church polity and aimed to set forth "a true description out of the Word of God of the visible church."[21] Its significance lies in the fact that it treated adult membership exclusively.[22] No mention is made of the Covenant of Grace and the relationship which the seed of believers sustains to God and the church.

The so-called *Second Confession of the London-Amsterdam Church* appeared in 1596. Quite distinct from the idealistic picture drawn in the other document, we find here a rather detailed treatment of several knotty problems in Congregational polity. The emphasis throughout is substantially identical with previous Separatistic writings, although the outlines are clearer. The officers are necessary not only for the careful supervision of adults but also for the training of the seed of the church in the Lord's ways.[23]

Anabaptism and the Pilgrim Fathers

Beside the early Brownist congregation and the church of Ainsworth and Johnson at Amsterdam other Separatists also came to the Netherlands. The best known of all these groups was the congregation of Scrooby. Their Congregationalism triumphed in New England some twenty five years later.

The early history of the group is obscure. About 1602 a certain John Smyth gathered at Gainsborough, half-way between York and Boston, a small congregation of Separatists. Nearby was the village of Scrooby, where there was also such a group. Their old teacher had been a certain Richard Clyfton. When John Robinson came to that neighborhood in 1606, he was appointed pastor. By this time Smyth, pastor of the neighboring church at

Gainsborough, had already left for Amsterdam. There he did not unite with the church of his former tutor, Francis Johnson, but established another English Separatist congregation. No doubt the reason for this lay in the large number of refugees who had come over during those years. Both churches lived side by side on friendliest terms. By the spring of 1608 the entire Scrooby congregation with its pastor also reached Amsterdam. About this time a heated controversy was raging among the brethren on the use of Bibles and prayer books, the value of the translated Scriptures, and especially the composition and authority of the consistories. Smyth had insisted that only the Hebrew and Greek originals could be considered the Word of God. Thus the originals had to be read in the services, then translated for the people, after which the exhortation could follow. Moreover, he claimed that the distinction between ruling and teaching elders was unbiblical. Soon afterward Smyth embraced the position of the Anabaptists, which cast yet more reproach on the Brownists. Joseph Hall used the opportunity to point out how Separatism consistently led to Anabaptism. "There is no remedy, you must go forward into Anabaptism, or come back to us; all your Rabbins cannot answer the charge of your rebaptized brother John Smyth: if we be a true church you must retain us; if not, you must rebaptize. If our baptism is good, then is our constitution good. He tells you true, your station is unsafe, either you must go forward to him or back to us."[24] Thus when Smyth baptized himself and gathered that group about him which must be regarded as the mother church of all English Baptists and their descendants, he demonstrated how close many of the positions taken by the Separatists bordered on those of the Anabaptists.

Because of their intimate relations with the other Separatists and their unwillingness to become party to the religious strife, the Scrooby folk under the leadership of Robinson moved to Leiden. Here the little church flourished and under the leadership of their able pastor laid the foundations for what was later to become American Congregationalism.

Robinson wrote several works on church polity. Because of social and economic pressure these Englishmen longed to settle in a place where the customs of the homeland could be practiced and its language freely spoken. Thus they determined to migrate once more, this time to America, where they hoped for complete religious liberty as well as an environment wherein their children could grow up as true sons and daughters of England. In order to settle in America they needed a charter. Realizing that they were in disfavor, Robinson and his people drew up the *Seven Articles* of 1617.[25] In it the position was defended that they had separated themselves from the English State Church but were in no way averse to cordial relations with other Reformed bodies. In the second note the authors stated their definite agreement with the doctrines and practices of the French Reformed churches. With the Dutch churches they agreed in doctrine but not in practice. Thus they declared, "We doe administer baptisme only to such infants as wherof ye one parente at least is of some church, which some of ther churches doe not observe; though in it our practice accords with their publick confession and ye judgments of ye most learned amongst them."[26]

The above statement and the *Mayflower Compact* are the only official declarations of the Pilgrim Fathers which have come down to us. The latter was in no wise a creed. However, it did prove that the Pilgrims realized the necessity of putting their Christian ideals into practice in social and political life. In that statement they committed themselves to the idea of the voluntary covenant. Walker claims that this was the result of their mild Barrowism or Congregationalism. Says he, "That system recognized as the constitutive act of a church a covenant individually entered into between each member, his brethren, and his God, pledging him to submit himself to all due ordinances and officers and seek the good of all his associates. In like manner this compact bound its signers to promote the general good and to yield obedience to such laws as the community should frame. The Separatist Pilgrims on the Mayflower constituted a state by individual-mutual covenant just as they had learned to constitute a church; and therefore the Mayflower Compact deserves a place among the creeds and covenants of Congregationalism."[27]

With this we can close our introductory survey. It has been demonstrated that the men who first settled New England were influenced by two widely divergent types of Protestant thought. Both used the covenant idea and terminology but in a vastly different way. Among the Anabaptists this was not directly drawn from Scriptures, although later on in attempting to reinforce their theories certain writers sought to relate them to Biblical teaching. The use of the covenant was limited to church government. The Reformed on the other hand made no direct use of the covenant idea in developing their church polity but made an exhaustive study of the Scriptural teachings and formulated their doctrinal theories in its light. The reason for this difference is deep rooted. The Anabaptists stressed individual piety and Christian practice. The Reformed stressed doctrinal conformity and strictly in harmony with this the Christian conduct. Thus the early settlers of New England were indebted to the Anabaptists for their conception of the church covenant and to the Reformed for their teaching on the Covenant of Grace and related subjects. The question challenging the Congregationalists was whether the two conceptions were homogeneous, and if not, which of them was to be victorious at the expense of the other.

Part Two

DEVELOPMENT OF THE COVENANT IDEA IN NEW ENGLAND THEOLOGY

Chapter 3.

The Early Puritan Conception of the Covenant

AMERICAN church history manifests a development which, when compared with that of other parts of the Christian world, is both unique and well-defined. Smith in his work on the subject summarizes this in an admirable way by mentioning the following leading characteristics, "First, it is not the history of the conversion of a new people, but of the transplanting of old races, already Christianized to a new theatre, comparatively untrammeled by institutions and traditions. Second, Independence of civil power. Third, The voluntary principle applied to the support of religious institutions. Fourth. Moral and ecclesiastical, but not civil power, the means of retaining the members of any communion. Fifth. Development of the Christian system in its practical and moral aspects rather than in its theoretical and theological. Sixth. Stricter discipline than is practicable where church and state are one. Seventh. Increase of the churches, to a considerable extent through *revivals* of religion, rather than by natural growth of children in an establishment. Eighth. Excessive multiplication of sects; and divisions on questions of moral reform."[1]

All these have played their part in the historic development of the churches of New England, where American ecclesiastical life has undergone perhaps its most significant changes. In studying the idea of the covenant the fifth, sixth and seventh characteristics mentioned by Smith will be amply substantiated, whereas several of the others will also become more or less apparent. It cannot be denied that of all the Protestant groups coming to America the Congregationalists showed the greatest degree of

77

willingness, if not eagerness, to pattern their ecclesiastical and civil life according to the system inherent in their cherished ideals. Among these, and the most comprehensive of them all, was the idea of the covenant by which all of life was to be related to and regulated by the revealed will of God. The ambition of these early pioneers was to establish in the wilderness a holy commonwealth in which the theocratic ideals would be realized as never before in the history of Christ's church.

Because this practical objective lay at the basis of their ambitions, they viewed the covenant not merely from the aspect of personal religious life but made it as well the foundation of their civil and ecclesiastical government. Thus in a general way the term "covenant" was used in three senses, which, though divergent from each other, were closely interwoven in the minds of the colonists.

The Covenant as a Civil Compact

The idea of the covenant was used first of all as the basis for the body politic. Realizing that in all things they stood under God's rule, the early settlers sought consciously to place His revealed will at the center of their lives. Thus the men of the Mayflower compacted among themselves with God for the establishment of the civil order in their colony.

In connection with this use of the covenant idea it ought to be stated at the outset that this constituted somewhat of a departure from the use to which it was put among the Separatists and Puritans in old England. Although in the mother country these men cherished and sought to realize the ideal of the holy commonwealth, it was not until they had freed themselves from the trammels of existing institutions, both civil and ecclesiastical, that they could apply their energies sufficiently in this direction. All of life was to be under the direct rule of God. And the Pilgrims, gripped by that lofty and comprehensive religious ideal, began their political history in America with a solemn agreement between themselves and God. The document has been recorded for us by William Bradford.[2] In it they affirm that the planting of their colony was undertaken for the glory of God and the advancement of Christianity as much as for the honor of king and country. The standard by which they would make laws was the benefit of the colonists in general. To seek the common welfare was pledged by all who signed the document, and all who did put their names to it did so voluntarily.

It has been quite generally affirmed, and not without some show of reason, that the political theory of the Pilgrims and Puritans was a development of Calvin's ideas practiced in Geneva.[3] Although large elements may be traced back to him, the theocratic development in New England has a history very definitely its own. In working out their ideas the colonists opposed vehemently the conceptions of Anglicans and Presbyterians, who championed the ideal of a state church. Although church and state were to be kept separate according to the best of the accepted theories, in practice this did not happen. Because the civil compact insisted on giving God His rightful place in all of life, the colonists could not easily separate religion from the supervision of the state. The theocratic ideal made close collaboration between them imperative in daily life. Thus the *Cambridge Platform,* although insisting, "As it is unlawful for church-officers to meddle with the sword of the Magistrate, so it is unlawful for the Magistrate to meddle with the work proper to church-officers,"[4] gave the civil authorities much influence in religious matters. The proponents of the *Platform* came dangerously near to a State Church with its consequent supervision of religious affairs by political officers, when they admitted, "It is the duty of the Magistrate, to take care of matters of religion, and to improve his civil authority for the observing of the duties commanded in the second table. They are called God's. The end of the Magistrate's office, is not only the quiet and peaceable life of the subject, in matters of righteousness and honesty, but also in matters of godliness, yea of all godliness."[5]

That the three usages of covenant terminology paralleled each other very closely is affirmed by Walker. "The Church Covenant gave form to the Covenant of Grace, and the Civil Covenant gave power to the Church Covenant."[6] In theory New England was a holy commonwealth dedicated unreservedly to carrying out the will of Almighty God. In this way much of the political theory of the Puritans was derived directly from the Old Testament. In fact, one of the most influential treatises on political organization, written by John Eliot of Roxbury on the subject of *Christian Commonwealth; or, The Civil Polity of the Rising Kingdom of Jesus Christ,* advocated the system of the Old Testament under God as the supreme Ruler and King.

Throughout the history of the colonies the covenant idea remained popular enough, so that for a time even towns were organized on this basis. As an example we may cite the case of Guilford, then called Menunkatuck. Their covenant drawn up when the settlers were on board their ship reads much like the Mayflower Compact in that all pledged themselves to seek the welfare of each other. The close relation between the civil compact and the church covenant in the minds of these early Puritans is evident from this document which mentions the "gathering together in a church way."[7]

The close relation between church and state, and thus between the two types of covenants, was further augmented in the Massachusetts Bay colony when the General Court of 1631 prescribed that the franchise would be limited to those who had entered the church covenant. Thus it was determined that "for the future no one shall be admitted to the freedom of the body politic, unless he be a member of some church within the limits of the same."[8] The same law was effective in the New Haven, where the theocratic ideal was more strictly adhered to than anywhere else in New England.[9] At the outset the leaders of that colony placed church and state on the same footing, in so far that the laws for both institutions had to be directly ordered by the Word of God. The compact in force there was even more distinctive than that of the Plymouth colony. Since Thomas

Hooker opposed any such limitation of the franchise in his Connecticut settlements, it can be understood that the men of New Haven violently opposed the union of the two western groups in 1664. To them it spelled the end of the holy commonwealth in covenant with the Lord of all the earth.

The Church-Covenant

The second usage of the covenant idea and terminology concerned the organization of the churches. It was the most radically Separatistic element which entered the colonies at the first, and its development and triumph have given to Congregationalism in New England its unique character.

The church at Plymouth, the first ecclesiastical organization in those parts, set the pattern which all the rest followed. Since the origin of its church life in America is shrouded in mystery and obscurity, it is necessary to trace some of the leading ideas of John Robinson, pastor and leader at Scrooby and Leiden, on this score. Although he never set foot in America, his ideas molded the polity of these congregations. From the very first he had been an ardent Separatist. In his first work of note, written about 1610 and entitled *Iustification of Separation from the Church of England. Against Mr. Richard Bernard his Invective, Intituled; The Separatists schisme,* he set out to prove the inconsistency and error in which they involved themselves who refused to break with the English State Church. It was a logical and clear treatment of the nature, functions and government of the church of Christ. His definition already reflected his whole attitude towards the question of Separatism. For him the church was "a company consisting though but of two or three separated from the world whither unchristian, or antichristian, and gathered into the name of Christ by a covenant made to walk in all the wayes of God knowen unto them." This body also "hath all the power of Christ."[10] He stressed unity in the Christian walk of life rather than conformity in doctrine. The basic conception of the covenant was that of voluntary agreement, which could be entered by any who desired to separate himself from the world. Each of these covenanting companies was regarded as wholly independent of the other.

Robinson did not emphasize creedal agreement in the church. In fact, he was inclined to minimize it in the light of his emphasis upon Christian conduct. Doctrine according to him could easily be a hindrance to Christian development. In his farewell message to the departing Pilgrims, he deplored the unwillingness of many Lutherans and Calvinists to go beyond the very words of their early leaders. "A misery much to bee lamented; For though they were precious shining lights in their times, yet God hath not revealed his whole will to them."[11] Therefore he admonished the departing brethren to receive only "whatsoever light or truth shall be made known to them from his written word." This emphasis on the Bible, almost to the exclusion of written creeds, came to be a prominent characteristic of the New England churches. It bears out the fact that the colonists were more interested in the practical than the theological aspects of the Christian religion, an emphasis easily traced in their development of the covenant idea.[12]

With the coming of the Puritans to the shores of Massachusetts the colonization of New England began in earnest. Instead of being a mere handful of immigrants strengthened only at rare intervals, in the new group there was found a strength of numbers never paralleled in the colonial history of America. Yet though their strength far exceeded the Pilgrim Fathers numerically, the latter were to influence them profoundly and give direction to their church polity. Doctrinally the two groups were homogeneous. Both were Calvinists of a rather pronounced type and accepted the Bible as normative for faith and practice. However, in their views of church constitution they differed widely at first. The Pilgrims firmly believed in separating themselves from the Established Church of England because of its many corrupt practices. To them membership in that institution was tantamount to a denial of the call to separation which came to every true Christian. The Puritans on the other hand would remain with the Establishment and sought in this way by their united influence to reform it from within. They remembered that during the stormy religious history of the sixteenth century the constitution and liturgy had been altered radically at least four times. Thus they looked hopefully for another period of reform and refused to take the pessimistic view of that church held by the Separatists. In spite of the reverses suffered since the accession of James I in 1603 and the elevation of Laud to the bishopric of London by Charles I in 1628 those who migrated to America as Puritans were by no means ready and willing to break with the church. Their sole aim was to escape the power of the ecclesiastical courts and the High Church bishops and settle in a place where they might with impunity discard such liturgical elements of the English State Church services as they considered superfluous or superstitious. Yet the Puritans before many years had elapsed also separated themselves and began their own church life in America.

The first permanent settlement made by the Puritans was at Salem. They arrived late in June of 1629 and by the twentieth of July had formulated and agreed upon a church covenant. Herein they did not regard themselves as separated from the English Church. Rather they viewed their church life as bound by every legitimate tie to the church in the mother country. Before a year passed, however, Salem had become pronouncedly Separatistic in its tendencies. The radical change becomes apparent already in the episode involving Winthrop, Johnson, Dudley and Coddington, whose request to partake of the sacrament of the Lord's Supper with the congregation was refused. The. Rev. Mr. Skelton also refused to baptize the child of Coddington, who had been born during the passage from England. This strange attitude evoked much criticism. Even John Cotton, soon to become the foremost minister in New England, wrote from his home in old England reprimanding Skelton. The reason adduced by the pastor for this strange action was that none of the men were members of any particular Reformed congregation, even though they were members in good standing in the Church of England. Cotton claimed that "it added wonder to my grief" upon hearing that Skelton was willing on the other hand to welcome to communion a member of Mr. Lathrop's Separatistic congregation in Southwark. Salem's move in the Separatistic direction was repeated in several other quarters.

The development of the covenants at Salem gives a good picture of what became the general practice among New England Congregationalists relative to their church covenants. At the time of organization a brief and simple statement was accepted by all. It read: "We covenant with the Lord and with one another, and doe bynd ourselves in the presence of God, to walke together in all his waies, according as he is pleased to reveale himself unto us in his Blessed word of truth."[13] This was deemed sufficient to meet the demands of the times. On doctrinal matters there was complete uniformity. The statement should not be construed to mean the exclusion of doctrine from the life of the church. On the contrary, all who desired to unite with the Salem group on the basis of church covenant were examined regarding "knowledge in the principles of religion and their experience in the wayes of grace, and of their godly conversation amongst men."[14] Only such who could meet these three demands were adjudged fit members of the church. Thus a large number of the colonists, even at the beginning, had no place within the church covenant.

The early years of Salem's history were filled with contention and strife. Especially the coming and going of Roger Williams left the congregation in a distracted state. However, under the able leadership of Hugh Peters the church took on new life and increased in numbers. One of his first acts was to lead the church to a solemn renewal of the covenant of 1629. This was enlarged greatly by nine new articles dealing more or less with questions which had arisen in connection with the disturbances occasioned by Williams. The opening words are very characteristic and give a pattern widely followed, "Wee whose names are here under written, members of the present church of Christ in Salem, having found by sad experience how dangerous it is to sitt loose to the Covenant wee made with our God; and how apt wee are to wander into bypathes, even to the looseing of our first aimes in entring into Church fellowship: Doe therefore solemnly . . . . renewe that church Covenant we find this Church bound unto."[15] Doctrinal issues had not yet arisen to any significant degree. However, during the long ministry of Edward Norris the Quakers came to disturb the peace with their ideas. Thus when John Higginson became pastor the covenant was again renewed and a new article was added in which the members pledged themselves "to take heed and beware of the doctrine of the Quakers."[16]

A much more significant addition was made in 1665, when the congregation definitely committed itself to the Half-way Covenant practice. Higginson ardently advocated the new theory by which he supposed the influence of the church would be greatly extended among the colonists. It declared that all baptized members were members in the covenant fellowship of the visible institution. When the church was ready to declare that all baptized members could claim that same rite for their offspring, Higginson prepared his *Direction for a publick Profession in the Church Assembly after private examination by the Elders.*[17] The work was patterned after the Westminster Catechism and embodied the type of Calvinistic thought current in all of New England at that time.[18]

The Charlestown-Boston covenant is also very significant. It consisted of a very simple statement of desire to unite as a congregation under Christ the Head of the Church.[19] A creedal basis is entirely wanting, and the colonists pledged themselves doctrinally only in so far as the "Rule of the Gospell" and "His holy Ordinaunces" required.

From this it is evident that the settlers made much use of the church-covenant. The emphasis fell almost exclusively on the believer's voluntary acceptance of the promises of God. The objective basis of spiritual life in the church was not clearly perceived and therefore neglected. The new emphasis on the Separatistic ideal with its demand for conscious spiritual experience as requisite to church membership led the early settlers to champion the "pure church" ideal, which would limit membership to the consciously regenerate. Without a doubt this more than anything else caused them to lose sight of the distinctive relation in which children of covenanting parents stood to the visible church. This led to a heated controversy soon after the settlement of America between the Puritan leaders in the old and the new world on the question of the Scriptural basis and necessity of church covenants. Among large numbers in the homeland the idea was never very popular. Many could find no Scriptural warrant for Robert Browne's contentions and attacked them vigorously. In 1634 John Cotton wrote his *Questions and Answers upon Church Government* to defend the idea and practice. One of the objections was that the New England churches sealed these covenants with unnecessary oaths. To this charge Cotton replied in his *Defence of the Answers made unto the Nine Questions or Positions, sent from New England.*[20] The English Puritans also feared that their brethren in America would insist that church covenant was indispensable to the organization of the true church of Christ. Therefore in 1637 they sent a letter requesting the opinion of the ministers of New England on their position. By the time Richard Mather wrote *An Apologie of the Churches in New England for Church-Covenant* the idea and practice became more general in England also. However, it never gained the wide-spread popularity there which it attained in the new world. The appearance of Thomas Hooker's *A Survey of the Summe of Church-Discipline* marked the triumph of Congregational polity in the colonies. By that time the Anabaptist "pure church" ideal together with the emphasis on the voluntary church covenant were almost universally accepted in New England.

The Doctrine of the Covenant of Grace

In the third place the New England Puritans used the covenant idea in their construction of a theological system. The idea of the Covenant of Grace they carried over with them from England. This doctrinal emphasis was largely in accord with the line of development from Calvin through Amesius (Ames), whose *Medulla S. S. Theologiae* was very popular among the preachers. Such men as Richard Baxter and John Owen were widely read, and the ideas of Turretin and Herman Witsius were highly recommended during the history of the churches. The last had published his views in 1677 under the title *De oeconomia foederum Dei,* which was translated into English at an early date and served as one of the chief theological texts for students preparing for the ministry.

Although the idea of the Covenant of Grace was often referred to and used, there was from the beginning no unanimity of opinion on several of the practical aspects of the doctrine. In fact the disagreement gave rise to the Half-way Covenant theory and practice. On the main issues there was agreement, especially since the Synod of 1646-1648 adopted the Westminster symbols with the exception of those parts which dealt with church polity. Instead of referring to scattered references in the works of several New England ministers, we shall consider the views of one of the most representative as well as influential men of that period. Since his conception of the Covenant of Grace was similar to that championed by most of his contemporaries, it may well serve us as a guide.

Of all the men of the first generation in America none wrote more profusely on the Covenant of Grace and its implications for the Christian life than John Cotton. Especially three of his treatises call for our attention. The first appeared in 1645 under the title *The Covenant of God's free Grace, most sweetly unfolded, and comfortably applied to a disquieted soul, from that text of 2 Sam. 23, ver. 5.* In it he approached the covenant as a source of comfort for the child of God. It alone could give support in "tempestuous stormes arising from Satan and the world without, or the distempers of their own hearts within."[21] It was in reality a sermon stressing that though David and his house failed in their covenant obligations, God's covenant endured forever with them. In developing the idea of the eternity of the covenant Cotton did not stress the basis of the promises as much as its administration among men. Thus he also contrasted the Covenant of Grace with the Covenant of Works.[22]

Not long afterward he wrote a second treatise on the same subject, this time considering the position occupied by children of believing parents. It arose out of a discussion with a son of former parishioners of his in Lincolnshire, England, who had fallen in with some who denied the validity of infant baptism. In this book, *The Grounds and Ends of the Baptisme of the Children of the Faithfull,* Cotton advanced the usual arguments though some were presented in an unique way. Christ, he claimed, commanded infant baptism, because children of believers were His "disciples." In considering the place of infants in the covenant the question was bound to arise: In how far do those who later apostatize from God share in the blessings and promises of the covenant? In line with this was the further question, How can anyone maintain both the doctrine of the perseverance of the saints and the immutability of the covenant and the position that the covenant can also be broken? Cotton realized at once the necessity of distinguishing in some way between two types of covenant membership. "There is a double state of grace, one adherent, (which some not unfitly call federall grace) sanctifying to the purifying of the flesh, Hebr. 9:13, another inherent, sanctifying the inner man. And of this latter there be two sorts, one, wherein persons in Covenant are sanctified by common graces which make them serviceable and useful in their callings, as Saul, Jehu, Judas, and Demas, and such like hypocrites. Another whereby persons in Covenant are sanctified unto union and communion with Christ and his members in a way of regeneration and salvation. In respect of adherent or federal grace, all children of a believing parent are holy, and so in an estate of grace. In respect of inherent common graces, Saul, Jehu, and Judas, and Demas were sanctified of God unto their several callings for the service of his peoples, as Apostates may be, Hebr. 10:29. Now there is no doubt but men may fall away from adherent federal grace, as also from inherent common graces; and yet without any prejudice to the perseverance of sincere believers . . ."[23] He maintains however that all are received into the formal relationship and are bound by God to yield themselves to Him and use the means of grace "so they might come to enjoy the sure mercies of the Covenant."[24] The blessings are promised to all but effectually bestowed upon the spiritual seed only. However, when the carnal seed "falls short of the grace of God" this proceeds not "from defect of the Covenant, but from their prophane refusall of it."[25] The weakness lay in Cotton's inability to give any assurances that God's promises would be fulfilled on the basis of His own Word. Thus parents and ministers lived in doubt as to the spiritual state of children until these came to profession of Christian experience.

In further explaining the position of children Cotton held, "We doe not say, that the children of believers are holy with that holinesse which accompanyeth regeneration, and mortifieth originall corruption, but onely with that holinesse whereby they are admitted to the means of grace, with promise of efficacy to the elect seed, and offers thereof to the rest, so farre as to leave them without excuse."[26] The mischief was, of course, begun. Cotton realized the problem which he was facing. Thus he felt that he could not give substantial value to God's covenant promise to the infants of believing parents, unless he could qualify them further as "elect seed." Knowing on the basis of experience and the Scriptures that not all baptized children later gave evidence of subjectively possessing the grace of God, he emasculated the significance of the promise until the fruits of election would manifest themselves in the later lives of the children.

This also accounts for the approach taken by him in his well-known *Spiritual Milk for Babes, Drawn out of the Breasts of*

Both Testaments.[27] It was a catechism for the youth written with the express purpose of providing spiritual nutriment for the children as they were learning to read. All agreed that the covenant promises might afford a ground of comfort and hope to adults who were experiential believers. However, these same promises were never valued as giving an objective ground of hope for their children. This is evident from some of the verses included for the edification of young Puritans. Of what comfort could the covenant position be, when such verses were included as the following?

> *"There is a dreadful fiery hell,*
> *Where wicked ones must always dwell;*
> *There is a heaven full of joy,*
> *Where goodly ones must always stay;*
> *To one of these my soul must fly*
> *As in a moment, when I die."*[28]

The high ideal was to awaken powerful religious convictions and experiences in children at a tender age. Not realizing that there is a parallel between nature and grace evident in the maturing of children within the covenant, Cotton and others with him looked for these adult experiences. Therefore they taught the youth:

> *"In the burying place may see*
> *Graves shorter there than I.*
> *From death's arrest no age is free*
> *Young children too must die:*
> *My God may such an awful sight*
> *Awakening be to me."*

There followed the familiar rhymed Dialogue between *Christ, Youth, and the Devil,* in which death was pictured as taking hold of the sinful and terrified child. Nearly always was the morbid side of religion in evidence. In the children's catechisms very little if any of the joy in Christ was found. The preachers thought it their God-given responsibility to frighten children, supposedly in gracious covenant with God, into religious enthusiasm.

Several of Cotton's works were published posthumously. One of the more important was *The Covenant of Grace*, which was later enlarged from his notes and published under the title *A Treatise of the Covenant of Grace*. Of all his works it is the most complete and systematic presentation of the material. In it he sought to give a fundamental interpretation of religious life from the aspect of man's covenant relationship to God. He approached the Covenant of Grace from its ideal form. Three contentions are elaborated as the main theses: 1—God gave Himself unto Abraham as the chief end of the Covenant of Grace; 2—God received Abraham and his seed, both physical and spiritual, as His peculiar people; 3—The Mediator and Surety of this Covenant is Christ through Whom and in Whom the covenant is realized.

Cotton affirmed that when God gave Himself, He gave everything. "All the creatures of God must stoop unto the people of God, when He is in covenant with them."[29] On this basis the whole structure of the spiritual aristocracy of New England with its insistence on the holy commonwealth could be raised. Although there were "conditions," these in no way vitiated the gracious character of the covenant, for "the Lord doth undertake both His own and our parts."[30] The distinction between the Covenant of Works and the Covenant of Grace was not always clearly made. Sometimes the former was identified with Sinai. As champion of pure Calvinism against Arminianism he countered the theory of election on the basis of foreseen faith as really an attempt to secure salvation by some Covenant of Works. However, God did ordinarily bring people first under some such Covenant of Works, he maintained, in order that he might terrify men's souls "with a sense of their palpable wickedness."[31]

Cotton insisted that the true Christian never rested upon his own imperfect faith but only in the Lord Himself. Even the promises were only an approach to God in Christ.[32] This question was raised especially during the disputes with Anne Hutchinson. On this score some suspected Cotton of a type of Antinomianism.

In regard to the position of infants as seed of the covenant Cotton elaborated greatly. He did not feel free to support the contention of Peter Martyr, "If they die when they are Infants they are certainly saved."[33] However, he did grant that they were in some sense holy and thus in covenant with God.

In the third branch the author took up the subject of Christ as Mediator and Surety of the covenant. According to him there is no way for us to make ourselves acceptable to God. We can neither place nor maintain ourselves in communion with Him. This is the function or office of Christ. Thus Cotton affirmed, "Therefore know that in all the duties you perform, you must, as it were, be dressing a meal for Jesus Christ, and be content to feed *after him,* and *upon him,* who is the *beginner* and *maintainer* of the covenant for us; and will perfect all the powerful blessing of it, in us and for us, in his own time."[34]

Cotton's conception reveals both the strength and the weakness of the usual Puritan construction of this doctrine. Coming from an environment in which the State Church theory was accepted and much of religion had degenerated into a merely formal relation to the church and its ordinances, the Puritans stressed by way of reaction the personal experience and appropriation of grace. Cotton more than many others was true to the idea of the sovereignty of God in the work of salvation as administered in the Covenant of Grace. Very positively he and others rejected any compromise by which man would be urged to place himself in some convenient way to receive eternal life as the highest good. Their deeply spiritual experience of the grace of God through Christ had caused the Puritans to forsake their homeland and enabled them to endure with a fortitude born of unshakeable confidence in the providence of God the disappointments and tribulations of the early years of colonization in a howling wilderness. The reality of God's presence and the conviction that they were His chosen succoured and sustained them. Without that dynamic faith they could never have planted, as they did, the Christian church and community on the bleak shores of New England.

However, the weakness of the Puritan position, best exemplified in Cotton, may not be overlooked. It was the weakness of one-sided emphasis rather than of positive error. Throughout his works, as well as those of others, the significance of the covenant promise of God as an objective reality was forgotten in an eagerness to stress the personal experience of comfort and joy in the Lord. Lest they should fall into the error of the homeland, they sought to discover who were in the covenant by virtue of election. Not perceiving clearly enough its historical manifestation, these men virtually pledged themselves at the outset to a double standard of membership within the visible church. The development of this theory became the history of much of New England Congregationalism during the two centuries following the death of Cotton.

Chapter 4.

The Beginnings of Change

NEW ENGLAND'S original uniformity in matters of doctrine did not maintain itself for a long period. Several factors contributed significantly to the undermining of the original ideas of the founders, not the least of which were the growing number of enthusiastic dissenters and the decline of fervent personal religion among the second and third generation colonists. These two factors together with the inconsistency which the Pilgrims and Puritans manifested in championing the Reformed faith while upholding the Separatist church ideal, caused them to modify their original ideas on the Covenant of Grace and its relation to personal piety and church government.

In the Puritan colony of Massachusetts Bay, which far exceeded that of Plymouth in numbers, wealth and influence, these divergences of religious thought first became evident. That settlement was by no means a democracy, the very thought of which was abhorrent to such men as John Cotton and Governor Winthrop. Within their "holy commonwealth" they aimed at religious uniformity of the most rigid sort.[1] Thus one of the ministers in an election sermon said, "'Tis Satan's policy to plead for an indefinite and boundless toleration." Another declared, "All familists, Antinomians, Anabaptists, and other Enthusiasts shall have free liberty to keepe away from us."[2] However, the dissenters, despite to vigilance of civil and ecclesiastical authorities, refused to take this "free liberty" and very early came in numbers sufficient to disturb the peace of the churches.

Early Controversies and the Covenant

The first enthusiastic dissenter was Roger Williams, an ardent opponent of the liturgy and hierarchy of the English State Church. His Separatism became evident immediately upon his arrival in Boston, when he refused to become the teacher of that church on the grounds that he "durst not officiate to an unseparated people."[3] His strong denunciations of the semi-Separatism of the churches involved him into trouble which finally led to his banishment. After having left Boston and Plymouth, he came to Salem for a second time. This led to his banishment in 1634.

The reason why the Massachusetts General Court banished him was a double one. His views on the unscripturalness of infant baptism conflicted with those of the majority. Moreover, his emphasis on full religious liberty threatened the foundations of the theocracy. To deny infant baptism in New England went hand in hand with insisting upon toleration. By separating the children from the church, it subverted the ideals of the early colonists of a life ordered in all things by God's covenant. This was expressed in a letter of the Rev. Thomas Cobbet of Lynn to Increase Mather, "And I add theyr very principle of makeing infant Baptism a nullity, it doth make at once all our churches, & our religious Civill State and polity, and all officers and members thereof to be unbaptized & to bee no Christians & so our churches to bee no churches; and so we have no regular powers to choose Deputies for any General Court, nor to choose any Magistrate."[4] The significance of Williams for the development of the covenant idea is rather negligible. He did not adopt the rigid form of Anabaptism until he removed to Rhode Island. However, his protest against the holy commonwealth struck at the very heart of the New England covenant idea which underlay all authority in church and state.[5]

Before the case of Roger Williams was settled, Boston found itself embroiled in another controversy. This was led by Anne Hutchinson, a woman of no mean ability. The two fundamental issues in the conflict, which was popularly called the struggle with the Antinomians, are stated by Welde in his *A Short Story of the Rise, Reign, and Ruine of the Antinomians*. They were 1—the doctrine of the indwelling of the Holy Spirit in the heart of the believer, and 2—the assurance of justification apart from good works. The believer, Mrs. Hutchinson held, was in immediate personal union with the Holy Spirit. Therefore the consciousness of being a child of God depended in no way upon the presence of good works as the fruit of faith. The consciousness of justification was sufficient. Thus a person might be assured of his salvation and share in the Covenant of Grace while still living in a state of sin. On this basis she distinguished between the Covenant of Works and the Covenant of Grace. Those who argued for the existence of assurance of faith from the betterment of morals, delight in divine worship, or anything short of conscious union with God through the indwelling Spirit were said to rest upon a Covenant of Works. To those in the Covenant of Grace these matters were worse than useless. Immediate and infallible testimony of the Spirit within the heart was alone of value.[6]

Because the early Puritans stressed the necessity of self-examination, Anne Hutchinson found a fertile field for her ideas in Boston. Since not all in the visible church could be regarded as possessing a saving position in the Covenant of Grace, it was incumbent upon all to look for the evidences of regeneration. Most Puritans took the position that such assurance was grounded upon the lively exercise of personal faith bearing the fruit of good works. Mrs. Hutchinson wanted only the "powerful application of a promise by the Spirit of God." So far did the advocates of this position go, that they urged the excommunication of all who were not ready to renounce entirely sanctification as evidence of their good state before God.

Not until the party of Mrs. Hutchinson became involved in the intricacies of colonial politics were the theories opposed. The election of Sir Henry Vane to the governorship provoked the quarrel, since it gave the others opportunity for criticizing him as one who held to the new theories. Towards the close of 1636 the strife became public, and Mrs. Hutchinson had the temerity to declare that all the ministers of the colony with the exception of John Cotton and John Wheelwright were under the Covenant of Works, not having received the "seal" or "second blessing." Wheelwright went so far as to denounce all under the Covenant of Works as "antichrists." When the leader refused to retract her position and sought to support herself by laying claim to divine revelation, the Court sentenced her to banishment. The group then settled Newport in Rhode Island, whence many of their Anabaptist sentiments filtered into Massachusetts Bay, much to the chagrin of the authorities.

At the Ministerial Convention of 1637 the four major points of the controversy were discussed: 1—the order of things in our union with Christ; 2—the influence of our faith in the application of His righteousness; 3—the use of sanctification in evidencing our justification; and 4—the consideration of the Lord Jesus Christ by men yet under a "covenant of works."[7] The whole discussion set the pattern for self-examination by members of the church-covenant as to whether they had part in the true Covenant of Grace. By far the great majority of ministers and colonists, especially after this controversy, stressed the subjective and personal side of the gospel at the expense of the objective.

The most influential opponents of Congregational doctrine and polity were the ever-present Baptists. They sought to develop more consistently the positions which they found within the churches themselves. The ministers feared them very much, however, since they viewed Anabaptism in the light of the Munster tragedy with its revolution, antinomianism and anarchy. They were further convinced that all who repudiated infant baptism and refused to take oaths sought to undermine the whole social order. And since this was often accompanied by a denial of the right of the state to judge in religious matters, the leaders of the colony felt that God required them to banish such impious heretics.

The hotbed of Antipaedobaptist principles was historic Salem, which had witnessed more than its share of religious dissension and conflict. Roger Williams had stayed long enough to sow the seed of his convictions. Lady Deborah Moody and her followers, people of similar ideas, came from that town.[8] Its court arraigned William Witter in 1644 for having declared infant baptism to be "a badge of the whore." He was later whipped "for saying that they who stay whiles a child is baptized doe worshipp the dyvell." What Salem was to Massachusetts Bay, Scituate was to Plymouth colony. There several insisted upon immersion as the only valid mode of baptism. Not long after the settling of Rhode Island there were rebaptisms in Seekonk, later called Rehoboth, in the colony of Plymouth. Yet in spite of all the opposition the Anabaptists throve.

At no time was the ever-recurrent danger of Anabaptism more forcibly impressed on the minds of the Congregationalists than at the defection of Henry Dunster, first president of Harvard. The significance of the story for us lies in the fact that now for the first time the Puritans admitted the seeming inconsistency of maintaining a Reformed body of theology and a Separatist theory of church polity. Dunster insisted that only visible believers should be baptized. John Norton agreed, only to add in the same breath ". . . . but (we) say infants of believing parents in church-state are visible believers."[9] Only in this way could they uphold infant baptism and the pure church ideal at the same time. However, this position virtually repudiated the position that children were entitled to baptism by virtue of the covenant promises. Thus it became increasingly clear that the leaders were ready to straddle the fence to maintain their two incompatible ideals of a pure church and a holy commonwealth.

A much more doctrinal dispute was occasioned by the appearance of William Pynchon's *The Meritorious Price of Our Redemption.* He openly repudiated the accepted substitutionary theory of the atonement and taught that Christ's death was a "chastisement."[10] Neither was there any imputation of Adam's guilt to all men and Christ's merits to the elect. He championed the theory that every man faced the problem of sin and obedience to God personally. John Norton sought to reply to this attack in his *Discussion of that Great Point in Divinity, the Sufferings of Christ*. He maintained "That the Lord Jesus Christ, as God-man, and Mediator, according to the will of the Father, and his own voluntary consent, fully obeyed the law, . . . in a way of obedient satisfaction unto divine justice, thereby exactly fulfilling the first covenant."[11]

Although Norton was in harmony with the majority of Reformed theologians, Richard Baxter in his *Aphorisms of Justification* declared that Norton "corrupted Christianity" by stressing the covenant idea in his defense against Pynchon. The majority in England and New England, however, agreed with Norton. The difficulty was that too often Adam was regarded as merely "the father of the human race" and "the root of mankind."[12] In this way the physical relationship was made determinative. Charles Chauncy in his twenty six sermons on justification also stressed this to the neglect of the idea that Adam was also head of the Covenant of Works. This emphasis on physical descent rather than on representative relationship was later carried through by Jonathan Edwards in his theories concerning the sinfulness of the human race. Thus the problem of the pollution of sin easily overshadowed that of its guilt. The net result was that the Satisfaction theory of the Atonement, so intimately bound up with the covenant conception, could later on be exchanged for the Governmental theory.[13]

The Problem of the Unbaptized Children

Another cause for the shift in emphasis was caused by the debate on the subjects of baptism. Very early in the history of the colony there was a tendency to restrict the administration of that sacrament. In an effort to preserve the purity of the church and to develop it along the lines of Separatism, Skelton at Salem refused to baptize the child of Coddington who was not a member of a Separatist church. Although the incident together with the rebuke of John Cotton exerted no direct influence upon the development of the covenant idea, it did signal the power of the pure church ideal. This was further demonstrated by the many restrictions placed upon adults who otherwise might have found their way to full membership in the churches. Without exception the churches demanded not only a credible profession of faith and a godly life but also insisted upon a clear statement of Christian experiences. This latter was a sine qua non for the visible believer. Thus the leaders virtually raised to a normative level the Christian experience of those who had undergone persecution for the sake of their faith. It was not long before this standard became unattainable for the generation which had not tasted the bitterness of religious persecution and hence had not been strengthened in their convictions by such fiery trials. When these grew up and married, a grave problem faced the churches. Their children could not be baptized, because they had not entered into voluntary church-covenant. And they could not enter that church-covenant for themselves, because they could not enter that church-covenant for themselves, because they could not attain to the high level of spiritual experience which the church authorities demanded. Hence the question arose whether these children might be baptized, in spite of the seeming lack of faith and experience on the part of their parents. If not, then the ideal of the holy commonwealth could never be realized.

The first recorded case of this sort appeared in the Dorchester church. There a grandfather appeared before the elders to request baptism for his grandchild on the grounds that the parents of said child were not able to make the required profession. The elders referred the matter to the Boston congregation and its officers for advice. The case was publicly debated, and the decision favored acceding to the request. The reason was stated by John Cotton and the two ruling elders of the church, Oliver and Leverett, in a letter to the sister congregation. "Though the child be unclean where both parents are Pagans and Infidels, yet we may not account such Parents for Pagans and Infidels, who are themselves baptized, and profess their belief of the

Fundamintal Articles of the Christian Faith, and live without notorious Scandalous Crime, though they give not clear evidence of their regenerate estate, nor are convinced of the necessity of Church Covenant . . . We do therefore profess it to be the judgement of our church . . . that the Grandfather a member of the Church, may claim the privilege of Baptisme to his Grand-Child, though his next Seed the Parents of the Child be not received themselves into Church Covenant."[14] When the grandfather assumed responsibility for the nurture of the child, it was baptized, and New England was on the road to making profound changes in its conception of the covenant and the church.

These ideas, championed by John Cotton, were in the main adhered to by the early ministry. However, it took several decades for them to crystalize into a definite theory and practice. To the end of his life Cotton championed the right of baptized but noncovenanting parents to demand the sacrament for their offspring. "Though they be not fit to make such profession of visible faith, as to admit them to the Lord's Table, yet they may make profession full enough to receive them to Baptisme."[15] Here lie the roots of the breakdown of the antithesis between the regenerate and the unregenerate. The two sacraments were definitely divorced from each other. This modified idea began to spread through the colony, so that Thomas Allen of Charlestown advocated the extension of the rite and George Philips of Watertown argued more positively for the abiding church membership of all descendants of covenanting parents. Richard Mather went so far as to state, that as long as those parents "do neither renounce the Covenant, nor doth the Church see just Cause to cast them out from the same."[16]

The consequences of this open defense of the new way by John Cotton and the Boston elders were twofold: first of all, because of differences of opinion several conferences and a synod were convened, and secondly, during the next two decades there became evident in all the colonial churches a rising tide of opinion in favor of the wider administration of the sacrament.

The Cambridge Synod

Not everyone was agreed that the extension of baptism was scriptural and assured the welfare of the churches. The growing divergence of opinion led the Massachusetts General Court to issue a call for a synod in which the subject was to be discussed. Here it is to be remembered that the covenant idea was constantly viewed under the double aspect of its implications for church doctrine and polity. On the latter there was by no means an unanimity. Some leading men still championed Presbyterian principles in preference to Separatism. Thus in Hingham Peter Hobart managed the internal affairs of the church along the lines of Scotch polity,[17] and in Newbury Thomas Parker and James Noye wished to do away with the right of consultation and assent which Congregationalism left entirely in the hands of the local church. At this time Presbyterianism was making rapid headway in England, and this in turn influenced the religious sentiments of the colonists. Although John Cotton had already given an elaborate exposition of the leading Congregational principles relative to church covenant in *The Keyes of the Kingdom of Heaven,* it was felt that a more official statement should be made. This was drawn up by Thomas Hooker in *Survey of the Summe of Church Discipline,* which was officially sanctioned at a meeting held in Cambridge on July 1, 1645. In Hooker's work, which was really a reply to Samuel Rutherford's *Due Right of Presbyteries,* there are especially two matters of importance. First of all, in regard to the composition of the church he unmistakeably affirmed the pure church ideal of Anabaptists and Separatists. "Visible saints are the only true and meet matter, whereof a visible church shall be gathered, and confoederation is this form." By visible saints he meant those who gave evidence of their regenerate estate. The infants were not excluded but rather comprehended in the church "under their Parents Covenant according to I Cor. 7:14."[18] Hooker emphasized the personal appropriation and confession of God's promises by the parents instead of the objective covenant relationship as the ground for baptism.

Secondly, Hooker proved himself the inveterate opponent of the wider administration. "Whether persons non confederate, and so (in our sense not Members of the Church) do entitle their children to the seal of Baptisme, being one of the Priviledges of the Church,"[19] he replied in the negative. Children as children never have the right to baptism, but it is bestowed upon them by their parents. He seems to have been one of the very few who realized the direction in which the new theory would take the churches. Thus he sought to uphold the subjective personal emphasis characteristic of much of early Congregationalism.

This brilliant defense by no means established unanimity. Besides the conscientious objections of those who held to a modified Presbyterianism, there were others who for the sake of practical objectives desired a change. They were convinced that the close relation between church and state led to a government dominated by the spiritual aristocracy. Since the Massachusetts law of 1631 had limited the franchise to covenanting members of the church and since the church maintained such rigorous tests for membership, only comparatively few in the colony had any voice in political matters. This political motive was negligible in most of the discussions and was soon overshadowed by another. Many of the leaders felt that the restriction of the use of baptism would lead to the progressive paganization of the colonies and the loss of the theocratic ideal. Thus the Congregational ideal was attacked on two fronts; politically, because it resulted in the extreme limiting of the franchise,[20] and religiously, because it refused baptism to a growing number of children in the colony.

All this led the General Court in its May session of 1646 to issue a call to the churches for a synod. New England was in a period of religious ferment. The Court, realizing the growing dissatisfaction as well as did the clergy, looked forward to the coming synod and earnestly hoped that definite positions would be taken.[21] For several reasons the final sessions of this body were not held until 1648. By that time a creed and platform of church discipline were adopted.

New England in spite of the many charges levelled against it on this score was no creedless colony. It, too, emphasized the necessity of making profession of the fundamentals of the Christian faith. However, it allowed latitude, since it never stressed precise quoting of creeds. Individuals and churches were allowed to formulate their own creeds. Instead of creating disharmony, this promoted true peace, according to Cotton Mather.[22] None the less, the New England church officially approved the Westminster symbols on September 30, 1648. Their teachings on the covenant became a definite part of official New England doctrine.

The decision taken by synod explicitly stated that in matters of church polity it did not agree with Westminster but referred the congregations to the Cambridge Platform of Church Discipline. This has been called by one writer "the most important monument of New England Congregationalism, because it is the clearest reflection of the system as it lay in the minds of the first generation on our soil after twenty years of practical experience."[23] Again, the church was said to be constituted by "visible saints only."[24] The proper form of church constitution was the "visible covenant, agreement, or consent wherby they give themselves unto the Lord."[25]

The admission of members to the local congregations was, of course, left up to the discretion of the officers. However, an examination was required. None disclaimed the necessity of examining personal Christian experience, also on the part of the baptized youth as they attained unto maturity.[26] By insisting upon such a profession, the churches in no wise sought to invalidate the promises and privileges attendant upon baptism. Of them it was affirmed, "They are in covenant with God, have the seale thereof upon them, viz., Baptisme; and so if not regenerated, yet are in a more hopefull way of attayning regenerating grace, and all the spiritual blessings both of the covenant and the seal; they are also under Church-watch, and consequently subject to the reprehensions, admonitions, and censures thereof, for their healing and amendment, as need shall require."[27]

From all this it is evident that the covenant idea was prominent in the minds of the leaders. Certain basic questions were not yet settled. The rather general statements of Confession and Platform left room for wide disagreement on certain practical issues. Although already in 1648 many were clamoring for the wider practice, the strength of the opposition caused the synod to hesitate. The fact that it spoke of warnings directed to recalcitrant covenant youth proves that its members were not oblivious to the growing need for defining church censures as applicable to members by baptism. The pastors and elders were not blind to the problem occasioned by the rapidly growing number of non-covenanting members in the churches. As the situation was aggravated, they considered the situation again and again. Between the Cambridge Synod of 1646-1648 and the Ministerial Convention of 1657 many were won for the new position.

The Rising Tide in Favor of the Wider Administration of Baptism

John Cotton's defense of his position relative to the Dorchester case also gave rise to a shift in emphasis among many of the early leaders. Although the Cambridge Synod had presented the churches with an officially recommended and endorsed creed and platform of church polity, it had not solved the practical problem whether children of non-covenanting but baptized parents might receive the sign and seal of the covenant. Gradually in the discussion which ensued party lines were drawn. In favor of the older practice were John Davenport and a large number of lay leaders in the churches. In favor of the newer practice were such leaders as Richard Mather and John Norton. Those who championed it thought that thus they could more effectively guard the sanctity of the Communion Table. They feared that if the lines of baptism were too tightly drawn, two grave if not disastrous consequences for the churches in New England would result. The first was that some desiring baptism for their children might be led to enter into the church covenant without having sufficiently examined themselves for the proper evidences of saving grace. The second danger, even more threatening, was that many, realizing the impossibility of entering the church estate, would allow their children to grow up unbaptized. Thus in course of time the majority of the younger generation would be outside of the church, and the ministers would never realize the ideal of a holy commonwealth.

Several possibilities were therefore open to them. The first suggestion came from Childs and his fellow-petitioners in 1646. Following Episcopal and Presbyterian tradition in the homeland, they would admit to Communion all who possessed knowledge of the gospel truths and led an exemplary moral life.[28] That custom was not altogether unknown in the colonies, as Lechford testified in 1642. However, this form, practiced also at Newberry, was not approved, since it signified an abandonment of the Congregational principle that the church should exist only of visible or experiential believers.[29]

The second possibility was to deny these people any right to church membership and thus to deprive their children of baptism and church care. To this position many had theoretical as well as practical objections. Many feared the increased paganization of the land as a result of this policy. However, still more did the leaders feel that the adults in question were members of the church covenant in some sense. Now there was no possibility of excluding them from church fellowship except by death, excommunication because of grave offence, personal withdrawal, or removal to another congregation. Since these members were not guilty of any heinous breach of the moral law, there was no ground for excommunication. The only charge which the ministers could level against their position was that they confessed a lack of God's regenerating grace. And surely, since it was entirely in the province of the sovereign God to give or withhold this, such members could not be blamed for their spiritual condition.

At this juncture a grave weakness in early Congregationalism became apparent. Their overemphasis on divine election at the expense of human responsibility led them to condone, if not to excuse, the halfheartedness of many birthright members. To this must be added their strong insistence upon personal assurance of regeneration. Very likely the Puritans had come under the hypnotic spell of the Anabaptist dualism of nature and grace. They made too sharp a distinction between the moral and spiritual life of man. To them these two were virtually exclusive. Thus they dared not grant the possibility that the moral life evident in many New Englanders and praised by the leaders might conceivably be and perhaps was the fruit not of the common operations of the Holy Spirit but of His saving and regenerating presence in their hearts.

Therefore they chose to follow another path. They began to propagate a theory which would allow the so-called unregenerate and uncovenanting baptized members to remain in the church and transmit their degree of membership to their children. However, they refused them all admittance to the Lord's Supper and any voice in the government of the congregation. The compromise was thoroughly illogical and inconsistent with their own position. Strictly taken, these members could derive little if any real benefit from their position, for it was openly acknowledged that they were devoid of regenerating grace.

With the erection of this half-way house between the true church and the world many were concerned. Richard Mather was one of the most influential exponents of the new theory.[30] He insisted that "the Gospel extends not the external covenant beyond the immediate Parents."[31] However, although historical faith was not sufficient ground for partaking of the Lord's Supper, it was enough for making use of baptism. The latter, he argued, was for all members of church covenant, whereas the former had to be restricted to the members of the eternal Covenant of Grace.

The same position was taken by Thomas Shepard in his *Church Membership of Children and their Right to Baptism.*

He spoke of a double seed within the covenant, an elect seed and a "church seed." Hence there must be a double covenant, the one "external and outward" and the other "internal and inward."[32] Those in the outward covenant did have the privileges of being reckoned with the Lord's family, of receiving the gifts of forgiveness, unless they refused them, and of giving them a new heart, if they would but repent and believe.

There were objections that such a conception of the covenant and church vitiated the principle that the church was subjectively "holy," as the Congregationalists taught. Shepard replied that this was not an inward but only a federal holiness.[33] That unregenerate and unbelieving people could be members of the church without fear of discipline was openly taught. "It is clearer than the day that many who are inwardly, or in respect of the inward covenant, the children of the devil, are outwardly, or in respect of the outward covenant, the children of God."[34]

John Norton was more interested in the doctrinal than in the practical aspects of the question of the nature of the covenant. His *Orthodox Evangelist* is one of the oldest elaborate theological works of the New England ministry. In it he spoke of the double way in which every man partook of Adam's sin, "by participation and imputation."[35] Thus he discussed Adam as the father of the race and as the representative of man. Norton was a supralapsarian. He spoke of sinful man almost exclusively in his capacity as either elect or reprobate. The basis of salvation lies in the Covenant of Redemption "between the Father and the Mediator."[36] On this basis the Covenant of Grace was regarded as absolute and unconditional, so that faith is " a Condition improperly . . . whose performance by the Covenantee, is absolutely undertaken for."[37]

In a similar manner Thomas Shepard discussed the doctrine of man's fall in Adam. He expressed the legal relationship in an apt figure. "We were all in Adam, as a whole country is in a Parliament man, and though we made no agreement to have Adam stand for us, yet the Lord made it for us."[38] He continued the pattern by speaking of the redemption through Christ as effectuated in a covenant way. His satisfaction was "the price paid to the justice of God . . . according to a covenant made between Him and the Father." Because of this covenant agreement "Christ stood in the room of all whom mercy decreed to save."

Thomas Hooker, who passed away before the problem became acute in the churches, has in several works set the pattern for self-examination.[39] He paved the way, unknowingly without a doubt, for the double standard of church membership by placing the demands for personal covenanting and assurance of faith so high, that few could ever hope to attain unto a comfortable persuasion of the presence of saving grace within their hearts. Although he spoke of the objective means of grace in *The Poor Doubting Christian Drawn to Christ*,[40] he drew out the details to such lengths, lest faith appear to be too simple and common a matter.

By 1650 it was already apparent in which direction the churches were rapidly moving. Every indication was that the new way would be almost universally accepted by the churches. The greatest obstacle lay with the constituency. Cotton Mather, himself a zealot for the new theory, has described the opposition in his characteristic way, "Very gradual was the procedure of the churches to exercise that church-care of their children, which the synodical propositions recommended; for although the pastors were generally principled for it, yet, in very many of the churches, a number of the brethren were so stiffly and fiercely set the other way, that the pastors did forebear to extend their practice unto the length of their judgment."[41]

Chapter 5.

The Synod of 1662: The Half-Way Covenant Adopted

NEW ENGLAND Congregationalism has made its most unique contribution to the development of the covenant idea in the formulation and practice of what has commonly been called the Half-way Covenant. The consequences of its adoption are a permanent warning to all Protestant churches, especially of Calvinistic origin, who wrestle with the question of the relation between the objective and subjective aspects of the Christian faith.

The presence and necessity of certain norms and standards for ecclesiastical life are generally acknowledged. These are contained in the body of doctrine, church polity and liturgy to which the churches adhere. However, since the Christian religion emphasizes that at its heart lies personal experience of communion with God in the face of Christ Jesus, an external agreement with formal standards can never be recognized as sufficient guarantee that the individual is in possession of the highest fellowship.

Since the Congregationalists sought to maintain the pure church ideal and thus desired to make the visible church conform as closely as possible to the invisible, the problem became very acute for them. The question has been much debated whether this aim of having a pure church, an ideal so greatly cherished during the early history of the churches, was repudiated, when for practical reasons the ministry adopted a double standard of membership in the churches. The fear which haunted many was that apart from this expedient the churches would die a lingering death because of the lack of interest in things religious displayed by the second and third generation colonists. To prevent this

110

disaster the majority were convinced that the church was forced to take measures which would insure its hold upon the masses. This question was already being discussed in the days of the Cambridge Synod. However, this new way was not officially adopted until 1662.

Preparatory Steps for the Synod of 1662

To understand properly the significance of the propositions adopted by the Synod of 1662, it will be necessary to trace somewhat the historical background. The rise and development of the Half-way Covenant practice was not occasioned by political considerations. Indeed, Dr. Robert Childs and six others protested in 1646 against the limitations of the franchise.[1] In accordance with the laws then obtaining in Massachusetts the only solution lay in a change within the church and its standard of membership. Some of the men openly advocated a form of Presbyterianism which in those days virtually conceded the idea of the co-terminous church and state. The complete triumph of the Separatist church ideal in the *Cambridge Platform* rendered further agitation on this score futile. Thus after 1648 the debate was purely religious and ecclesiastical in its scope. The pressing question was the position of the baptized but noncovenanting members in the church and their right to transfer their own status in the church to their offspring.

Soon after the sessions of the Cambridge Synod it was almost universally felt that the congregations ought to settle on some uniform practice. This need became clearer when the Rev. Thomas Cobbet and his Ipswich church adopted the new way officially. This stirred the General Courts in the colonies to action.[2] As a result the Ministerial Convention of 1657 was convened. More than anything else it paved the way for the ultimate triumph of the Half-way Covenant five years later. Thus ministers insisted that all children of covenanting parents were members of the church by divine arrangement. Where this could be proved, the children should be baptized. Such who were members by virtue of their parents' covenant could not be excommunicated, except by the Lord Himself who had confirmed such membership. Children in minority were said to have covenanted with the Lord in infancy by virtue of their parents' act. When adult, they were obligated to covenant for themselves. This act was defined, "To covenant in our own persons according to the sense of this question, is nothing else but an orderly and Church profession of our Faith, or a personall publick and solemn avouching of God, in an Ecclesiasticall way, to be our God. . ."[3] On the surface this seemed to safeguard the holiness of the church. However, such leaders as Shepard, Rogers and others had defined the ecclesiastical position of the majority in such a way that all who thus covenanted needed no more than historical faith. Those who desired to partake of the second sacrament were admonished to examine their hearts in addition for the presence of regenerating grace. Though in theory the ministers admitted that both sacraments were signs and seals of the Covenant of Grace, they separated them in practice. Federal holiness was deemed sufficient for baptism, but personal holiness as the fruit of regeneration was required in the case of the Lord's Supper.[4] Only those who stubbornly refused to "covenant" in this way could be excommunicated. Moreover, this formal barrier was later on removed. Thus the rite of baptism was externalized, as is evident in the case of the Haverhill church which voted to allow parents who were members by baptism to present their children for the sacrament without even professing their interest in the covenant and its promises.[5]

The results of this meeting were formulated by Richard Mather in a series of answers to twenty one questions. The Massachusetts General Court does not seem to have taken cognizance of the decisions, but the Connecticut General Court voted to send copies of the result to all the churches. Political disturbances in England at that time caused the courts to emphasize the need of religious unity in New England. The protracted debates were ruffling the spirits of many. Therefore the authorities sent a pointed order to the various churches to meet in synod on the second Tuesday of March, 1662, to discuss these questions, "Quaest I. Who are the subjects of baptisme. Quaest 2. Whither according to the Word of God, there ought to be a consociation of churches, & what should be the manner of it?"[6]

The Propositions of 1662

The organization of the synod interests us very little. All the leading ministers of the Bay colony were present. It was evident from the beginning that unanimity could not be expected. The group was sharply divided. Of the seventy present at the opening sessions at least eight or nine violently opposed the Half-way theory. However, the vast majority approved the new way. The exact phraseology of each proposition was debated and finally fixed on the synod floor. The crucial ones were the fourth and especially the fifth, which granted the right unto baptism of all children of persons themselves baptized and willing to profess an intellectual adherence to the teachings of the church. Chauncy said of the fifth, "There hath been three expressions of this proposition, and this swerves further off from Scripture then both the former."[7]

Walker contends that the opposition, though intellectually strong, was weak because of the glaring inconsistencies in its theory. The basis upon which he contends for this is that Chauncy or one of his friends proposed the third statement which professed the birthright membership of children of covenanting parents. According to the majority this virtually conceded the principles of the Half-way Covenant. However, Walker forgets that the minority did not so much contest the right of those infants to the sacrament as they did the privilege of the admittedly unregenerate parents to transfer their legal standing in the church-covenant to their offspring.

The question was a vexing one. Jonathan Mitchell, who drew up the *Preface to the Propositions* of 1662, wrote, "How hard it is to finde and keep the right middle way of Truth in these things, is known to all that are aught acquainted with the Controversies thereabout. As we have learned and believed, we have spoken, but not without remembrance that we are poor feeble frail men, and therefore desire to be conversant herein with much humility and fear before God and man."[8]

Seven propositions were adopted as an answer to the first question proposed by the Massachusetts General Court.[9] The men of the synod held that not all who were in the visible church received the true covenant blessings. Thus they sought to reconcile the place of the unregenerate and unbelieving in the visible church with their pure church ideal. They spoke often of covenant and federal holiness, but their definition was far from clear.[10]

A large part of the second proposition was devoted to a defense of the church membership of children of "confederate visible believers." They argued this from God's covenant with Abraham, the relation of such children to God and the church by virtue of federal holiness, the statement of Christ that the children were proper members of the Kingdom of God, which term "is not rarely used . . . to express the visible church," and "the whole current and harmony of Scripture" which demonstrates that children have always been a part of the church.[11] The third proposition affirmed that such children were necessarily under church care and supervision. In the fourth proposition the presence of two types of church members was admitted. They argued the legitimacy of this from the "different nature of Baptism and the Lord's Supper." According to them Baptism sealed "covenant-holiness, as circumcision did," but the Lord's Supper was "the Sacrament of growth in Christ . . . which supposeth a special renewal and exercise of Faith and Repentance in those that partake."[12]

The controversy virtually centered around the fifth proposition. In it was defined what the early Congregationalists understood by "confederate visible believers." All were agreed that there were "degrees" of church membership. However, all parents, if they were "but in the lowest degree such," were required to present their children for baptism. Thus although repudiating the idea of the national church, the congregations were definitely proceeding in that direction.

The members of synod realized that another question would have to be settled, before the practice could become universal. The churches were forced to face the problem of the presence of baptized members who upon attaining maturity did not unite with the church as members in full communion. Synod declared that their membership did not cease, even though they evidenced no faith and repentance. The leaders sought to prove that "in Scripture persons are broken off, onely for notorious sin, or incorrigible impenitency and unbelief, not for growing up to adult age."[13] Was an adult who refused to enter church covenant guilty of unbelief and therefore subject to church censure? Indeed not, the fathers answered, for although such a one was devoid of saving faith, he did believe with an historical faith.

Whether this defense of the sufficiency of historical faith for church membership was in harmony with the original views became the storm center of the debate which followed upon the adjournment of synod. Many of the laymen, particularly, argued that this was a repudiation of New England's first principles. This much was sure, the churches had taken an official stand. Church membership had been defined, and a place was guaranteed to infants and children within the boundaries of the "pure church." Although the theory of "regenerate membership" in the visible church was practically overthrown, the ideal of the holy commonwealth which had inspired so many to leave England for the wilderness was theoretically still intact.

Since the decisions had not received unanimous approbation, further debate continued. Instead of subsiding, however, the discussions increased. Hardly had synod adjourned, when the presses in the new world found themselves taxed to capacity because of the wealth of polemic material demanding immediate publication. The old party lines, which had forced the General Court to convoke a synod, were greatly sharpened.

Synodists and Anti-Synodists

The men of the opposition opened the first round of fire in this phase of theological strife, when Charles Chauncy argued against the propositions in his *Antisynodalia Scripta Americana.*[14] He had already championed the strict position indirectly in his *Plain Doctrine of Justification of a Sinner in the sight of God.* In his views he virtually identified the Covenant of Grace with the Covenant of Redemption, thus leaving no room for human responsibility. He cautioned parents against thinking their children free from the bondage of sin by virtue of the covenant.[15] Warning against what he calls the "Jews great delusion," he wrote, "Yea, more godly parentage makes a Childes condemnation much worse, whilest he lies still in his natural estate."[16] The awful fear which haunted him was that when the godly parents should die, the Lord would come in judgment to "wipe New England as a man wipes a dish, wiping and turning it upside down."[17]

He opposed the Half-way Covenant on the ground that it compromised the ideal of regenerate church membership. Thus he accounted the fifth proposition entirely unscriptural. He also sought to limit the expression "seed" of the covenant to immediate descendants. "Where there is no federal holinesse, there is no right to Baptism, but where neither Parent is a believer, there is no covenant-holiness. . ."[18] Visible unbelief, which he defined as "non-manifestation of making profession of the Faith and the fruits thereof," was good ground for maintaining that the covenant was no longer in force in such a family.[19] This could only be upheld on the ground of a radical distinction between the Covenant of Grace and the church-covenant, a position championed by all the opponents of the synodical propositions. "We must distinguish betwixt the Covenant of Grace and the church-covenant, which differ very much: for the covenant of Grace belongs only to the Elect and true Believers, which the Church cannot infallibly judge who they are; but the Church-covenant . . . requires mutual consent of them that are admitted into communion to walk with God according to the Gospel."[20] Because of this radical differentiation, the covenant promises to the children were of little value until the fruits of election, faith and repentance, became manifest. "The Children in question are in a state of Neutrality for the present, and such Christ counts to be against him. . . ."[21]

Much the same position was taken by John Davenport,[22] who had debated with the leaders of the Dutch churches on the nature of the Covenant of Grace.[23] He virtually identified it with the Covenant of Redemption. It is apparent that he sought as much as possible to reserve the sacraments as seals of the Covenant of Grace for those only of whose regeneration he possessed some reasonable assurance. Both his *Profession of Faith* and *The New Haven Catechism* give evidence of the large place which the covenant idea received in his theological position. He strongly stressed the voluntary nature of the church-covenant, by insisting that only such children who later covenanted for themselves were in any sense in covenant. This too was the position of Nicholas Street of Plymouth colony.[24]

The dependence of the covenant membership of children upon their parents was emphasized by all the Anti-synodists but by none more strongly than by Increase Mather.[25] "Infants cannot claim right unto Baptism but in the right of one of their Parents or both: where neither of the Parents cannot claim right to the Lord's Supper, there their infants cannot claim right to Baptism."[26] In fact he went so far as to affirm "that their membership is Conjunct with and Dependent upon the Membership and Covenant of their Parents, so as to live and die therewith." He refused however to proceed with formal excommunication of those who refused to come to full profession and covenant. His opposition to the Half-way Covenant was grounded on the fear that "it hath in it a natural tendency to the hardening of unregenerate creatures in their sinful natural condition, when Life is not onely Promised but sealed to them by the precious Bloud of Jesus Christ."[27]

The first reply to the Anti-synodists came from the pen of John Allin under the title *Animadversions upon the Anti-Synodalia Scripta Americana.* He feared that the opposition would strengthen the position of the Antipaedobaptists.[28] The two issues at stake he formulated very clearly. The first involved the right of the infant-seed to the sacrament and the second the grounds for excommunication from the visible church. On these two all the supporters of the new way were in principle agreed.

Many objected to the position of the Anti-synodists on the ground that it was contradictory, since it allowed that the baptized parent was at one and the same time " a member and yet no member." However, Allin and his confederates, in spite of their emphasis on the unity of the Covenant of Grace, had to distinguish between the outward and inward dispensations.[29] The standard accepted for church membership was clearly stated, "To make a person a Member of the visible Church, the matter is not whether he hath Faith and Grace really or not; if he hath such qualification as the rule of the Word accepteth for Faith in the visible Church, we can go no further."[30] Here the mischief was begun. By such a definition of the requisites for church membership, many could enter full church-covenant and yet be regarded by themselves and others as yet without grace. The same was admitted by Cotton when speaking of the regenerate state of church members on the basis of the theory of the pure church. He claimed that he was not speaking of what the members were in reality but only of what they were federally and thus claimed to be.

That the whole theory of the Half-way Covenant borrowed largely from the Old Testament is evident from both Allin and Richard Mather. The latter sought an answer to the question of grounds of excommunication in the Old Testament rules and regulations. He also argued strongly against the position of Davenport who claimed "that they are discovenanted, by not performing that whereunto they were engaged by the Covenant."

The further discussion turned out to be mere wrangling on what was meant by covenant position and covenant-interest. What should be remembered is that Mather as well as the rest of the Synodists insisted that such adult but non-covenanting members were indeed not "immediately fit for the Lord's Supper." To prevent the presence of such unregenerate members at the second sacrament, Jonathan Mitchell argued for the Half-way practice. Had he lived, he would no doubt have been greatly surprised to note that his own position would in course of time lead precisely to this sad condition within the churches.

One of the last polemical writings which came out of the controversy was Increase Mather's *First Principles of New England concerning the Subject of Baptisme and Communion of Churches.* In it he collected, partly out of printed works and partly out of unpublished manuscripts of the first generation preachers, opinions on the two subjects. He admittedly directed his attention largely to the brethren of "Anti-synodalian perswasion" and spoke to them of his recent conversion to the new way. From the material adduced it is evident that the very first ministers in the colony wrestled with the question of harmonizing the pure church ideal with the conception of a holy commonwealth. In his work *Discourse concerning the subjects of Baptisme* Mather virtually externalized church membership. Thus he spoke of the "visibility of faith" which gave no assurance concerning a person's true interest in spiritual things. It soon became apparent to the defenders of the new way that "the bare having of Baptisme does not alwayes keep true Religion."[31] To their grief they were to learn that instead of solving the problem of church membership, they had merely created more questions and difficulties than before. The next century and a half found these churches embroiled in one debate after another concerning the significance and qualifications for membership in the visible church.[32]

Several tragic consequences of adopting the Half-way Covenant soon became apparent. The first was the birth of incessant strife in many congregations. The majority of the ministers favored the new way, but large numbers of the laymen heartily opposed it. Rather than disturb the peace of the churches, many sought to leave the question unsettled. Even such a zealot as Richard Mather confessed on his death-bed that he had been defective as to the practice out of fear for the dissenters.[33] When the political situation in England called for a united front in the colonies, the General Court decided that where the membership could not agree, second congregations might be formed.[34] As soon as toleration was practiced, interest in the controversy subsided.

A second consequence, much more far-reaching in its results than the first, was the adoption of a suitable form by means of which such baptized but non-covenanting parents could affirm their personal "interest in the Covenant." Thus these were required "to own the covenant," which in practice came to mean that they professed to the presence of historical faith in the teachings of Scripture and the churches, willingly placed themselves and their offspring under the supervision of the ecclesiastical authorities, and promised to make proper use of the means of grace. Since no such form had been prescribed by Synod, it was left up to the several congregations how they would develop this. Wherever such forms came into vogue, they were usually drawn up by the local pastor and used either with or without official sanction of the members. One of the earliest forms used in the ceremony of "owning the covenant" was that of the Salem congregation.[35] Among the best known and most consistent was the form long in use in Boston's Old North Church, of which the Mathers were ministers for a long period.[36] These forms give evidence that the ministers and members were by no means satisfied with such half-way membership on the part of many. Diligently the pastors were to admonish those who embraced their church state in this way to seek for more fruit in their lives. The churches were still interested in upholding as normative the intense spiritual experience of the first fathers of the colony. In so strongly emphasizing the experiential, the Congregational churches in New England departed from the traditional Reformed conception of the qualifications for church membership.

It could be predicted that on such a basis the position of children in the church was purely formal. New England had never held out a large measure of hope for the little ones on the basis of God's covenant promises. These were constantly overshadowed by an emphasis on inherent sinfulness as the result of their relationship to Adam. Even in the lives of the very youngest the religiously inclined among the parents and ministers looked for hopeful evidences of regeneration. Cotton Mather was simply following the New England tradition, when he related in glowing terms the religious experience of especially devout children who died at a tender age. Without the presence of something akin to adult experience and insight, the child was hardly ever regarded as being in a hopeful way.

This emphasis worked havoc in the churches. With increasing insistence the leaders taught that there was "no certain, but onely a probable connexion between federal Holyness and Salvation." Hence it was comparatively easy for them to allow those who were merely federally holy to continue as church members. If God did not choose to grant them a vivid experience of regeneration and conversion, they would acquiesce in their fate. Surely it could not be expected of them to force the will of God, who plainly elected some and rejected others according to His own inscrutable purpose. Intimately associated with this was another evil. Because the churches affirmed the sovereignty of God in the way in which they did, many used it as an excuse for being content with half-way membership. Increasingly the ministers complained that the people no longer sought salvation earnestly and prayerfully. Thus although the churches were assured of a permanent place in the community, they had to be content with an increasing number of those who were to all appearances devoid of any interest in the gospel message.

New England religion came under a cloud. It was the cloud of a deterministic conception of God's gracious operations with His covenant people, which now was breeding indifference and spiritual complacency. It is not easy to determine whether the Half-way Covenant was the cause or the result of the decline in religious interest so manifest since 1660. To a certain extent it seems to have been both. From these days on until the time of Jonathan Edwards the ministers uttered their lamentations and prophesied their woes over the spiritually unfortunate but materially prosperous and complacent settlements.

Chapter 6.

Stoddardeanism: The Half-Way Covenant Modified

THE Half-way Covenant as accepted by the Synod of 1662 did not bear the much-desired fruit. What the Puritan leaders had so fondly hoped for was by no means realized. Instead of a growing interest in the church and a deepening piety among the inhabitants of the land, New England experienced a time of grave laxness and gross indifference. The masses who perhaps would have dreaded a complete break with the church under the old system were now quite well satisfied with their partial admission to church privileges.

Some further results of this new way will have to be traced here in order to understand how the theory was modified in course of time. The most significant consequence was that during the next half century many of the churches openly acknowledged historical faith, or an intellectual acceptance of the Scriptural truths taught in the churches, as the only requisite to full membership. This decision was the result of the fearful religious decline suffered by the colonies during the period from the Synod of 1662 to the Great Awakening.

Religious Decline and Reforming Synod

"A little after 1660 there began to appear a Decay; and this increased to 1670, when it grew very visible and threatening, and was generally complained of and bewailed bitterly by the Pious among them; and yet more in 1680, when but few of the first Generation remained."[1] This picture given by Thomas Prince

123

in 1743 clearly portrays the subtle rise and general nature of the religious declension.

Its first characteristic was the rise of a somewhat new type of preaching. Although the doctrines were zealously expounded and defended, they had become harsh and cold and intellectual. Too much of religious teaching bore no relationship to the life and experience of the colonists. The first colonists, having suffered much for their faith, had the vital experience of God's presence in their lives. They realized their complete dependence upon His grace at all times and in all things pertaining to their physical and spiritual well-being. However, with the growth of the colony prosperity increased, and the second generation enjoyed many luxuries which their fathers lacked. Thus they did not seem to need God. In the wake of this transition there followed the growing tendency to preach morality instead of religion. The Christian came to be more and more identified with the decent, industrious and prosperous citizen. Thus the difference between the church and the world upon which the first fathers had insisted was rapidly forgotten.[2]

Besides, there was also in the colony a large element of the population which had relatively little sympathy with old Puritan teaching and practice. They were the descendants of the servants of the first colonists. Walker says of them, "They were relatively a numerous and positively a debasing factor in the life of the Colonial towns and villages."[3] The ideal of the holy commonwealth guaranteed them some relation to the visible church. However, this could only be done at the expense of the former insistence upon genuine experiential religion.

The chief fault, however, lay with the churches themselves. Although from the beginning they had insisted upon careful church watch and discipline, this was not carried out. Nearly every writer after 1662 mentioned the fact that acknowledgedly unregenerate people were openly admitted to the church. This went hand in hand with the neglect of the office of elder. This concomitant of the religious decline in the New England churches has too often been neglected by historians, although Cotton Mather does not fail to mention it.[4] Although at first ruling elders were elected to serve with pastors and teachers, this custom fell into disuse. To justify this the leaders held that the Scriptures taught that the oversight of the flock was entrusted to the pastors. It was impossible, however, for the pastors alone to keep careful watch.

It need not surprise us that the decline grew in proportion as the Propositions of 1662 were put into practice. One writer has called the Half-way Covenant practice "at best, a compromise between the methods of the Established Church of England, and those of the free churches of New England. In the course of time it did away with the Puritan principle of a church made up of regenerate persons."[5] Since the ministers could no longer look upon their church members as children of God, their preaching shifted in its emphasis. The ideal of the pure church could not be upheld, and thus church discipline became lax. All these factors contributed to the growing apathy towards the gospel and its demands on the part of the majority.

The immediate results were a series of lamentations and prophecies of woes by the clergy who professed deep concern about the "prosperity of New England's Zion." The best opportunity for such a message was in the election sermons once every year.[6] Depicting the deplorable situation, Increase Mather wrote, "If the begun Apostacy should proceed as fast the next thirty years as it has done these last, surely it will come to that in New England (Except the Gospell itself Depart with the Order of it) that the most Conscientious People therein, will think themselves concerned to gather Churches out of Churches."[7] Little did Mather realize that his prophecy was to be almost literally fulfilled.

Because the whole church was aware of the growing decline, the Massachusetts General Court convoked the "Reforming Synod" in Boston on September 10, 1679. The need for reformation was discussed in the light of two questions, "What are the

Evils that have provoked the Lord to bring his judgments on New-England?" and "What is to be done, that so these evils may be reformed?" The decisions were recorded in *The Necessity of Reformation with the Expedients subservient thereunto, asserted, in answer to two questions* and have been preserved for future generations in Cotton Mather's *Magnalia Christiana Americana*.[8] These men were convinced that God had been using shipwreck, conflagrations, wars with the Indians, sickness, and other calamities as punishments and chastisements upon the colonists. The root cause of all New England's sins was "spiritual and heart apostacy from God."[9]

In suggesting remedies the Synod was very explicit. They insisted first of all that the officers of the church should keep careful watch of the faith and order of the congregations. This meant above all guarding the holiness of the Lord's Table.[10] Furthermore, they insisted on discipline as "Christ's ordinance both for the prevention of apostacy in the churches, and to recover them when collapsed."[11]

However, the best solution in the estimation of the leaders was the solemn renewal of the church covenant. For this they found Scriptural precedent in the stories of Asa, Jehoshaphat, Hezekiah, and others. This followed a rather conventional pattern in the churches. After a time of fasting and prayer the minister was to read the covenant of the local church. The people were to express their readiness "anew to declare their 'most explicit consent' unto the covenant of grace, and most explicitly to engage a growing 'watchfulness' in such duties of the covenant as were more peculiarly accommodated unto their present circumstances." In some churches only communicants and in others the entire congregation expressed assent. In the form usually read to the church the congregation was exhorted to confess its sins and to acknowledge the need of repentance and its inability to keep the covenant without the help of the Holy Spirit. At the close of the service the members pledged themselves to three specific duties: 1—the reformation of their own hearts and lives,

2—the education of their families by precept and practice, and
3—the purifying of themselves from the "sins of the times."[12]

This expedient suggested by the Reforming Synod did not
succeed in stemming the tide of religious indifference. There
was very little permanent religious reawakening in evidence.
Very likely the tremendous social upheaval through which the
colonies were passing constituted a formidable factor in the
growing externalization of religion. Schneider has written,
"The Puritan thrift soon produced Yankee prosperity, and the
Yankee prosperity produced urban aristocracies. The precari-
ousness of the frontier gave place to the security of the towns.
Luxury crept in. The younger generation could afford to rest
a bit on their fathers' oars. They had not undergone the moral
discipline of the frontier. To them New England was home,
not a howling wilderness. Consequently their fathers' strenuous
standards began to irritate them, and the philosophy of God's
wonder-working providence began to take a hollow sound."[13]

Thus the orthodox sought to make the doctrines still stricter
and harsher. In order to prevent the loss of the sense of sin,
which was basic to New England Calvinism, the preachers forgot
to relieve their descriptions of human depravity with the Biblical
stress on divine grace. Consequently many among the leaders
became indifferent to the heritage of the fathers. Arminianism
with its conceptions of man's ability to accept the gospel entered
the churches about the turn of the century. Since so few
professed real spiritual experience, the preachers busied themselves more with moral and social issues.

The direction in which the churches were moving is evident
from the reorganization of the churches. When the Brattle St.
church was founded in spite of the opposition of the Mathers,
the result was the loosening of the hold of the conservatives upon
Boston's ecclesiastical life. It also opened the way for modifications in Half-way Covenant theory, since it admitted to baptism
children of those who were not even willing to covenant with
the church in any sense. Also, religion in the families was fast

dying out, according to the Rev. Samuel Torrey, who insisted, "Surely, here and hereby, Religion first received its death's wound."[14] In spite of all the pleas of the conservatives, New England turned a deaf ear to the calls unto repentance. As it waxed fatter and richer and older, its religious interests waned. Again it became imperative that the preachers who were solely in control of the ecclesiastical machinery find some practical solution to their problem of maintaining the holy commonwealth in the face of the religious decline.

Stoddard and the Communion Question

The man who made respectability, gradually accepted as the standard in New England's social life, the norm for church membership was the Rev. Solomon Stoddard.[15] He was the pastor of Northampton, New England's most fashionable and influential church outside of Boston. Although on the edge of the wilderness, it never lost contact with the outside world. It did not take long for the customs and fashions of London and Paris to reach this remote corner, and so zealously did the people follow these that Edwards, the successor of Stoddard, found it necessary upon more than one occasion to inveigh against the worldliness of the community.[16] Stoddard was a zealous and pious pastor. In the Connecticut valley he was accounted the leader, and Dwight tells us that he "possessed probably more influence than any other Clergyman in the province during a period of thirty years."[17]

Stoddard's position was the logical and necessary outcome of the Propositions of 1662. He allowed the unregenerate to enlarge their use of church privileges and ordinances. The Synod of 1662 had allowed the children of such to receive baptism on the basis of parental affirmation of interest in the covenant. This gave legal standing in the church. This sad state caused the number of communicants in the churches to decline at an alarming rate, since the majority were satisfied as long as their children received baptism. In order that the churches might still main-

tain their hold on the people of the land, the ministers began
to emphasize as never before the use of the means. Although
it was recognized that only the Lord could change the sinner's
heart, he could place himself in a more or less favorable situation to receive divine favor. These included regular attendance
upon public worship, prayer and a decent life. To this list
Stoddard would add Communion as still another "converting
ordinance."

Although the first public statement appeared in 1700, the principle was known and perhaps also practiced earlier. Stoddard
claims to have advocated it as early as 1679 at the Reforming
Synod. In fact, he claimed responsibility for modifying one of
the proposals of that body in such a way that it would be con-
sonant with his theory. He refused to demand a "relation of the
work of God's Spirit upon their hearts" as requisite to Communion.[18] All that was required was a profession of faith and
repentance. As early as 1677 Increase Mather bewailed the presence of "teachers in our Israel, that have espoused loose large
principles here, designing to bring all persons to the Lord's
Supper, who have an historical faith, and are not scandalous in
life, though they never had an experience of a work of regeneration in their souls."[19]

This policy gained ground and was defended by Stoddard in
his *Doctrine of the Instituted Churches Explained and Proved
from the Word of God*. Insisting that the proper procedure for
the churches in face of the growing delinquency was to admit all
members of blameless conduct and ability to examine themselves to the Supper, he argued that such members not only had
the right but also the obligation to come to the second sacrament. By this means he sought to obviate the difficulty caused
by the presence of so few communicants in the churches. Too
many stayed away under pretext that they were yet "in an unconverted state." Stoddard surrendered the Puritan conception
of the sacraments as the privilege of the experiential saints only
by claiming that the Lord's Table was a "converting ordinance."

In his first work on the subject he expressed several views entirely at odds with the traditional conceptions of New England.[20] He claimed that explicit covenanting was unnecessary, that the churches and their officers need not be assured of the regeneration of the members, and that the ministers' call lay not in the free election by the people but in the ceremony of laying on of hands. For the sake of the outward prosperity of the churches he was willing to make several concessions. Yet that he did not stand alone in his tendencies toward the Scotch ideal of the national church is proven by the fact that in 1705 the Massachusetts clergy was ready to adopt a system of associations and councils.[21]

Stoddard's Controversy With the Mathers

This attempt to embrace a larger number of inhabitants within the church by the double expedient of changing the qualifications for attendance upon Communion and the reorganization of the churches met with strong opposition. Many were not yet inclined to surrender the ideal of a church of elect saints. These, led by the Mathers, opposed Stoddard. The exponent of pure Congregationalism in those days was the Rev. John Wise of Ipswich.[22] The later development of the church idea in New England cannot be understood apart from his theories, which also influenced the American Revolution. The matter of communion privileges was even more heatedly debated in the controversy between Stoddard and the Mathers.

Stoddard had postulated the fundamental issue very clearly, when he asked, "Whether such persons as have a good conversation and a competent knowledge, may come to the Lord's Supper, with a good conscience, in case they know themselves to be in a natural condition?"[23] By the term natural condition he designated the state of such who were strangers to the experience of regeneration insisted upon by the first generation as necessary unto church membership. Stoddard answered, "They may and ought to come, tho they know themselves to be in a natural condition; this ordinance is instituted for all adult members of the church who are not scandalous and therefore must be attended by them; as no man may neglect prayer, or hearing the Word, because he cannot do it in faith, so he may not neglect the Lord's Supper."[24] Stoddard shifted from the strongly subjective and experiential basis required for partaking of the Lord's Supper to the thoroughly objective one of church membership. His theory virtually admits of too low a regard for the sacrament. Although this tended to bring the two sacraments, so radically divorced by the Synod of 1622, together again, it did so at the expense of true spirituality. In this way Stoddardeanism was a further concession to the spirit of the times. With his innovation the idea of the covenant underwent a profound change, in that membership in it was completely externalized.

To understand the change, it will be necessary to review the differences between him and the Mathers. Stoddard had defined visible saints as "such as make serious profession of the true Religion, together with those that do descend from them, till rejected of God."[25] This sounded much like the Propositions of 1662. However, it was a new interpretation of church membership. Mather contended in his *The Order of the Gospel, Professed and Practised by the Churches of Christ in New England* that the churches of the Reformation had stood high spiritually only so long as they maintained the sanctity of the Communion Table. In defining visible saints he stressed explicit covenanting, personal testimonies of experience, and reception in the church by the whole congregation rather than by the officers only. He thus sought to restore the old system of admission to privileges of church membership.[26] When these two views were compared, party lines were quickly drawn. The new view gained ground especially in the churches of the Connecticut valley.

The controversy broke out anew, when the Mathers, Increase and Cotton, wrote an introduction to John Quick's *Young Man's Claim unto the Sacrament of the Lord's Supper.* In it they emphasized the fearful consequences which would accrue to those who partook without earnest self-examination contending that those who partook while unregenerate heaped to themselves God's eternal wrath. Thus they said that they "would not for Ten Worlds, run the Hazard of bringing the Blood of so many souls upon our Heads, as we might, if we should bid men in their Known Unregeneracy to come unto the Tremendous Mysteries."[27]

To this attack Stoddard did not reply until 1707, when he preached his famous sermon on "The Inexcusableness of Neglecting the Worship of God, under a Pretence of being in an unconverted Condition." He emphasized two points, viz., 1—"That Sanctification is not a necessary Qualification for Partaking in the Lord's Supper" and 2—"that the Lord's Supper is a converting Ordinance." In this sermon he maintained that in the Lord's Supper a special type of grace was given by which a man could be converted. It has been asserted, and not without some ground, that his insistence upon having the unconverted come to the Table was based upon his own experience.

Immediately after the appearance of the above sermon Mather took up the cudgels and wrote his *Dissertation Wherein the Strange Doctrine, lately published in a sermon the tendency of which is to encourage unsanctified persons (while such) to approach the Holy Table of the Lord, is examined and confuted.* All the powers of logic and argument were summoned in defense of the Propositions of 1662. He claimed that both of his opponent's contentions were heterodox and dangerous in the extreme. Since the Lord's Supper was instituted only for the "friends of Christ," no unregenerate person might partake. His arguments included the following. The New Testament ordinance was foreshadowed by that of the Old, and since no unholy person might partake of the latter (Lev. 26:11, 12), the New Testament church had no right to admit the unconverted.[28] The old distinction between external membership in the church by virtue of baptism and true membership by virtue of personal experience, officially recognized in the Half-way Covenant theory, was pressed forward in the second chapter. Mather, although rightly protesting against the indiscriminate administration of the Lord's Supper found with Stoddard,[29] lost sight of the unity of the two sacraments. He claimed that unsanctified persons are not really in covenant with God, since they are by their own admission destitute of grace. Only faith in Christ, called "Justifying Faith," gives a right to the sacrament. Thus the rite of baptism became a mere form expressing the initiation of the children in the visible church. There was no assurance of the gift of divine grace unto them.

Mather did recognize the possibility of being converted at the Table. However, he disputed the view that this gave a right to the unconverted to be present at the administration.[30] He moved on rather dangerous ground when he sought to reduce Stoddard's argument to the absurd. The latter had held that only certain types of ungenerate might partake, namely those who were not guilty of scandalous behavior and who could examine themselves. Now Mather sought to demonstrate that if the Lord's Supper was a converting ordinance, the scandalous needed it most.[31] When Stoddard contended that even the strictest supervision of the Table did not guarantee the presence of regenerate only, Mather replied that this fact did not constitute an excuse to relax supervision and watch as Stoddard was ready to do.

Under withering fire from such a formidable foe Stoddard held his ground. The very next year he published his answer, *An Appeal to the Learned, being a Vindication of the rights of Visible Saints to the Lord's Supper, though they be destitute of a Saving Work of God's Spirit on their Hearts*. In it he held that "Sanctifying grace is not necessary to the lawful attending" of any of the rites of the Christian religion. To partake of the second sacrament would serve as a check upon a man's behavior and thus place him in a more favorable position to receive God's grace.[32] This constituted in principle a very grave departure from the Reformed faith, since it denied the inherent depravity of man and his inability to do anything to receive the favor of God.

Although Mather was by far and away the more logical of the two and at the same time presented a far greater array of Biblical texts, Stoddard really gained the victory. In spite of many glaring inconsistencies and inaccuracies, his theory made a strong appeal to the clergy who sought to remedy the slow but steady decline in the churches. It seemed to fit the need of the times. Little did they realize that this externalization of the individual's relation to the church and to God undermined the whole structure of Calvinistic theology to which they were committed. In the west particularly it was adopted, and soon the distinction between members in full communion and those by church covenant was ignored.[33]

Without a doubt Stoddardeanism did much to further the loss of spirituality. Church discipline was neglected to such an extent that only those who were guilty of heinous offenses against public morality were rebuked. The half-way members received all the privileges of full members. And lest they be offended, the ministers were forced to modify their preaching. In fairness to the ministers it ought to be added that the difficulty lay with the people as much as with them. It is true that total depravity and inability were preached to the neglect of repentance and faith. However, as Schneider points out, there was abroad in New England among people of all classes a new spirit not at all inclined to believe in total depravity and to seek the greater glory of God in all of life.[34] Some have held that Stoddardeanism was responsible for Unitarianism. In view of the geographical distribution of the churches, this cannot be maintained. Unitarianism made its chief inroads along the seaboard, when the theory of Stoddard was not widely practiced.[35] The type of spiritual life found in the churches at that time has often been characterized as a 'low Arminianism."[36] Trumbull says, "Numbers of them (the ministers) were Arminians, preachers of a dead, cold morality, without any distinction of it from heathen morality, by the principles of evangelical love and faith."[37] Without a doubt this period was the lowest in degree of spirituality in the history of the first two centuries of New England Congregationalism. Both in theory and practice the gospel had lost its hold on the masses. The type of preaching was either a moralistic Arminianism or an emasculated Calvinism, which in its unbalanced stress on election forgot the covenant idea which would have given room to human responsibility. Foster is quite right when he epitomized the error of those days thus, "And doctrinally considered, the cause of all was the doctrine of inability, so preached as to deplete the churches, by discouraging repentance and faith."[38]

Chapter 7.

Jonathan Edwards: The Half-Way Covenant Attacked

THE outstanding characteristic of the eighteenth century was the gravitation of human society and its outlook from the religious to the secular. So tremendous were the changes which made for this shift that the religious leaders sensed almost immediately the dangerous currents then becoming manifest. Thus they set themselves consciously and conscientiously to counteract these fatal tendencies. Among the great men who ranged themselves against this emphasis was Jonathan Edwards. His rare combination of experiential piety and penetrating logic enabled him to lift New England's organized religious life out of the sad state into which it had declined since the Synod of 1662. Yet in doing so he unwittingly divorced it too radically from the concerns of secular life by making it the interest of the individual as he stood face to face with God.[1]

The name of this religious leader has been connected most commonly with the rise of that new religious phenomenon known as revivalism. It emphasized conscious conversion as the only true method of approaching God. When this became the standard for entering the fellowship of the church, the covenant conception which gave children of believers an organic place in Christ's church was neglected. Thus beginning with Edwards the covenant idea, which was never too firmly grasped by the New England churches, was gradually forgotten.

The Theology of Jonathan Edwards

To understand Edwards' views on the covenant it will be necessary to trace some of his fundamental conceptions.[2] He was a Calvinist; so he considered himself, and so the world since his

136

time has generally judged him. His chief aim was to suppress the "low Arminianism" which had taken root in the churches. To achieve this goal he modified the Calvinistic doctrines in several directions.[3] First of all, in developing his ideas Edwards held that the sinner had the "natural ability" to do the will of God, so that his inability was not the result of "lack of power" but of "lack of inclination." Although this left intact the traditional emphasis on the necessity of regeneration, it lessened the significance of Christian nurture. This theory, developed at length in *A careful and strict Enquiry into the modern prevailing Notions of the Freedom of the Will*,[4] stressed the voluntaristic tendency so evident in all his works. Somewhat related to this was his second contention that virtue was disinterested benevolence or "disinterested love to being." This was a conscious attempt to salvage the waning glory of God. In the third place he sought to bring consistency into the views regarding the chief end of man and creation. Thus he taught that divine action in salvation and punishment flowed from the same source, which was God's wise benevolence to the created order. To preserve the unity of the race, to account for the universality of sin and to maintain his position that all sin is by its very nature voluntary Edwards resorted to a new theory of the transmission of Adam's sin to all his physical descendants. The unity of the individuals with the race he represented as the result of God's immediate creative activity, which he regarded as continuous. The first and fourth contentions especially had bearing upon the idea of the covenant.

Especially in his attack on Arminianism Edwards developed his own theory of the will. The basic disagreement between the Calvinists and the Arminians on this score was whether the freedom necessary to human responsibility required the freedom from necessity, or to use Edwards' words, the freedom from necessity of consequence. To solve the problem Edwards distinguished between moral and natural ability. Wherever there is no lack of strength and no physical obstacles to hinder the performance, we have what he termed "natural ability." Moral ability and inability took into consideration the deeper and internal desires and refusals (lack of inclination) to act in accordance with duty.

On this basis he argued that no man could be justly held for natural ability, since its causes lie outside of man's personal being. With moral inability the question is quite another. Because the moral quality resides within the nature of the act and not at all in its causes, the person must be held responsible, whether he is at liberty to will the act or not. To clinch the argument he claimed that vices are denounced because of moral qualities resident in them and not because of the occasions giving rise to them. Thus he separated moral character entirely from freedom, which question according to him was an afterthought. Thus though the moral character is fixed (inability being universal), the individual is responsible. Behind the acts of man he recognized motives, to which he ascribed causative power| As long as these were directed away from and contrary to God, man's whole life would be sinful.[5] Thus he sought to prove Calvinism with its doctrines of depravity, necessity of regeneration and divine sovereignty intellectually tenable. However, the unconscious emphasis on logical consistency worked havoc when further developed by his successors.

His tendency to draw away from the covenant idea is further demonstrated by his theories concerning universal sinfulness. These he developed in *The Great Christian Doctrine of Original Sin Defended*. The two main elements concerned the depravity of human nature and the imputation of Adam's sin. The latter was really his chief interest. To claim that he chose for mediate as over against immediate imputation, thus maintaining a form of Realism instead of Federalism, hardly seems to do justice to some passages. Rather, he took his stand apart from these controversies and injected into Christian theology a novel conception.[6] He concluded that man was born into the world in such a condition which would necessarily lead to sin. The condition was by its very nature unfit for holiness, and could thus be termed "depraved." He did accept the idea of Adam's federal headship. However, the first transgression was not imputed to make it the sin of all men, but was "imputed because it is the sin of all men, for they committed it in Adam." All sin, Edwards maintained, was voluntary and thus consisted in choice. To uphold this he developed the idea of the identity of every individual with Adam. After the primal sin, the Holy Spirit withdrew himself. Consequently Adam and all his descendants are sinful. "The first depravity of the heart, and that imputation of that sin are both the consequences of that established union; but yet in such order that the evil disposition is first and the charge of guilt consequent, as it was in the case of Adam himself."[7] In order to justify this Edwards had to teach that all created things are directly dependent upon God who is pure being. He upholds them from moment to moment as if they were being constantly created. The continuance of consciousness, so essential to conscious personal identity, is really the continued creative activity of God. The same divine will possesses the power to make Adam and any other person identical at the same time, because He chooses to regard them as the same person. Thus the race is virtually reduced to one person, which is a species of realism. Thus the unity is no longer grounded in an organic relation. This sounded the death-knell for a vital covenant conception, since in Edwards natural and organic relationships made room for speculative theories.

The real intent behind Edwards' labors was laudable indeed. The orthodoxy of New England was largely formal. The Half-way Covenant had taught the people that they could have acceptable relations with God apart from the special operation of the Holy Spirit. Unconsciously Stoddardeanism fostered the notion that the performance of religious duties might lead to spiritual renewal.[8] Thus there was a great trust in the external means without a conscious dependence upon the Spirit. The Christian life was in danger of being regarded as an inheritance passed on from parents to children. Against this Edwards militated. The roots of his theories lay in his profound faith in and practical experience of God's sovereignty. Therefore he could never view morality as a substitute for genuine piety of the heart. This was already evident in his first published sermon on *God Glorified in Man's Dependence*. Herein he affirmed, "Faith is a sensibleness of what is real in the work of redemption; and as we do really wholly depend on God, so the soul that believes doth entirely depend on God for all salvation, in its own sense and act. Faith abases men and exalts God, it gives all the glory of redemption to God alone."[9] This insistence upon salvation as solely the fruit of divine grace became increasingly evident in the two controversies into which he was drawn while pastor at Northampton.[10]

The Theory and Consequences of Revivalism

The first controversy concerned the nature and validity of revivals, which were largely occasioned by Edwards' preaching of the gospel of divine sovereignty.

Revivals as a phenomenon in American religious life did not begin with the labors of Whitefield and others during the Great Awakening of 1740. Neither did they first appear on the scene during the early reawakenings of spiritual life in Northampton under Edwards. Already during the long pastorate of his grandfather there were definite periods of renewed interest in spiritual things called "revivals." In 1672, 1682, 1695, 1711, and 1717 the town experienced what that aged pastor termed "harvests." However young Edwards was the first to give an accurate description as well as a rather complete evaluation of the phenomenon.

His first work on the subject was *A Faithful Narrative of the Surprising Work of God in the Conversion of Many Hundred Souls in Northampton, Mass., A.D.* 1735. In it he traced the earlier degeneracy of the town and the gradual awakening during a series of his sermons on Justification by Faith.[11] Tracing the course of the revival he wrote, "The town seemed to be full of the presence of God. It was never so full of love, nor so full of joy, and yet so full of distress, as it was then."[12] He cherished the fond hope that "more than 300 souls were savingly brought home to Christ in this town in the space of half a year."[13] According to him there were many varieties of religious experience, some awakened gradually and others instantaneously. Throughout the emphasis fell on the sovereignty of God in the work of grace, especially in the records of the children converted.[14] His definition of conversion is very significant, "Conversion is a great and glorious work of God's power, at once changing the heart, and infusing life into the dead soul; though that grace that is then implanted does more gradually display itself in some than in others."[15] It is evident that he made no clear-cut distinction between regeneration and conversion. Here he followed the Puritan tradition which made little distinction between the gift of new life and its first conscious operation in the sinner brought "under conviction." Describing the aftermath, Edwards wrote, "It began to be very sensible that the Spirit of God was gradually withdrawing from us, and after this time Satan seemed to be more let loose, and raged in a dreadful manner."[16] This continued until 1740, when the great revival spread over large sections of colonial America. Once more Edwards occupied a position of prominence. This time he took up his pen to give a more eloquent and systematic exposition of the work of revivals. A series of three works on the subject appeared, bearing the titles, *Some Thoughts concerning the present Revival of Religion in New England* (1740), *The distinguishing Marks of a Work of the Spirit of God* (1743), and the best known *A Treatise concerning Religious Affections.*

Revivals, he affirmed, were to be regarded as the work of the sovereign God by which He stirs up His church. He bestows the necessary saving grace where and whensoever He will. In spite of the excesses which form an undeniable part of the movement, it is the true and proper method by which the church is reformed and revived. According to their nature and purpose revivals result in a radical reform of individual and social life, caused by fear of sin and its consequences as well as a realization of the work of Jesus Christ as the only ground of salvation. In these discussions

Edwards nowhere touches upon the subject of the position of children of believing parents in the churches. He strongly champions the ideal of personal commitment as necessary unto salvation. Because of his strong stress on the will and emotions, which for him belonged properly to the activity of the will, he expected even of children a definite and conscious conversion to God before cherishing any hopes concerning their spiritual state.[17] This is further evident from other works, chiefly his sermons. After having exhorted the aged and the young people in his *Sinners in the Hands of an Angry God*,[18] he turned to the children with these words, "And you children that are unconverted, don't you know that you are going down to hell to bear the dreadful wrath of that God that is now angry with you every day and every night? Will you be content to be the children of the devil, when so many other children in the land are converted and are become the holy and happy children of the King of Kings? And let every one of you that is yet out of Christ and hanging over the pit of hell, whether they be old men and women or middle-aged or young people or little children, now hearken to the loud calls of God's word and providence. . . ."[19] All unregenerate persons were placed on one level, and the same conscious experience of God's converting Spirit was demanded in the form of a conscious surrender to the divine will.

At the close of the last-named book there was a lengthy reference to the covenant. This concerned not the Covenant of Grace but the church-covenant. Thus he sought to emphasize the necessity of true covenanting from the heart rather than the external form found in so many of the churches in his day.[20]

The tremendous awakening of 1740 had some consequences which Edwards rejected. Everywhere men began to imitate him and other leaders by seeking to induce religious frenzy in the congregations. On this score the new movement encountered strong opposition from the intellectuals in eastern Massachusetts. These were led by the brilliant Rev. Charles Chauncy, whose *Seasonable Thoughts on the Religion of New England* was designed as a refutation of the chief contentions of Edwards. He sought to disprove the validity of revivals by pointing out the excesses of which many preachers and people were guilty.

In championing revivals and their technique Edwards at one and the same time upheld and broke down the Puritan tradition. This is evident, if we remember that at the outset this tradition contained two incompatible elements. The Reformed emphasis on organic relations, which was weak at its best in their theories, was wholly discarded by him. The Anabaptist individualistic piety and church polity triumphed. Thus in spite of his heroic defense of certain Calvinistic positions, he overthrew the Calvinistic heritage of the churches by championing revivals as the true method of church reformation. This is further evident from other consequences. First of all, they occasioned the outbreak of new enthusiasm for Congregational piety in Eastern Connecticut under such men as Nathan Cole and others. They reacted to the firmly entrenched conservatism around them and insisted on vigorous evangelism.

Closely connected with this was the rise of the conventicles, which in several places threatened the position of the organized church.[21] Especially where the pastors opposed the enthusiasm and emotionalism of the new movement, the laity met in homes for mutual edification. Here often the preachers were mercilessly criticized as unregenerate.[22] Out of these groups, which became increasingly prevalent during the last half of the eighteenth century, many Baptist churches were organized.[23] From this it is apparent that there was no longer any unanimity among the Congregationalists on the score of doctrine. Those who opposed the revivals were either old-school Calvinists who feared the rise of an evangelical Arminianism and the liberals who had passed beyond the stage of "low Arminianism" to positions where they were influenced by Socinian ideas which filtered in from abroad. In the course of the controversy the New Lights, who favored the revivals, withdrew from the churches and organized new fellowships for the regenerate, where the pure church ideal in its radical form was championed.[24]

Such a consistent and thoroughgoing application of the theory that only consciously regenerate people constituted the church of Christ led necessarily to the denial of the Scripturalness of infant baptism. This happened in several cases.[25] Thus the covenant relationship everywhere was neglected. To maintain the position of children in the church became one of the chief concerns of the Edwardean School. However, the more its leaders argued, the more they compromised with the Baptist position. The net result was a tremendous increase of Baptist churches during the Second Awakening some decades later. In evaluating the influence of the revival movement upon the history of the churches Walker says, "It was not only a tremendous quickening of the Christian life, it changed the conceptions of entrance on that life in a way which profoundly affected the majority of American churches to this day . . . It emphasized the conception of a transforming regenerative change, a "conversion," as the normal method of entrance into the kingdom of God. It gave general diffusion to the Baptist or Congregational view of the church as a company of experiential Christians. It laid little weight on Christian nurture."[26]

The Controversy on Qualifications for Communion Attendance

The truth of Walker's statement that the revivals made conscious conversion the requisite for full membership is borne out by the history of Edwards' second controversy at Northampton. It grew out of the first and led to the break between him and the congregation. The revival experiences were in line with his conviction that all true Christians were deeply impressed by God's glory manifested in His saving grace. Many who joined the churches in times of revival, however, did not manifest this characteristic. In consequence he decided that something would have to be done in the direction of preventing the profanation of the Lord's Table. Because his religion and that of many others had been fanned into flame, he expected such vital fellowship with God to be requisite for full church membership.

These new ideas he championed in his *Humble Inquiry into the Rule of the Word of God concerning the Qualifications requisite to a complete standing and full communion in the Christian Church.* In the preface he acknowledged that several of his theories clashed with those held by his esteemed grandfather. At the outset he merely opposed the extremes of Stoddardeanism and the Half-way Covenant theory. He at the same time strongly opposed the position of the Separatistic groups who claimed to be lineal descendants of early Congregationalism. Of those who became schismatic because of their revivalism he wrote, "I have no better opinion of their notion of a *pure church* by means of a *spirit* of *discerning,* their *censorious outcries* against the standing ministers and churches in general, their *lay-ordinances,* their *lay-preachings,* and *public exhortings,* and *administering sacraments,* their assuming, self-confident, contentious uncharitable *separating spirit.*"[27] In this new work Edwards made the distinction between "members of the *visible church in general* and members in *complete standing.*"[28] To the first class belonged the children and such adults who had no right to the second sacrament. This might only be done by "visible professing saints." Here he made the legitimate distinction between the right in foro ecclesia (on the basis of visible profession and conduct) and in one's own heart.[29] The church had to judge on the basis of the former[30] Thus only those might be allowed at the Table who openly acknowledged and owned God's Covenant of Grace, described by him as the covenant "of espousals to Christ; on our part it is the giving of our souls to Christ as his spouse."[31]

Edwards repudiated the distinction between an external and an internal covenant. He claimed, however, that one could be member of the Covenant of Grace either externally or internally, depending on whether or not one was subjectively in possession of saving grace.[32] All baptized persons had to profess their faith before being allowed to come to the second sacrament. "When those persons who were baptized in infancy properly own their baptismal covenant, the meaning is, that they now, being capable to act for themselves, do professedly and explicitly make their parents' act, in giving them up to God, their own. . ."[33] Thus all public covenanting, too, was regarded as a giving up of oneself to God, which implied renouncing the world. What Edwards sought to do was to make active faith as the fruit of God's saving grace requisite for attending Communion. Thus he vigorously opposed Stoddardeanism. Those whose minds were willing to accept Christ but whose conduct was not in harmony therewith he claimed "are not truly pious" but have "guile, disguise, and false appearance."[34] He claimed that the disciples admitted only such who claimed possession of saving grace. Although scandalous persons were found in the earliest churches, these always crept in unawares, he contended.[35]

On this basis he emphasized the necessity of self-examination. Everyone should judge before attending Communion whether he had personally found Christ as his Savior and Only Good.[36] Communion was "a mutual solemn profession of the two parties transacting the covenant of Grace, and visibly united in that covenant; the Lord Jesus Christ, by his minister on the one hand, and the communicants on the other . . . Thus the Lord's Supper is plainly a *mutual* renovation, confirmation, and seal of the covenant of Grace."[37]

The author anticipated certain objections to his theory. If some would claim that the Israelites never were required to manifest visible holiness before coming to the Passover, Edwards replied that in the New Testament the ethical and spiritual demands were higher.[38] He sought to overthrow Stoddardeanism[39] by insisting that their main premise that in the church there is an external covenant with external promises and obligations was unscriptural.[40] Further he discussed the necessity of baptism to church membership and attendance upon Communion. He repudiated any magical conception of the grace thereby signified and sealed.[41] It seems as if he considered the covenant line broken off after one generation of unconverted. This was in harmony with his emphasis upon the child's position in the church on the basis of an act of the parents on its behalf.[42]

To this treatise he appended an interesting letter from Thomas Foxcroft of Boston, dated June 26, 1749. In it the five fundamental questions which had arisen in the course of the sacramental dispute are taken up. The true Protestant doctrine was set forth in the following propositions: 1—Self-examination demands that the communicant search his life for the presence of "real godliness" and not merely the "truth of grace;"[43] 2—Those who know themselves devoid of real grace may not partake of the Lord's Supper;[44] 3—Coming to the Supper, one must profess "saving faith and repentance . . . which are the terms of the covenant of grace;"[45] 4—Although it is necessary to have "the special exercise of faith which fits for the Lord's Supper," this is not essentially different than that which is required for baptism;[46] 5—The parent who presents his child for baptism by that act virtually renews the covenant for himself.[47]

Opposition to this strict position was immediately forthcoming from the camp of the Stoddardeans. The chief antagonist was Solomon Williams[48] who wrote *The True State of the Question concerning the Qualifications Necessary to Communion.* He defended the thesis, "All persons whom God has taken into the external Covenant are bound to the external Duties of it, except such as God hath expressly excluded; but he hath expressly excluded none but ignorant and scandalous Persons. From hence it follows that if there be any unconverted Persons in the external Covenant, 'tis their Duty to attend."[49] Williams further maintained that the Supper was according to its very nature a "converting Ordinance only to Church Members." The new element injected into the controversy at this point concerned the validity of speaking of an external covenant. This became one of the chief issues in the further disputes between the Edwardeans and the successors of Williams.[50] Here is evident the fruit of the Half-way Covenant, for now many insisted that many church members were not in the Covenant of Grace but still as "unregenerate were in covenant with God." Convinced that in the "external covenant" there were external privileges and duties, Williams contrasted these with the fruits of the "internal covenant." The latter enjoyed all the flavor which the term had enjoyed in the hey-day of colonial Puritanism under the influence of the Westminster standards.

It did not take long for this external covenant to become the storm-center of debate. One of the results was that in many of the discussions the "Covenant of Grace" was made meaningless by the endless refinements of theologians.

Edwards replied in his *Misrepresentations corrected, and Truth vindicated, in a reply to the Rev. Mr. Williams' Book.* He claimed that Williams misrepresented the whole struggle between himself and the Northampton church. Here the controversy took a strange turn. Both Edwards and his opponent held that only visible and professing saints might partake of the Lord's Supper. But on this basis the latter supported the idea that unsanctified persons might attend,[51] for, said he, "This profession of godliness must be in words not of a determinate meaning . . ., obliging us to understand them of saving religion."[52] The absurdity and danger of this position provoked a sharp reply from Edwards. It became evident that they used virtually the same terms. However, the content which each poured into these was vastly different.[53]

Another question closely related to the controversial issue was: In what sense are those who are baptized and are members of the church but remain and die in a state of unregeneracy in the Covenant of Grace?[54] Edwards admitted the presence of "multitudes of unsanctified persons" in the churches of his day and held "in that sense they were God's covenant people that by their own binding act they were engaged to God in covenant; though such an act, performed without habitual holiness, be an unlawful one."[55] Since much of the argument was occasioned by a neglect of the Scriptural teaching, he devoted large sections of the footnotes to this material. The chief end of all human society was the glory of God, which could be achieved by aiming in every circumstance of life at the special design for which each was intended. Thus the purpose of the church was "to exhibit before the world real Christianity" or "to promote religion."

On this basis the church is to judge individually of its members.[56] However, it may not form an opinion respecting the person's spiritual state before God. That was a matter between the individual and God.

Treatise on "The History of Redemption"

In connection with this study of the covenant concept one of the more obscure writings deserves mention. *The History of the Work of Redemption* was an attempt to trace the idea throughout the Biblical revelation and church history.[57] In it Edwards consistently used covenant terminology without making the idea truly determinative. The appearance of this type of thought can be explained, if we remember that the theological ideas of Coccejus and the Federal School in the Netherlands found their way to New England through the works of Turretin and others. It is interesting to us, since it demonstrates that at this time the covenant idea was not yet forgotten.

The first revelation of the Covenant of Grace is to be found in Genesis 3:15, where Christ is presented as having "immediately stepped in between an holy, infinite, offended Majesty and offending mankind."[58] The essence of the promise was the assurance that the seed of the woman would destroy man's enemies. This theme is developed throughout.[59] The real promise of the Covenant of Grace was Christ Himself. Therefore David was said to have prized the covenant so highly, because he saw therein "God's greatest smile."[60] His statements of the purpose of Christ's incarnation and the nature of His atonement harmonized with Westminster. Christ was thought of as having fulfilled the Covenant of Works for His people, so that they might be saved by grace.[61]

In the times after Christ God was concerned with the establishment of His Kingdom. In this period Edwards distinguished four dispensations: the destruction of Jerusalem marking the end of the first, the conversion of Constantine the end of the second, the destruction of the Antichrist the end of the third, and the destruction of all the ungodly at the end of the ages the end of the last. This last dispensation was characterized as "accompanied with an advancement of the church into that state of the glorious prevalence of truth, liberty, peace and joy, that we so often read of in the prophetical parts of scripture."[62]

The book aimed at being a Biblical theology and a philosophy of history based on the covenant idea. Throughout there is little that may be regarded as new. In treating the material the author forgot too much the historical aspect of the covenant. His emphasis was individualistic and thus did not do justice to organic relations.[63] Without a conception of the covenant which takes its rise in the organic relation in which the members of the race stand to their head, and again the relations between that head and God, and finally the relations obtaining between the three persons of the Godhead, the whole idea of the covenant becomes no more than an anthropomorphic representation of God's dealings with men, which must sooner or later lose its hold on religious thought and life.

Though Edwards sought to reinstate Calvinism in the New England churches as the source of spiritual vitality, he failed, largely because his successors developed his several deviations from earlier theologians rather than the main body of his thought. Thus in several respects Edwards' labors mark a turning point in the history of Congregational thought. In summarizing his significance the emphasis must fall upon his attack on Stoddardeanism and the Half-way Covenant practice in vogue for nearly a century. In doing this he rendered priceless service. As regards his conceptions of the nature and constituency of the church and the place of the means of grace there is little originality. Throughout he championed the Congregational ideal of a church consisting of the regenerate.[64] This virtually excluded the children from the Covenant of Grace, of whom he could not affirm regeneration in the sense of his definition. Although he upheld the New England tradition of infant baptism, he seems to have based it too much on the considerations of external church membership. Thus he stressed the "obligations" of the children more than their "privileges."

For this very reason instead of restoring the covenant conception to its true and legitimate place in the church on the basis of the original confessions after having successfully attacked the false theories prevalent in his days, Edwards did perhaps more than anyone else toward preparing for the complete and final eradication of this idea from New England religious life. He was chiefly responsible for completely "Congregationalizing" the Congregational church, since his ideas on revivalism and qualifications for church membership signalled the ultimate triumph of religious individualism and voluntarism in New England.

As Bronkema points out in his *The Essence of Puritanism,* Congregationalism arose out of English Puritanism, a phenomenon peculiar to the English Reformation. To understand it requires an appreciation of the English temper and mind which is practical (voluntaristic) instead of theoretical (intellectualistic). Hence it never developed its own theology but borrowed from others. Contact with the Calvinists gave it a Reformed body of theology. However, its pure church ideal and its emphasis on experientialism was inherited from the Anabaptists. This left little room for the organic conceptions so strongly embodied in the Calvinism of Scotland and the Netherlands. Edwards by stressing the legitimacy of revivals steered the churches still more in the individualistic direction.

In spite of his strong defense of characteristic Calvinistic doctrines such as election and original sin, he had no eye for organic relations. In fact his theism has been attacked on the score of stressing too much the immediate and direct working of God. Though not denying the presence of natural and spiritual laws, these were virtually obscured. This idea carried over in the revival technique lost sight of the use which God made of His own ordinances. To this Horace Bushnell reacted so strongly nearly a century later. All this demonstrates that the Puritans never gave whole-hearted allegiance to the Calvinistic construction of the relation between nature and grace, creation and redemption.[65] There was always a tendency toward Anabaptist dualism. The aversion to art and culture among many, the strong tendency toward a legalistic construction of ethics and the separation of religion from daily concerns may be mentioned as evidences. Furthermore, there was an unprecedented emphasis on the soteriological aspect of Christian doctrine so characteristic of all groups who do not grapple with the underlying issue of the connection of nature and grace.

In spite of the weaknesses which cleaved to his construction, however, one cannot conclude any study of Edwards without profound admiration for the manner in which he opposed the dead formalism which had held sway for decades and replaced it with a dynamic and living conception of man's religious relation to God.

Chapter 8.

The New Divinity — The Half-Way Covenant Overthrown

ALTHOUGH New England had for some time been losing its uniformity on doctrinal matters, it was not until the middle of the eighteenth century that these differences crystallized into well-defined groups. Four of them constituted the pattern of religious and ecclesiastical life during the fifty years following Edwards' dismissal from the Northampton church. Three were schools of thought within the Congregational fold, while the fourth consisted of those whose radical enthusiasm and support of revivalism had caused them to break with the established church. The growing liberal party, generally characterized by the name Arminians, found its chief support in the old seaboard towns. Equally strong in opposition to the new ideas and methods of church reformation were the old-school Calvinists. They followed in the footsteps of the Half-way Covenant supporters, especially as these had come under the influence of Stoddardeanism. The new group, which supported the revivals and was destined to become the most influential, came to be known as the New Divinity or Edwardean School.

The rise of this new theological party, which in some respects aimed to be more Calvinistic than Calvin himself, was the direct result of the Great Awakening. Its avowed aim was to steer a safe middle course between the reactionary anti-revivalists and the enthusiasts who tended strongly in the direction of the Baptist positions.[1] Perhaps no other group of American religious thinkers has been more misunderstood and consequently maligned than these spiritual successors of Jonathan Edwards. Bates in his *The American Faith* has called them, "a veritable

153

intellectual bureaucracy, . . . stiff-necked theologians, . . . and infinitely subtle formulators of meaningless technical distinctions."[2] On the face of it this criticism may appeal to those who fail to understand their approach to the controversies of their age. However, the criticism is manifestly unfair. Here were men who wrote voluminously, and their works were read by their contemporaries. They made a tremendous impact upon their generation and for upwards of seventy five years controlled the theological development of New England. Their influence spread far beyond the narrow confines of the Connecticut valley where most of them lived and labored all their lives.

During this period the idea of church membership underwent a radical transformation. Although these men attempted to uphold the Congregational emphasis on personal experience, the relation of members to the church was gradually externalized. In so far as the technique of revivalism triumphed, individualism ran wild in the churches. Several modifications introduced by the New Divinity led to the loss of the Calvinistic heritage. Their emphasis on speculative theories concerning the will caused the organic conception of the individual's relation to the covenant and church to perish as much as did the radical contentions of the Baptists.

The theological development of these years may be grouped around four major controversies. The first discussed the question or original sin and infant responsibility. The second concerned itself with the nature of the Covenant of Grace and sought an answer to the question whether or not there was an "external" or "graceless" covenant. The third dealt with the use of "means" in the Covenant of Grace. The final discussion carried through the argument begun by Edwards and Williams on the qualifications for admission to the Lord's Table.

Controversy Concerning Original Sin

As noted before, Jonathan Edwards did most of his original work while in virtual exile among the Housatonic Indians at Stockbridge, Mass. There he also wrote the two treatises *The*

Christian Doctrine of Original Sin Defended and *A Careful and Strict Inquiry into the Modern prevailing Notions of that Freedom of the Will*. In the former he treated the two significant problems of the depravity of the race and the imputation of Adam's primal sin.

Carefully but irresistibly he argued that sin was universal. He did not identify it with external acts but demonstrated that it was a tendency or "propensity"[3] in man's constitutional nature by which he is unsuited for his environment. In answering the second question he rejected the Calvinistic conception of the immediate imputation of the guilt of Adam's first transgression on the basis of the unity of the human race which rested upon the federal headship of the first parent. Instead he advocated his theory of creatio continua, in which God was said to regard all men as one with Adam and therefore guilty.[4]

The conclusion of the matter was that all sin was regarded as voluntary. Men were sinners because they lacked the Holy Spirit and thus had no communion with God, which alone could keep them free from iniquity. What Edwards really did was to place the corrupt constitution prior to the imputation of guilt. Since he did not ascribe positive sinfulness to that nature as such, his position was not identical with that of the school of Saumur.[5]

This unique and original defense of the unity of the race and the universality of sin and guilt had several far-reaching consequences for the development of New England theology. The denial of Adam's federal headship contributed greatly to the loss of the organic covenant conception. To this was added his insistence on creatio continua, which removed the whole problem into the realm of metaphysics and did not a little toward weakening and finally destroying belief in original sin. Human responsibility seemed to be rendered more certain in the preaching but at the expense of divine sovereignty.

Reaction did not come from those who objected to Edwards' theory. However, some refused to agree with its practical implications, for they realized that the results for infants were the same under this new teaching as they had been under the Puritan doctrine. In both cases all children were regarded as responsible for Adam's sin and thus under God's condemnation.

The opposition arose when an anonymous publication appeared, entitled *A Winter Evening's Discussion upon the Doctrine of Original Sin . . . wherein the notion of our having sinned in Adam and being on that account ONLY liable to eternal damnation is proved to be unscriptural, irrational, and of dangerous tendency*. It seems that Samuel Webster of Salisbury, Mass., was the author of the dialogue. He argued the question on its practical grounds.[6] Since God is the "holiest, justest, and kindest being in heaven and earth,"[7] it is impossible to believe such a horrible doctrine as that championed by Edwards. All three attributes ascribed to God would prevent one from subscribing to the idea that God made infants "heirs of hell," thus "making them first to open their eyes in torments; and this all for a sin which certainly they had no hand in."[8]

The intense emotional background of the revivals, so utterly foreign to the conservative intellectualism of the earlier Puritans, was now being utilized to oppose the traditional doctrines. Webster thus could lean almost exclusively on the concept of God's goodness to the exclusion of His sovereignty and justice, which had been the themes of several earlier revivalistic sermons. Thus the author championed the innocence of all infants.[9] There was no room for the imputation of Adam's guilt in any sense, for "sin and guilt (so far as I can see) are personal matters, as much as knowledge."[10] That Adam "should stand as a federal head or representative for all his posterity, so that if he sinned, he and all his posterity should be condemned to hell fire for his first transgression"[11] was inconsistent with human reason. In fact, the author throughout made more use of rational arguments than he did of Scripture.

There is an inconsistency in the dialogue. Though claiming to reject complete the idea of federal headship, Webster held that all men did suffer for the folly of Adam's sin. In fact, that first sin was somehow connected with the sinfulness of all men.

This was perhaps an obscure remnant of his earlier Calvinism which he himself hardly recognized. However, that he was attacking the heart of the old theology he admitted openly. He spoke quite convincingly of "our compassionate heavenly Father"[12] and urged his readers to a degree of doctrinal toleration unheard of in Puritan history. Since everyone, he claimed, was agreed on the fundamentals of divine love and wisdom, the atonement through Christ, and the blessed resurrection of the dead, such a matter as original sin ought to be deemed "a very little thing."[13] Plainly Webster had used Edwards' theory of the voluntary nature of all sin to advance the age-old Pelagian contention that if sin is truly voluntary, there can be no imputation of guilt from one person to another mediately or immediately.

Those who still adhered to the old Calvinistic position realized that Webster attacked their conception of the way of salvation. Therefore only a brief period elapsed before Peter Clark, pastor of the church at Danvers, Mass., replied with his *The Scripture Doctrine of Original Sin, Stated and Defended. In a Summer Morning's Conversation between a Minister and a Neighbour. Containing Remarks on a late anonymous Pamphlit, intitled, "A Winter Evening's Conversation."* . . . This was the attempt of one who still loved the old doctrines to vindicate them in the eyes of such who might otherwise be tempted to yield to the seemingly more humane position of Webster. Clark openly admitted concerning original sin, "This is a doctrine most disagreeable to the proud heart of man, as it tends to beat down that conceit he is apt to entertain of the goodness of his nature."[14] And yet the facts of experience and the teachings of Scripture, according to the author, left no room for doubt. The universality of human apostasy, affecting as it does "the whole species, must originate in some cause or principle, that extends its influence to the whole kind."[15] That he can find only in the fall of Adam in Paradise. However, to Clark's mind there is no federal connection between Adam and the race. "Natural generation" is sufficient to account for the universality of sin and the depravity of the race. Instead of taking Edwards' approach basing man's sinfulness on the unity of the race, Clark distinguished between the imputation of natural acts and that of moral acts.[16] In this way he sought to maintain the guilt of all.

Clark did not, however, give any prominence to the theory of imputation. He averred that it was more necessary to believe in human sinfulness than in the imputation of Adam's first sin to the rest of the race. "This latter . . . is a matter of faith; being made known to us only in the Holy Scriptures. The former is a matter of sense and experience; yet not so fully manifested, as when the light of Scripture is brought to our hearts."[17]

Thus it became evident that all who believed in the voluntary nature of all sin as defined by Edwards and his contemporaries either denied or ignored the imputation of Adam's sin. On his own basis Clark insisted that "there is no reason to conclude" that infants would suffer the torments of hell purely on the basis of Adam's first transgression. However, he was quick to add, "The Almighty has not thought it fit so far therein to gratify our curiosity as to acquaint us with the method of his dealing with infants."[18] His rather strange construction was an attempt to formulate a theory of original sin which would be more palatable to the popular taste of his day. Sentiment and "reasonableness" rather than Scriptural consistency constituted the bases of his contentions. Individualism had gained another victory over the organic view of the unity of the race. Behind much of the speculation on the eternal state of those dying in infancy we see the weakness of much of New England theological theory. Although the early Calvinists in those churches clung tenaciously to the theories of original sin and imputation, they did not balance the same with the Reformed conception of the covenant which insisted on salvation through Christ promised in the way of the covenant.

Immediately the liberal party, headed by Charles Chauncy of Boston, seized upon the fact that the Calvinists were virtually surrendering their doctrine of original sin and thus exposing their whole theological structure. In his *Opinion of one that has perused the "Summer Morning's Conversation"* . . . *in two things principally* he contended that Clark had made it virtually impossible to believe in imputation. In fact, he went so far as to accuse Clark of virtually deserting the doctrine which he claimed to be supporting. It was painfully apparent that Chauncy was right. On the basis of Clark's contentions one could no longer claim to be a Calvinist. His reconstruction of the doctrine introduced irreconcilable elements into Calvinistic theology, which of necessity must hold to the depravity of infants and their liability to eternal punishment in some way or another.

By this time the controversy had taken such a serious turn that the peace of the churches was being disturbed. The Edwardeans then stepped into the arena of debate. In 1758 Bellamy wrote *The Wisdom of God in the Permission of Sin,*[19] and one year later Hopkins wrote *Sin through Divine Interposition an Advantage to the Universe.*[20] From the titles it is clear that the controversy had taken a new turn. The writers were no longer concerned with the infants only but rather sought to justify the necessity of eternal damnation as proper punishment for sin. It was out of this question which lurked in the minds of many that the Universalist trouble was born. At the time of its outbreak the ideas of federal headship and imputation had lost their influence in New England theology.

Controversy Concerning the Nature of the Covenant of Grace

More or less directly related to the subject of the Covenant of Grace was the question raised in connection with the appearance of certain pamphlets concerning the existence of a so-called "graceless" or "external" covenant. To this those then might profess adherence who felt themselves destitute of regenerating grace but nevertheless desired a place in the church.

The chief advocate of this theory was Moses Mather, who in 1759 wrote a treatise of some sixty pages on *The Visible Church in Covenant with God.* In it he defended the position that by uniting with the church one merely agrees intellectually with the church-covenant, which bears no necessary relation to the Covenant of Grace. The signs and seals used are then only those of the "external" covenant. Only upon this basis could infant baptism be vindicated according to him. In contrast with the confessions of faith and plan of discipline current in the Congregational churches, all of which openly declared for the Covenant of Grace as the sole basis of ecclesiastical life and insisted upon the sacraments as holy signs and seals of saving grace and understood profession of faith in terms of a "cordial subjection to Jesus Christ,"[21] Mather sought to prove from Scripture that church membership involved no more than sharing the outward covenant.[22] This latter offered no hope of grace and thus left its members, if they did no more than live up to its outward demands, in the clutches of eternal death.

According to his interpretation this was the covenant with Abraham, with the Israelites at Sinai and with the converts in the early church. Its purpose was to serve as a means to the final end of establishing the Covenant of Grace.[23] Thus he could define the visible church as "a congregation in which there is no visible profession made of real Christianity,[24] i.e. of friendship to Christ, or of Christian grace, or of anything but what is consistent with a state of total enmity to God and Christ, and all spiritual good."[25] A new ground for infant baptism was also propounded. He affirmed that membership in this formal, external, graceless covenant gave a right to the sacrament.

The chief opponent of Mather's ideas was Joseph Bellamy.[26] He is best remembered for his paradoxical statement, "The more unable we are to love God, the more we are to blame."[27] Thus instead of freeing him, man's inability increased his blame according to the New Divinity.

In opposition to Mather, Bellamy sought to restore the old Congregational ideal of the "pure church." In his *A careful and strict Examination of the External Covenant* he pointed out that the new construction was fraught with even greater spiritual dangers than the Half-way Covenant expedient of 1662. His purpose was to defend the "plan" on which the New England churches were founded.[28] This he stated in three propositions. "I. That those who are qualified to offer their children in baptism are equally qualified to come to the Lord's Table; and that therefore the half-way practice which has so much prevailed of late in the country, is unscriptural. II. That baptism and the Lord's Supper are seals of the covenant of grace, and that therefore those who know they have no grace, cannot be active in the sealing of it, consistently with honesty and a good conscience. III. That there is no graceless covenant between God and man existing suited to the temper of graceless men, a compliance with which they might, as such, consistently profess and seal; and that therefore there is no door open for graceless men, as such, to enter into covenant with God."[29] In consequence, when speaking of the sacraments, Bellamy emphasized the spiritual activity of men[30] and spoke of faith as "uniting" the sinner to Christ and "entitling" him to pardon, justification and life.[31]

To clarify his position still more he also wrote *That there is but One Covenant . . . viz. the Covenant of Grace.* In this he argued against Mather that the covenant with Abraham was gracious because of the specific promise. He also demonstrated the inconsistency of Mather, who had written, "I will allow that none but such as profess the Christian religion and will endeavor to conform his practice to the rules of it, ought to be admitted into the church."[32] This played directly into Bellamy's hands, who demonstrated that professing and practicing the Christian faith were impossible without saving grace. It soon became evident that Mather's theory failed to provide a workable conception of the relation between the covenant and church membership on the one hand and the nature and function of infant baptism on the other.

The controversy continued. It now became the avowed purpose of the New Divinity men to crush the Half-way practice, which according to them had robbed New England of vital spirituality. The case against it had been so sufficiently proven, that Bellamy could write without fear of contradiction, "And since those ministers who are in this practice, do grant it to be unscriptural; which, so far as I know, all of them do; nothing now remains but to put them in mind, that the second commandment requireth the receiving, observing and keeping pure and entire all such religious worship and ordinances as God has appointed in his word."[33] The opposition came largely from the churches where the practice lingered on.[34]

Mather, of course, had again gone beyond Stoddardeanism. Instead of viewing the Lord's Supper as a "converting ordinance," thus implying that there was yet another step to be taken unto real membership in the visible church, he reduced church membership to a merely formal relationship to the human institution.

In order to deal this theory its death-blow Bellamy wrote a series of dialogues entitled *The Half-way Covenant, a Dialogue*. These are very significant for the development of the idea of church and covenant in New England.

In the first dialogue the author attacked the position of Increase Mather, who insisted upon a double standard of church membership, holding that until "more full and satisfactory evidences of regeneration and Christian proficiency"[35] were found in the case of the majority, they could not use the second sacrament.[36] This divorce of the two sacraments was according to Bellamy "setting up the commandment of men in place of the precept of Christ."[37] He criticized Stoddardeanism as having completely externalized church membership.[38] At that time again there were many in the churches who openly claimed to be devoid of grace.[39] However, the general theory was that such people were at least partially acceptable to God. To this Bellamy objected by stating, "One baptized in infancy, who in the sight of God practically renounces his baptism when adult, as all do who reject Christ, and continue impenitent, is not considered by God as entitled to the blessings of the new covenant, but as under the curse of the law."[40]

In the second dialogue "Parishioner" insists that if Bellamy ("Minister") is correct, all non-professing but baptized adults should be excommunicated.[41] "To drive this point will make sad work,"[42] Bellamy replies, although he is in agreement with the main contention. In the next dialogue the question of baptism on the basis of the graceless covenant is taken up. "Parishioner" here makes use of Mather's theory, who held that the promise of the parents to God required only "moral sincerity."[43] When the author upholds the higher standards of the sacraments as signs and seals of grace, the objector replies, "Sir, on your plan three quarters of the Christian world will be shut out of the church."[44]

The fourth dialogue was more doctrinal in content. Herein "Parishioner" voiced his objections to the Calvinistic doctrines of total depravity and the necessity of regeneration, since these excluded the possibility of holding that the unregenerate are in some measure holy and acceptable to God.[45] This paved the way for future discussions. Bellamy demonstrated that this was the logical outcome of Stoddardeanism and its successors.

Very evidently he followed his teacher, Jonathan Edwards, to a large extent.[46] Speaking of the false kind of holiness professed by "graceless men," that is by those who heard the gospel but remained impenitent, he affirmed, "For supreme self-love governs every apostate creature, who is totally destitute of true love, of disinterested benevolence to the most high God, the Creator and Lord of heaven and earth."[47] He concluded that Mather's theory was only an ill-concealed effort to compromise the position of the church still more in a time greatly devoid of divine grace.

Others also who came under the spell of Edwards' teachings bitterly opposed the Stoddardean positions. One who accused the spiritual successors of the Half-way theory of Arminianism was Jacob Green,[48] whose *Inquiry into the Constitution and Discipline of the Jewish Church — in order to cast some Light on the Controversy Concerning Qualifications for the Sacraments of the New Testament* exposed three grave errors in the churches of those days. The first was the radical divorce of the sacraments of Baptism and the Lord's Supper; the second, the interrogation into personal Christian experience together with a judging of the heart; the third, the admittance of "graceless persons" to the signs and seals of the Covenant of Grace. He spoke of the external and internal administration of the one covenant. In the "one covenant of Grace with Man" the unregenerate really had no place, although they did enjoy some blessings connected with its external administration.[49] He claimed that the church might admit to the sacraments only such as had a right unto them on the basis of God's Word, which demanded sincerity of heart.[50]

A controversy quite independent historically though connected by virtue of the material discussed was that which disturbed the historic Plymouth church during the pastorate of Chandler Robbins, an able pupil of Bellamy.

In 1772 John Cotton, the teacher of that church, wrote *The general Practice of the Churches of New-England relating to Baptism, vindicated.* He sought to uphold the Half-way Covenant practice of Increase Mather.[51] His contentions were "1st the whole visible church under the new testament is to be baptized. 2d. If a man be once in the church (whether admitted at age or in infancy) nothing less than censurable evil can put him out. 3d. If a parent be in the visible church, his infant child is also."[52] To those who refused to baptize infants of baptized but non-covenanting parents he declared, "You in effect excommunicate them all out of heaven; for there is no salvation out of the church."[53] In fact he went so far as to accuse them of "cutting off their heads" by refusing them the sacrament.[54]

Robbins insisted that Cotton had not argued honestly.[55] In his *Reply to Some Essays lately published by John Cotton, Esq., (of Plymouth) relating to Baptism,* he claimed that too many since the Synod of 1662 believed in two separate and distinct Covenants of Grace, each having its own sacrament. Robbins sought to reunite the two by emphasizing that they were not only signs but also seals of the same grace of God. The tendency in Cotton's position was toward a denial of total depravity, since the Half-way practice did not regard man as by nature entirely an enemy of God.[56]

Of course, the age-old question loomed large in the Plymouth controversy: What will become of the infants who remained unbaptized? Robbins stressed that "unscriptural methods" might never be used to remedy a sad situation.[57] Throughout he upheld the necessity of obeying the commandments of Christ. He claimed that one reason why the Baptists were making such tremendous gains in the Congregational churches lay in the fact that these latter had reduced infant baptism to a "mere ceremony."[58]

Controversy Concerning the Use of the Means of Grace

A subject very intimately bound up with the doctrine of the Covenant of Grace and the growth of children as members of the church by baptism unto spiritual maturity was that of the use of the means of grace. In the course of the discussion the place of children was forgotten, and the question was largely limited to the possibility of regeneration for those adults who made diligent use of them. This demonstrated a growing apathy toward the doctrine of the covenant and a rising interest in revivalism with its neglect of the children.

From the beginning the Puritan churches had strongly emphasized the use of the means. Along with the other Reformed churches they held that the sinner was regenerated in connection with the preaching of the gospel.[59] With the wide-spread appearance of revivals and the discussions which arose in consequence, it soon appeared that the two schools of Calvinistic thought stood poles apart. The men of the old school cherished a high regard for the means. The Rev. Jedidiah Mills of Ripton, Conn., spoke of the "precious means" of grace,[60] while others used expressions which virtually committed them to the position that the Word itself was a vehicle of divine grace.

Because of the tendency present among the Stoddardeans to regard the use of the means as an end in itself, the New Divinity men began to stress reliance upon them as very dangerous to spiritual life.[61] They insisted that there was no half-way house between the penitent and impenitent, the regenerate and unregenerate, the saints and the sinners. Reliance upon them might easily foster a postponement of full surrender to Christ and God. Although much of the speculation was highly theoretical, the practical consequences of the debates were far reaching. The revivalists preached the immediate operation of the Holy Spirit. Sudden and overpowering conversions were regarded as the most genuine. The results were that such a new emphasis led to neglecting the administration of the Word and sacraments.

The debate in its more vital stages was begun by Jonathan Mayhew, who belonged to neither party. He published two sermons on the subject of striving to enter in at the narrow gate.[62] God's message, he was convinced, required great zeal on the part of the sinner. Although he still maintained the necessity of the operation of the Spirit unto regeneration, he sought to prove that God would give the necessary strength to all who showed willingness to strive.[63] Apart from this exercise of the will, there were no requirements or conditions unto salvation.

Without a doubt Mayhew championed a species of Arminianism.[64] In spite of his insistence on the necessity of divine grace, he minimized man's total depravity. He did repudiate any meritorious character of such striving but went astray when teaching that the unregenerate could have desires and strivings after true holiness.[65]

Samuel Hopkins was the first to attack Mayhew and thus precipitated the quarrel on the question of the means between the Stoddardeans and the New Divinity. To understand his attack it will be necessary for us to remind ourselves of a few of his basic contentions. He taught that sin was "the necessary means of the greatest good."[66] Real love to God should be manifested in a complete disinterestedness and absolute surrender to the divine will. Furthermore, God made no promises to the unregenerate. Before anyone received promises, he had to surrender to God. He also rejected the doctrine of original sin. Although the sinfulness of Adam's posterity was connected in some way with the first transgression, man cannot be regarded as a sinner before God before he consciously chooses against God and for sin. "There is, strictly speaking, no other sin but actual sin."[67]

With such a theological position Hopkins reviewed and criticized Mayhew in his *Inquiry concerning the Promises of the Gospel*. In it he maintained that if the sinner truly possessed such strivings as Mayhew had described, these must come from the Spirit through regeneration. If the expression "desiring salvation" meant anything, it involved the deliberate choice of salvation. Unless the will responded to the gospel, there was no striving.[68] Hopkins further gave one of the first clear-cut distinctions between regeneration and conversion among the New England theologians. The former he considered "Divine illumination" or enlightenment by the miraculous correction of the perverse will.[69] Conversion was man's response to that work of the Holy Spirit. It, too, is instantaneous.[70]

Mayhew never replied to this attack. However, the old Calvinists saw in this position an attack on their theories. Thus several answered him.

The first of these was Jedidiah Mills, who published his *Inquiry concerning the State of the Unregenerate under the Gospel*. In it he sought to refute Hopkins' position that the unregenerate under the conviction of sin were in a more dangerous position than those who were entirely indifferent. His theory was based upon the presupposition of degrees of unregeneracy, some being in closer proximity to salvation than others. He was afraid that Hopkins would discourage those who were under conviction and thus cause them to neglect the means.

Hopkins took up the challenge afforded by the work of Mills by writing *The True state and character of the Unregenerate, stripped of all Misrepresentation and Disguise*. It was thoroughgoing in its application of the Edwardean positions. In it he claimed that the sinner was in no different position than Adam before the fall except that he lacked the Holy Spirit. Despite this lack man was in full possession of all his faculties, so that he had sufficient light to know God and understand His demands. Only the perversity of the will made it impossible for man to surrender to God. Thus the greater the degree of light, the more responsible man was. Those who with "clear light and conviction of conscience" remained obdurate were "more guilty, vile, and odious in God's sight" than others.[71]

William Hart of Saybrook sought to attack Hopkins by challenging the Edwardean conception of true virtue or real holiness in his *Brief Remarks on President Edwards' Dissertation concerning the Nature of true Virtue.* In it he demonstrated his own inability to understand the basic positions of the new school.[72]

Perhaps the most influential opponent of Hopkins was Moses Hemmenway. His two works, *Seven Sermons on the Obligation and Encouragement of the Unregenerate, to labor for the Meat which endureth to everlasting Life* and *Vindication of the power, obligation, and encouragement of the unregenerate to attend the means of grace,* constituted the most thoroughgoing defense of the old position. None of the strivings of the unregenerate were in any way meritorious, nor did any of the means have the promises of faith definitely and absolutely annexed to them. Yet it was the duty of all to attend them since "God has commanded them to do so, and it is their duty to obey."[73] He was ready to accept all the Edwardean theories except the distinction between natural and moral ability and inability.[74]

As a final reply Hopkins wrote *Inquiry into the Nature of True Holiness,* which was an elaboration of Edwards' conception of virtue as applied to the subject in hand.[75] True holiness he considered reasonable, since it was the greatest good in the universe because it unites intelligent beings into a most beautiful union. Thus true holiness consisted in love to being. This gave a new interpretation to sin as self-love, a position completely in harmony with the theory that the natural man was in full possession of all his faculties and needed only a change in the direction of the will by the operation of the Holy Spirit.

It was a glorious attempt to rescue the Calvinistic conception of man's creation and redemption for the glory of God from the oblivion to which it seemed doomed in New England's churches.

The basic question was that of the manner in which God generally worked the grace of regeneration. The old Calvinists sought to bind God more or less to His own means. The New Divinity with passionate earnestness desired to defend and vindicate His absolute sovereignty.

It could almost be foreseen in the debate that the old school was drifting in the direction of a mild Arminianism. In certain quarters the unregenerate were regarded as having the ability to turn to God by means of some pre-venient grace. Thus the sinner might ardently seek to become a saint, and though the evil inclination would prove to be an obstacle, God would work grace, since the soul truly waited upon Him. Thus although such were guilty before God and had a distaste for spiritual things, they possessed a "next power" to desire repentance. Concerning this Boardman writes, "Next power is a general sentiment or emotion which embraces a specific act or may embrace it. Self-respect and desire of eternal happiness may require honesty in business. With some men they do. They are thus the next preceding power or principle from which honesty flows, but self-respect and desire for eternal happiness do not embrace, as a part of themselves, a cordial relish of the service of God, are not a next power to it."[76] The basis for these distinctions lay in the "Taste Psychology"[77] developed by the leaders. It led to an emphasis on the inherent worth of the actions and desires of the unregenerate. On the basis of such works the unregenerate came to expect greater or saving grace. The Edwardeans refused to concede such distinctions and detracted from the works of many decent but professedly unconverted church-members of that day all value.

The results of the dispute led to modifications in the theory of human sinfulness on the part of both groups. The old Calvinists sought to maintain that a life of decency and order on the part of the unregenerate was generally more acceptable to God than a careless and profane conduct. However, they forgot the distinction between common and special grace and virtually made the first a stepping-stone to the second. Thus they veered in the direction of denying the absolute dependence of man upon the Holy Spirit for saving grace.

On the other hand the Edwardeans went to great and often amusing lengths in denouncing all use of means. Ezra Stiles has described this in a letter to Chauncy Whittlesey. Speaking of an independent Baptist minister at Newport, R.I., he wrote, "He preaches that it is sinful for the unregenerate to pray at all; to use the Lord's Prayer in particular, for if they said the truth, they would say, . . . 'Our Father which art in Hell,' our father, the Devil: that unregenerate are to use no means at all, there are no means appointed for them . . . they are more likely or at least as likely, to be seized by grace, not using than using means. Particularly as to attending his preaching, he asked them what they came there for, he had nothing to say to them, only to tell them they were heirs of damnation. . . None but saints were subjects of his preaching or ordination; and (he) forbid at length the promiscuous congregation to sing with them, or pray with them, — only a dozen or so now sing. . . So that he does the thing thoroughly, — he makes no pauses or reservations. Now this, at this time, is a very wonderful looking-glass."[78] It was indeed a very wonderful looking-glass, the more so since the men of the New Divinity were often forced into this and similar positions by their inexorable logic.

The Hopkinsians had become thorough-going voluntarists. All cultivation of nobler sentiments and better character was spurned. Though seemingly closer to the Reformed and Puritan antithesis between the regenerate and unregenerate, they fell into the danger inherent in their position of finding sin in specific acts rather than in an inward state and condition. Therefore it need not surprise us that the Calvinists in the Presbyterian and Dutch Reformed churches looked askance at this development of New England theology.[79] They regarded it as no less than a revival of that age-old enemy of the Reformed faith, Pelagianism or Arminianism. Gradually religious thought drifted during the period from Edwards to Emerson "from the Calvinism of transcendence to the Calvinism of immanence."[80] It cannot be proven that such a Calvinism of immanence is Calvinism in any true sense of the word.

In spite of some of their emphases the men of the New Divinity seemed to stress more than the old school Calvinists the necessity of working with the baptized children. Hopkins emphasized the relation in which such children stood to the church and thus to a certain extent went back to earlier Congregational positions. In his *System of Divinity* he devoted no less than sixty pages to an elaborate discussion of the nature and design of infant baptism. He stressed instead of God's covenant the active faith of the parents as the basis for such baptism. "That real holiness and salvation are secured to the children of believers by the covenant into which parents enter with God as it respects their children, if the parents faithfully keep covenant and fulfil what they profess and promise respecting their children when they offer them in baptism."[81] The covenant was regarded as conditional, for the holiness of the children was made dependent upon the faithfulness of the parents instead of God. "The church receive and look upon them as holy and those who shall be saved. So they are visibly holy, or as really holy, in their view, as their parents are."[82] Thus although claiming to be interested in the position of the children, he obscured the promises of God as the sole foundation and was in danger of reducing the covenant relationship to something purely natural, thus preparing the way for Horace Bushnell.[83] The danger which more and more threatened the men of the New Divinity was too great an emphasis on revivalism. Since many were so busy trying to persuade adults to conversion, they lost sight of the covenant relationship of the children to the church. In the minds of many the idea was fostered that children, too, could be saved only by experiencing the same violent, conscious, instantaneous conversion to God.

This tendency was largely developed when the theology of Cyprian Strong began to dominate the churches. He virtually denied the covenant interest of the children of believers and thus completed the process of eliminating them from the church, a process begun unintentionally by the Synod of 1662. His interest in the controversies concerning the nature of the Covenant of Grace and the use of means led him to discuss the relation of children to the church. This he did in his *Inquiry wherein, The End and Design of Baptism — The Qualifications for it — The Extent of its Administration — The Advantages arising from it. — The Standing of baptized Children — Whether Baptism in infancy do Entitle to Church Privileges in Adult Years — And the Discipline which the Church is to Exercise relative to Baptized Children, are particularly considered and illustrated.* This treatise must be regarded as one of the most powerful attacks upon the Half-way Covenant and its Stoddardean modifications.

His basic contention was that children are not baptized on the basis of a covenant relationship to God and the church at all.[84] Since this was the basic Anabaptist contention against infant baptism, he felt that he was overthrowing their position and bolstering the Congregational practice. Thus by insisting that only the experiential believer is in covenant with God, he overthrew the Calvinistic position of the church membership of children. To pacify the Baptists he wrote, "The objection will appear altogether groundless; for then it will appear, that neither *faith, repentance,* nor a single other *doctrinal idea* is necessary to prepare the way for administering baptism to an infant. . . It implies that the *parent* hath faith and doth dedicate such a child to God."[85]

In order to present a child for such dedication through baptism only two qualifications had to be met. First of all, the child must "be the child or property of him who offers it."[86] Moreover, the parent must himself be "really and completely in covenant with God."[87] This sounded the death-knell of the Half-way theory and practice. It also overthrew the main argument for that position, for now there was no danger of making New England and its children heathen by leaving them unbaptized. Strong claimed that all who were not adult believers in the true sense were heathen. "Persons will be heathen till they comply with the terms of christianity, whether they be baptized or not. They do not become christians merely by assuming the external badge of christianity. Baptism is a token that he who is active in it is a christian, but it does not make him such."[88] Thus the advantages of infant baptism accrued only to parents. It gave them a good conscience toward God, since it signified their full surrender to Him.[89]

The results of this position for the sacrament of infant baptism were far-reaching. Strong denied the children any real place in the church since they "are incapable of any activity in the transaction."[90] Thus he speaks of the connection as "mediate."[91] This was merely a development of what had been latent in the New England theory from the beginning. The first fathers already insisted that the children were members only by virtue of their parents' covenant. In order to enjoy the privileges such members had to make "personal profession, or enter personally into covenant with God."[92] The duty of parents according to Strong was the instruction of their children. When these became openly godless, the church publicly could discharge itself and the parents of any further duties in regard to the children.[93] Thus the immediate business of the church was always with the parents. Here, then, the Anabaptist theories of church membership finally triumphed over the Calvinistic doctrines. Infant baptism was reduced to a ceremony of presentation or dedication, and the covenant relationship of children to God was denied both in theory and practice.

Controversy Concerning Qualifications for Communion

The last of the many controversies of this period concerned the old question of qualifications for attendance upon the second sacrament. It was precipitated by the discussions of Hemmenway and Emmons on the problem of adult membership.[94]

Once more Hemmenway determined to defend Stoddardean-ism in his *Discourse concerning the Church, in which . . . a Right of Admission and Access to Special Ordinances, in their Outward Administrations and Inward Efficacy, (is) Stated and Defended.* In it he argued that Stoddardeanism was not identical with the Half-way Covenant theory in its views of the nature and efficacy of the sacraments. He was correct in maintaining that the newer position had virtually excluded the double standard of church membership introduced by the Synod of 1662.

Nathaniel Emmons replied in his *Dissertation on the Scripture Qualifications for Admission and Access to the Christian Sacraments: comprising some Strictures on Dr. Hemmenway's Discourses concerning the Church.* He claimed that Hemmenway always based his theories on the actual situation in the congregations rather than upon the Scriptural requirements. Though admitting the presence of a strange admixture of unregenerate and regenerate in every local church, Emmons insisted that only those who were truly in covenant with God might maintain church membership. His basic position was the voluntary nature of this religious covenant or contract with God.[95] "God can no more enter into covenant with men, without their personal consent, than they can enter into covenant with each other, without their personal consent."[96] He opposed the idea that God as Sovereign had the right to take His creatures into covenant relation without their previous consent.

The essentials of the covenant he found in the gracious purposes of God. These required faith on the part of man which "confirms the covenant and gives the believer an infallible title to the kingdom of heaven."[97] Although the Covenant of Grace is the result of the Covenant of Redemption, the distinction between the two must be carefully maintained. In the latter man has no part to perform, whereas in the former he has.

The chief point raised by both groups concerned the question of who were members of the covenant. Both defined these as "visible saints." However, the phrase was interpreted in different ways. Hemmenway insisted that visible saints possessed an external holiness which might be and often was opposed to real holiness. Emmons held that visible saints were those whose external holiness resulted from internal holiness. Only real saints had any business at the Lord's Table, since God always required sincerity in all religious acts. Strict self-examination was always required, according to Emmons.[98] Hemmenway, on the contrary, was satisfied, if those who partook had an interest in the covenant and lived a decent life.

Nearly half of Emmons' work was a refutation of the treatise of his opponent.[99] In arguing for infant baptism he agreed with Strong that infants are not members of the church. "We cannot allow, that baptized infants, whether sanctified or unsanctified, belong to the visible church."[100] The reason for this was, that they were "weak and ignorant."[101] Neither could they be members by virtue of their parents' covenant, for parents might covenant "*about* their infant seed, but *not for* them."[102] Since the church is by definition a "voluntary society, formed by a voluntary compact,"[103] they can by no stretch of the imagination be considered members. Nor do they belong by virtue of an act on God's part. Emmons averred that it "does not lie within the province even of divine sovereignty, to take any of the human race into covenant, without their own personal knowledge or consent."[104]

Thus the whole organic conception of the covenant broke down with the men of the New Divinity and left room only for an emphasis on human action and responsibility. The new theory of the will, advanced in the hope of making Calvinism acceptable to the men of the eighteenth century, caused the utter collapse of the Calvinistic doctrines of divine sovereignty in the work of human salvation and the Covenant of Grace.

The revivals had undermined the Reformed theory of the covenant and the church. Individualism and voluntarism were now the pillars upon which Congregationalism rested. It is not

surprising therefore that the Baptists gained ground so phe-
nomenally since the days of Edwards and were to consolidate
their position during the Second Awakening at the expense of
the Congregationalists. If the children of believers were not in
covenant with God anyway and had no special privileges and
positions in distinction from those born of unbelievers the sacrament could be of no significance to them or to their parents.
It has indeed degenerated into a "mere ceremony." Thus many
could find it easy to forget the "mere ceremony" and join the
Baptist fellowship.

New England also forsook the doctrine of God's sovereignty.
Although the men of the New Divinity sought strenuously to
maintain this at the beginning, their speculations on the nature
of the will and the intricacies of the Spirit's operations upon it
led them to a virtual denial of the same. Both parties felt the
tension of the problem with which they were wrestling. They
wanted to leave room for responsibility within the framework of
the Covenant of Grace. The old school Calvinists were in danger of curtailing the sovereignty of God by an undue emphasis
on the use of means. The new school Calvinists did the same
by rejecting the means and insisting upon a conscious surrender
of the will to God. The bitter end was a significant change in
their conception of God. The God who was worshipped at the
end of the eighteenth century bore little resemblance to the God
trusted by the first settlers. He was shorn of too much of His
power over the lives of men.

Chapter 9.

The Loss of the Covenant Conception

THE controversies between the men of the New Divinity and the old school Calvinists did not lead to the ultimate triumph of either group at the expense of the other. Although the theology of the former gained a firm foothold in many churches, there were always many who did not agree with it. Gradually the distinction between the two was erased, when new and more formidable questions arose in connection with the Universalist[1] and Unitarian[2] controversies. The rise of these groups caused both parties to neglect their differences concerning the covenant.

Causes for the Decline of the Covenant Idea

There are several reasons why interest in the question of the covenant declined. The first and most obvious was that the individualism of the revivals left no room for an appreciation of organic relations within the sphere of religion. Since the days of Edwards this new method of gaining new members for the church was regarded as indispensable. After each period of religious decline the leaders sought to apply the technique by which a reawakening was assured. This tendency was greatly augmented during the Second Awakening, which followed soon after the Revolutionary War.[3] The new spirit swept through the nation and left permanent impressions everywhere.[4] In the frontier districts it was accompanied by a strong stress on the emotions but took on a more staid appearance in New England. Here as well as elsewhere the Methodists and Baptists gained a numerical ascendency over the Congregationalists and Presbyterians which they have never lost since.[5] It is therefore not at all surprising that after such successful experiments revivalism became firmly entrenched in the American churches. The appeal to the individual and the insistence upon immediate and personal surrender to the gospel call became the accepted method of preserving the church.

The second reason why the covenant idea was forgotten is to be found in the neglect of the children of the church.[6] This necessarily followed in the wake of revivalism, which could never deal with those who were too young to understand the message of Christianity. In so far as children were included in the revival appeal the same experiences found with adults were demanded of them. Hand in hand with this neglect of the child's relationship to God and the church went the repudiation of infant baptism. The Baptists refused to administer the sacrament on the ground that they could not be in covenant with God, since the covenant was a mutual compact. Strong had compromised the Congregational position in his attempt to bolster it. However, he in principle had accepted the Anabaptist interpretation of the Covenant of Grace and the church-covenant. The child, in spite of all his religious education, would still have to pass through the deeply emotional experience of conversion as championed by the revivalists. The net result was a gradual neglect of the training of children.

The theological modifications introduced by the men of the New Divinity also did much to overthrow the covenant idea. What Edwards rather innocently had maintained concerning human responsibility on the basis of the distinction between natural and moral ability and inability had disastrous consequences. His successors developed it in such a way that sin and holiness were thought of only in terms of individual acts. Thus children, especially infants, could not be regarded as guilty and depraved before God.

Perhaps one of the most significant changes was the repudiation of the penal substitution theory of the atonement. This has had a very ancient and respectable history in the development of Christian theology. It triumphed in the theology of the Calvinists where the ideas of imputation, representation, substitution, atonement in the sense of legal satisfaction became the basis for the theological superstructure.

There had always been a tension between the legal and moral patterns on this score. Very often they had been placed antithetically to each other. In the Calvinistic camp the distinction was greatly sharpened as a result of the Arminian controversy. Out of this came the Grotian theory of the atonement.

For more than a century the Calvinistic pattern had been dominant in New England theology, but with the rise of Jonathan Edwards and the schools of thought which followed him, the emphasis fell on man's moral relation to God. Thus the governmental theory of Christ's atonement was widely accepted. In all this there was a rather imperceptible but very definite shift away from the Calvinism of the first fathers. Since the covenant idea as developed by the Calvinists sustains such an intimate relation to the forensic pattern in theology, it was inevitable that a change would obliterate the traditional theory of the covenant. And this is precisely what happened. The strict logic of the followers of Edwards finally succeeded in ousting not only the Half-way Covenant theory and practice[7] but also the whole structure of Covenant theology.

Triumph of the New Divinity in its Relation to the Covenant Idea

That the covenant idea was abandoned by many theologians about this time is evident to anyone studying their works. Also in this regard they spoke a different language than the early settlers.

One of the leaders of the churches during the first years of the nineteenth century was Leonard Woods Jr., a man of broad sympathies and catholic interests. He has been remembered largely for the significant role which he played in the establishment and development of Andover Seminary. Because he was able to satisfy both the old school Calvinists and the New Divinity, he was chosen to the professorship of divinity at the new institution.

In a general way his teachings were those of the Edwardeans. In his works there is a strong emphasis on human instrumentality, sometimes seemingly at the expense of stressing the necessity of the Spirit's operations. Although he expressed himself very cautiously, he seems to have regarded the Christian life and experience as the fruit of training and education. "From the beginning of the world, the character and condition of children have generally resulted from the conduct of parents. The peculiar character of a tribe or nation has commonly been derived from the character of its father or head. This extends to the religious as well as to the social and secular character. The history of the Christian church shows that after it has been once established in any place, it has depended on its continuance and increase, chiefly upon the success of parents in promoting the piety of their children."[8] Woods favored the use of revivals only to a limited degree. He objected to their extreme emotionalism, but nevertheless regarded the conversion experience at a more or less mature age a requisite for full membership in the churches.

It is evident that he had no place for the idea of the Covenant of Grace to seal God's promises to the seed of believers. Because the natural relationship of children to parents was strongly stressed, the danger of reducing the operation of the Spirit in the work of salvation was marked. That salvation was viewed quite largely as the outcome of the natural laws of education is evident from the use which he made of Knapp.[9]

Foster has claimed that the position of Woods was self-contradictory.[10] He held in the main to the conceptions of Westminster but plainly rejected the underlying philosophy of those creeds. It was this rejection which brought about the many changes of detail in his system, so that the uncompromising supporters of Westminster could not agree. Since he consistently avoided all ontological questions, he never could present a complete covenant theology. Moreover, he virtually repudiated the legal and forensic elements of Westminster. This made it all the more impossible for him to support the Calvinistic doctrines except formally. This change did much to prepare the way for Horace Bushnell.

Calvinistic orthodoxy as modified by the New Divinity is best represented, perhaps, by Timothy Dwight, grandson of Edwards.[11] In several respects he stands at the theological crossroads. Although he defended the traditional doctrines, these received a new emphasis. By this time the positions of the New Divinity had fairly well crystallized, so that it became evident that the Calvinism of 1800 was by no means that of 1600.

In his presentation there was no appreciation of the covenant promises of God to the child. The promise of God to parents, in so far as he spoke of it, was purely conditional. "The amount of the promise is, that their children will *generally*, when trained up in the way they should go, not depart from it."[12] The reason why such training was required lay not in the obligation of the parents towards God but rather in the presence of certain laws relative to growth and development in the human spirit. Thus he held, "The conscience is, at this period, exceedingly tender and susceptible, readily alarmed by the apprehension of guilt, and prepared to contend or fly, at the approach of known temptation. . . . The heart is soft, gentle, and easily won, strongly attached by kindness, peculiarly to the parents themselves."[13] The old Puritan emphasis on the inherent sinfulness and depravity of human nature is almost entirely missing. Salvation in the case of faithful training was viewed as resulting quite naturally and readily without any special, direct and saving operation of the Holy Spirit.[14]

This strong emphasis on training of children was quite generally neglected during the period which separated Dwight from Bushnell. Thus the latter could claim that he knew of none who had studied the matter of child training in religion so carefully as Dwight. No doubt the results of the Second Awakening greatly obscured this element in the teaching of Woods and Dwight.

One prominent New Divinity clergyman, however, deserves special mention as among the last to defend the traditional conception of God's covenant with man. This was Samuel Austin, for twenty five years pastor of the church at Worcester, Mass.[15] His most important contribution on this score was *View of the Economy of the Church of God.* It parallels the work of Cyprian Strong in that it took up many of the thorny questions which had arisen during the various discussions and controversies. Though refusing to add fuel to the "vehement debate"[16] between Baptists and Congregationalists, he aimed at developing a clear and consistent scheme of the church and covenant, since this lay at the root of the differences between the two.

He contended that there was only one gracious covenant, that of Redemption or Grace. No careful distinction was made between the two. This covenant forms the substance of God's revelation in the Scriptures. He argued for the unity of the two dispensations from Paul's figure of the olive tree in Romans 11.[17] In all dispensations the promises and objects of divine grace are the same.[18] All promises are absolute, for with God who swears by Himself there can be no contingence or reserve. Thus the covenant is not maintained upon the condition of human obediece, for "even their (human) own perverseness can not unsettle it."[19]

Those with whom God made His covenant were Abraham and his "seed." Austin went to great lengths in establishing his conception of seed. It was said to have both a literal and figurative meaning. To perpetuate his covenant God organized the seed into a "visible society."[20] Parents and children were thus constitutionally united. Even though the children were incapable of faith and repentance for the time, they were regarded as "born of God."[21] Thus there was an "indissolvable connexion with him and his people,"[22] and the infants were regarded as "compleatly members"[23] of the body of Israel. There is always a vast difference between the children of the church and the children of the world, since the latter are "strangers from the covenant of promise."[24] Thus Austin argued strongly against the positions of Strong on the place of children in the church.

Austin showed a far greater appreciation for the organic relations and thus counteracted the individualism of the revivalists, when he wrote, "It was the seed, as a mystical or spiritual society, rather than the individual, though the individual was comprehended, to whom circumcision sealed the promises of the covenant."[25] In continuing his emphasis on the close relation between the eternal and the historical, he maintained that circumcision "did not initiate"[26] into the covenant, thus definitely rejecting the theory of the Stoddardeans. "It did not place the subject in covenant; but was administered, because he was in covenant already. He was so by birth. Nay, he was comprehended in the covenant before he existed."[27]

On the basis of twelve arguments he sought to overthrow the Baptists contention that the children of believers have no right to baptism by virtue of the covenant relationship. The most essential was the second proposition which affirmed that infant membership was essential to the existence of the covenant, since the "seed" constituted the great object of promise. From this he deduced the challenging duties of Christian parents. He stated that the pious example of parents, prudent and energetic discipline and above all strict religious education were the essential means of "carrying into effect the promises of the covenant."[28]

He further defined the position of the infants as follows. "The membership of infants, though as complete as that of adult believers, is of a lower grade, not involving the same profession, not leading to the immediate enjoyment of the same privileges, nor binding to the same duties. Infants are complete members of the *family* into which they are born, but they are at present mere objects of care. They are incapable of services which devolve upon grown members of it. . . . They are complete members of the State. But they are not fit to be turned into soldiers, or clothed with office. . . . It is often asked, if children are born members of the Church, and are to be baptized as being such, Why are not all led to communicate at the Lord's Table? It might as pertinently be asked, if children are born members of the State, Why are not some of them sent ambassadors to foreign courts?"[29] The answer was self-evident. Since the partaking of the Supper required spiritual activity, it could not be expected or allowed since "Moral agents can never be bound any further than they have natural ability to act. . . . Children become obliged so far as, and no farther than, they become possessed of capacity."[30] On this basis he insisted upon the excommunication of all those who did not live up to their covenant obligations. He advocated a direct system of instruction, supervision and discipline for all members by baptism.

The last pages of his book were filled with warnings to the churches which practiced infant baptism. He chided them as in many cases not understanding the nature and purpose of the ordinance and charged them with having "criminally disregarded important duties of the covenant."[31] "The neglect of these duties," he went on to say, "has furnished the most plausible objection to infant baptism. The true principle upon which it rests, i.e. the absolute promise of God respecting a seed and their consequent membership in His Kingdom, has been perhaps of late but little understood, and but partially received. Hence little more attention has been paid to these children than to the children of the uncovenanted world. They have been baptized and then forgotten."[32] He went so far as to say, "Perhaps this is the primary reason why religion is in so low a state, and the church seems so much forsaken."[33] Thus he urged all parents and ministers to become conscious of the implications of baptism "as a seal of the covenant and a testimony to their membership."[34]

Austin dealt with the problems at hand more thoroughly than any of his contemporaries. Many of them were interested only in upholding the traditional ceremony of infant baptism in the churches. They presented the usual doctrinal arguments but failed to show where the life of the church was at stake.

Indeed, there were weaknesses in the position of Austin. He virtually identified the Covenant of Grace with the Covenant of Redemption. Thus the historical aspect was minimized. To him only the elect seed was in covenant with God. This had been the teaching in New England for generations, except for those who accepted the Stoddardean principle of an internal and an external covenant.

Very likely the strong emphasis on revivals in those days caused Austin's theories to be neglected. The emphasis on divine sovereignty was more and more falling into disrepute everywhere. Increasing accommodations were made by the successors of the early Edwardeans to the idea of human achievement in the way of salvation. New England's theology was rapidly changing from the "Calvinism of transcendence to the Calvinism of immanence."

Collapse of the Covenant Idea in Bushnell's Theology

It was to be foreseen that the extreme emphasis upon individualism in the revivals would lead to a reaction. Religion was in danger of losing all contact with life, because of the positions taken on conversion by many advocates of experientialism and emotionalism. Although the Second Awakening had done much good in its quiet way throughout New England,[35] it obscured the covenant relation of children to God and the church entirely. Religion was made the concern almost exclusively of adults. These were urged to enter in at the narrow gate of an intensely emotional experience of regeneration and conversion. Every child was regarded as a child of wrath and an heir of hell unless and until he could point to the required change in his life.

It was against this theory that Horace Bushnell militated.[36] In several respects he stood at the cross-roads of New England theological development. Buckham says of him, "Bushnell was in some respect almost as truly the father of the late constructive development of American theology as was Jonathan Edwards of the earlier."[37] In his day he stood very much alone, but many of the modifications which he introduced were developed by his successors. For this reason the constructive part of our study really ends with a discussion of his views. Although he called back the church to her duty towards the young, he did not base his theories respecting the religious education of the children of believers on the covenant idea. His strong stress on natural relationships and the "supernaturalness"[38] of man changed the whole conception of man's religious relationship to God. This caused the complete collapse of the covenant idea.

That there was much amiss with the revival theory and technique as developed in New England for over a century was becoming evident to many. The old theology in its consideration of the Christian life had starved all normal expression of the same. The revivals virtually limited religious life to one definite pattern to which all were required to adhere in self-examination. By writing *Christian Nurture* in 1846 Bushnell "did perhaps more than any other single agency to break down the extreme individualism of the old Puritan theology of America."[39] In criticizing this he wrote, "Our very theory is that men are to grow up in evil and be dragged into the church of God by conquest. The world is to lie in halves and the kingdom of God is to stretch itself side by side with the kingdom of darkness, making sallies into it, and taking captive those who are sufficiently hardened and bronzed into guiltiness to be converted. Thus we assume even the absurdity of human society and the universal prevalence of Christian virtue. And thus we throw an air of extravagance and unreason over all we do."[40]

What, then, did Bushnell emphasize? He fought for the idea of the church as a body of believers and the "organic unity of the family."[41] In the latter, when sufficiently under the influence of the Christian gospel, he saw the hope of the church on earth. Normally, he contended, the Christian faith passes from one generation to another and thus gives stability to the history of the church. Thus, although he did not reject the necessity of the work of redemption, he stressed much more the effective indwelling of the Divine Spirit in the life of man.

In his *Christian Nurture* Bushnell took up two major topics: the doctrine or theory of such nurture and its mode or practice. He held, "Man is a social creature, so that if we really deny organic power and dissolve even families into isolated units of free agency — if we hold our religion as a strict exercise of individualism, and never allow it to marry itself to our natural affections and our social instincts, still these social instincts remain with us, and the more they are baffled and kept out of action, the more sure they are to burst over, at last, all barriers, and seize, as it were by force, the indulgence denied them."[42] However, in attempting to give them a place, he came so close to identifying religion with them, that the supernatural element of Christianity was obscured. He rejected the Episcopalian theory of baptismal regeneration, but held that children should receive baptism as a seal of their relation to God, since "they are to grow up as Christians, or spiritually renewed persons."[43]

What his view of the child was becomes plain. Although he by no means rejected the presence of sin, he denied the traditional New England position that they were "children of wrath." He spoke of "the simple and ingenuous age of childhood"[44] and the child's "ductile nature to the truth and Spirit of God."[45] Therefore the child "is not to be told that he must have a new heart and exercise faith in Christ's atonement."[46] The parents instead must be living epistles of faith in God.[47]

In his *Growth, not Conquest* Bushnell gave an illustration of the use to which he put this organic conception of religious life. Concerning the church he held, "It is a creature whose vitality is spiritual life, and it can have its increase only by the same law which pertains to all organic living bodies, that is by development from within, not by external accretion."[48] What he most strongly condemned was the New England practice of his day, which he described as that of parents taking "their own children to be aliens, and even under the covenant — train them up to be aliens, and even tell them that they can do nothing right or acceptable to God till after their hearts are changed; or what is the same, till after they have come to some advanced age."[49]

Although he made some use of the old terminology and thus spoke of the covenant, he virtually rejected the old position entirely. He openly refused to base his ideas of child nurture on the covenant made with Abraham, giving as his reason that the words he would use would "settle into a meaning proper only to religious individualism."[50] Furthermore he claimed that he could not "go back and wade through this worn-out question (total depravity and the need of regeneration) to vindicate myself against objections from a doctrine as distant from me as the supremacy of the Pope, and shortly to be as distant from the world."[51]

Thus the idea of the child's covenant relationship to Adam, both naturally and forensically, was denied. The author spoke of the child as beginning "life under a law of hereditary damage, as to plunge himself into evil by his own experiment."[52] However, there was no "sin which he derives from his parents, but only some prejudice to the perfect harmony of this mold, some kind of pravity or obliquity which inclines him to evil."[53] Bushnell has been criticized as teaching the sufficiency of ethical culture. This is far from the truth. Any neglect of faith in God met with his strong disapproval, for "virtue unblessed by the nobler impulsions of religious inspiration"[54] could not bear the fruit of a Christian life.

However, he claimed that this Christian life would develop normally and naturally as the fruit of the training of Christian parents. Speaking of the unity of the family, he had in mind no vascular connection, nor solely direct teaching, but rather the whole atmosphere created by the parents.[55] He held that "the child is potentially regenerate, being regarded as existing in connexion with powers and causes that *contain* that fact. before time and separate from time."[56] The grace is "conferred by no casual act" but rests "upon the established laws of character in the church and the house."[57]

Against this position which virtually rejected the absolute necessity of regeneration by the supernatural operation of God's Spirit several objections were raised.

Among those who objected were the old school Presbyterians headed by Charles Hodge of Princeton. This group had always stood close to the Congregationalists by virtue of their common allegiance to the doctrines of Westminster. However, with the gradual drift away from the underlying philosophy of this creedal formulary since the middle of the eighteenth century on the part of the Congregationalists, the Presbyterians had been regarding the theological development in New England with suspicion. When Bushnell's *Christian Nurture* appeared, Hodge at once undertook to appraise it. He first mentioned those truths which he thought Bushnell again called to the attention of the churches. The first was "the fact that there is such a divinely constituted relation between the piety of the parents and that of their children."[58] The second great truth which he found was "that parental nurture, or Christian training, is the great means for the salvation of the children of the church."[59] Hodge also opposed very strongly the tendency prevalent in those days to forget the position of the children.[60]

Yet he could not agree with Bushnell. He asked the question: How does Bushnell account for that constituted relationship between the religion of the covenant parents and that of their children?[61] He claimed that only three possibilities existed. Either the connexion rested upon the covenantal promise of God, or it resolved itself into a law of nature accounting for the transmission of religion in much the same way as the transmission of other forms of character, or it was the result of the ritual or church system in connection with the administration of certain ordinances. Bushnell he claimed held to the second, and thus gave a naturalistic account of conversion or the effect of religious training. The statement which Hodge used to prove that Bushnell rejected traditional Protestant supernaturalism was the following: "What more appropriate to the doctrine of spiritual influence itself, than to believe that as the Spirit of Jehovah fills all the worlds of matter, and holds a presence of power and government in all objects, so all souls of all ages and capacities, have a moral presence of Divine Love in them, and a nurture of the Spirit appropriate to their wants."[62] Here, Hodge contended, Bushnell confused the workings of the Spirit in the realms of nature and grace. The basic question was whether God operated in spiritual life in any way other than through nature and the natural process. Whereas Hodge maintained the evangelical Protestant view that there was, Bushnell denied this, because he refused to be guilty of "hanging everything thus on a miracle, or a pure *ictus Dei. . . .*"[63]

Bushnell's views further elicited criticism from within the Congregational fold. The chief voice of the opposition was the Rev. Bennet Tyler, president and professor of Christian Theology at the Theological Institute of Connecticut. His chief objection, like that of Hodge, was that the new theory seemed to deny the absolute necessity of regeneration by the Holy Spirit. He attempted to refute the thirteen arguments for the new position advancd by Bushnell in *Argument for Discourses on Christian Nurture.* The significant element in this debate was the relatively little use made of Scriptural material. Bushnell's views really constituted an attack on the revival theory as the chief means of maintaining the church. Tyler, on the other hand, claimed that the American Puritans had always looked to them for the growth of their churches. Furthermore, he insisted upon the New Divinity theory of instantaneous conversion. "Every genuine conversion must, from the nature of the case, be sudden. However protracted may be the antecedent conviction, regeneration is always instantaneous. . . . The transition from one state to the other, must be instantaneous, whatever may be the circumstances under which it occurs."[64]

From Tyler's writings it is evident that the place of children in the covenant and the significance of this for the church was entirely lost. Although the children of the faithful may be in a "more hopefull way"[65] of receiving the gift of regeneration, they are still to be regarded as alienated from the life of God. "We are bound therefore to assume that every person is in his natural state, till he gives evidence that he has been spiritually renewed."[66] To reverse this judgment in the case of the covenant seed has "no scriptural warrant."[67] Thus the covenant promises were for the last time in New England emptied of all their significance.

There can be no doubt that Bushnell reacted rightly against the excessive individualism bred by the revivals and the machinery set in motion by many preachers to win a few souls for the kingdom of Christ. The divorce between nature and grace, the natural and supernatural, so characteristic of the Anabaptist leaven, had entered the New England churches and worked untold havoc, because it was coupled with the doctrine of total inability. Bushnell therefore sought to substitute a new approach to the child in the church. However, in so doing he virtually identified the realms of nature and grace.[68] Thus he based the religious life of the child entirely on the natural laws of education and failed to emphasize the necessity of the special work of the Holy Spirit. Because his definitions and descriptions of the beginnings of spiritual life were not always clear, his position met with the stubborn resistance of the orthodox. Adopting his theory it became increasingly difficult to maintain any valid distinction between Christians and non-Christians on the basis of a new birth. This was nothing less than denial of covenant distinctiveness. Thus the covenant concept could no longer have any meaning in the New England churches which once adopted the views of Bushell.

Part Three

EVALUATION OF THE COVENANT
IDEA IN NEW ENGLAND THEOLOGY

Chapter 10.

The Influence of the Covenant Idea Upon New England Religious Thought

THE major portion of our task has been completed. After having surveyed somewhat sketchily the foundations upon which the doctrines of the early American Puritans rested, we considered rather much in detail the various changes which the idea underwent during the development of New England theological thought. What remains to be done is to offer an evaluation of this. In order to do this it will be necessary to keep clearly in mind what influence this conception had upon the religious thought and life of New England during the two centuries from Cotton to Bushnell.

In brief, our contention has been that New England Congregationalism from its earliest beginnings can hardly be called a form of Calvinism in its generally accepted sense. Although in theology it was largely Reformed, its church polity and the underlying principles upon which it was based harmonized better with certain teachings of the Anabaptists. Because of the emphasis on personal experience and surrender to God, it was apparent very early in history that the Calvinistic conception of the covenant would have to be modified. With every change the Congregationalists turned farther and farther away from the doctrines which had been originally accepted. The most radical departure dates from the time of the revivals, under the influence of which individualism, voluntarism and experientialism in religion triumphed. When this emphasis dominated the life of the churches, there was no room for the uniquely

195

Calvinistic positions. Although the loss of the Reformed heritage in the churches of New England cannot be entirely attributed to the neglect of the covenant idea, this factor was far more significant than has often been recognized.

During the years which separated John Cotton from Horace Bushnell much was written about the idea of the covenant, and yet there was very little which can be called original in the various constructions. The greatest contribution made by the New England thinkers on this score was the Half-way expedient, by which they sought at one and the same time to maintain their theocratic ideal and their stress on experiential piety as requisite to church membership. Outside of certain variations among the men of the New Divinity little that was new was added to the ideas carried over from old England by the earliest settlers.

In this study of the development and loss of the covenant idea in New England theology we can witness a very definite change in and re-interpretation of some fundamental Christian concepts. This has also clearly paralleled the loss of the distinctively Reformed elements in Congregational theology.

The first and most obvious change during the two centuries from 1620 to 1847 is to be found in the idea of God.

Those who lived in the days of Horace Bushnell held to a conception of God which differed widely from that of the first American Puritans. In the positions of the men of the nineteenth century there is little room for a sovereign God whose every promise "is a promise of one Covenant or other."[1] The first settlers accepted the Calvinistic idea of God as absolutely sovereign. The attributes of deity which were stressed included His majesty, omnipotence, and sovereignty. This emphasis pervaded every religious doctrine which they championed. God was in a very special sense regarded as the sole author of salvation. To the very last detail this work was dependent upon His almighty will. The church was the "pure church" of those who were chosen by Him in Christ before the foundation of the world. Faith was a gift of His grace, not in any way to be merited by the sinner. It was bestowed in accordance with the desires of His will. All events in nature and grace alike were directly attributable to His intervention. Thus the Puritans did not only speak of God's special grace in bestowing salvation but loved also to dwell upon the thought of "God's wonder-working providence"[2] in behalf of His elect. He saved His own from the fury of the seas and the cruelty of the savages alike. Although there was a large place for the love and mercy of God revealed in the person and work of Jesus Christ, this was subordinated to the emphasis on His sovereignty. The Puritans have rightly been called a "God-intoxicated" people. However, this decided stress on the majesty of the Almighty made little if any appeal during the years upon those who considered themselves with a great deal of complacency as destitute of the saving grace which sprang from Divine election.

Thus in the course of history the Puritan God became more and more a "Deus absconditus" for the majority. Their unique stress on the divine will, quite unpredictable at any time, could very easily lead in the practice of life to a removal of God from daily concerns and cares. Not that any of them would have agreed to this in theory, however. To the very minutest detail life in theocracy was supposed to be regulated by the revealed will of God. But when many had lost the fervent Christian experience of the first settlers and possessed only a knowledge and appreciation of morality, a practical deism descended upon the land. The preachers preached the sovereignty of God perhaps even more strongly than before. The people, on the contrary, did not seem to know and understand this God. Thus the preaching in the days of Stoddard, the Mathers and immediately thereafter removed God still farther from the lives of many.

Jonathan Edwards sought to revive the traditional conception of God. In all his sermons he preached Divine sovereignty. However, in seeking rational substantiation for this idea of God, he modified the theory of the will of man in such a way that he prepared for the downfall of the conception which he sought to save. Still more, whereas in the days of John Cotton all of life was placed in covenantal relation to God, Edwards at times seemed to divorce religion from daily life. This was in large measure due to the fact that he saw the danger of confusing religion with morality, which had threatened New England for some decades. Moreover, in his various treatises he conceived of religion too much in terms of the individual's relation to God. In his concern for defining the Biblical theory of Christian experience, he lost sight of the relationships in which the individual stood. Thus religion to him came to mean largely the fellowship of the soul with God to the exclusion of the rest of life. As a result the broader and more inclusive view of some of the early fathers, who claimed that all of life constituted the rightful domain of religion and was in covenant relationship with God, was forgotten. By virtually restricting religion to the duties of the first table of the law, he unwittingly helped to secularize New England life.

This idea of God who concerned Himself only with the soul's personal relation to Him with little regard for the concerns of daily life and social relationships was continued by the men of the New Divinity. This false dualism between nature and grace lies at the basis of the whole revival movement. Those who championed it in New England were also exclusively concerned that those to whom they preached would receive a personal experience of salvation. Thus God no longer controlled the entire life of man in every relationship. The domain over which He ruled was that of the individual soul in fellowship with Himself, that and very little more.

It was apparent that New England, after some decades of preaching of this sort, would become ripe for a radical reaction. The secularization of life as progressively affected during the century between Edwards and Bushnell could not satisfy the needs of the religious man. Sooner or later the one-sidedness of the individualistic emphasis of the revivals had to be exposed. Men realized that God was not only concerned with the relationship of the individual to Himself but also with the relationship of the individual to his fellow-men and society. Had the New England temper been somewhat the same in the days of Bushnell as in the time of Cotton, there might have been a return to some form of the covenant idea. However, because life had become so strongly secularized, the natural sciences so markedly developed, and the democratic philosophy so dominant everywhere, man lost sight of his dependence upon God to a large degree. If the revivals had virtually divorced natural and spiritual laws, assigning to them spheres which never met and much less interacted, the men of the nineteenth century under the influence of Bushnell were in danger of identifying the two. Thus the distinction between nature and grace was obscured. Duties towards God were swallowed up in duties towards fellow-men.

All this reveals an allegiance to a new theory concerning God. He was no longer regarded as the Omnipotent Ruler who according to His special providence regulates the lives of His saints to the last detail. Rather, He became that benevolent and beneficent Being, who works not through special laws reserved for individuals standing in a special gracious relationship to Himself but rather through the laws of nature. Moreover, the methodology begun by Jonathan Edwards, who sought to demonstrate the rationality of the Christian religion, became dominant in all of theology. Not only did his successors come to seek proofs in that which was reasonable and intellectually defensible rather than in that which was in accord with Scripture; those who differed with them did the same.

God had through the centuries of profound speculation and stormy debate lost all of His sterner characteristics. He no longer ruled the individual directly by the intervention of His providence but rather through natural law which tended to obscure His position as ruler. Indeed, the religion in New England in the days of Bushnell was far from a thoroughgoing humanism or naturalism. Yet the tendency in both directions was in evidence. With the rise of the theory of organic evolution especially the latter was to receive a new and powerful impetus.

The doctrine of man also underwent some radical changes. At the heart of the covenant idea lay the fact that man was entirely and continually dependent upon the grace of God. Without God man was helpless. It was further impossible for man ever to fellowship with God, unless God first revealed Himself and opened the way. Apart from that first coming of God unto man, all religion in the sense of communion with the Eternal was impossible.

The Reformed teaching on the covenants had sought to make this very plain. Not only was this said to hold with respect to the race in the state of sin but also in the state of rectitude. Adam in that state of original righteousness and holiness could never possess the possibility of full fellowship with God apart from divine self-revelation in some form. This was done covenantally. In the Covenant of Works God showed Adam how it was possible for him to enter into a life of perfected and unbroken fellowship. The condition for this was obedience, tested by the probationary command of refraining from the forbidden fruit. The promise of such a life of communion was sealed by the sacrament symbolized in the fruit of the tree of life.

Still less could man in the state of sin ever rightly know and worship God apart from the revelation of grace. This was given in Christ, whose atonement on Calvary was regarded as a satisfaction for sin and fulfilment of the divine law. Thus Christ was considered the Mediator of a new covenant, the Covenant of Grace. This in turn rested upon the Covenant of Redemption made between the Father as representative of the Trinity and the Son as representative of the elect.[3] In this presentation of the gospel the legal relationships were dominant, quite often to the exclusion of the moral. Very definitely such a theory of the covenants was intimately bound up with the substitutionary theory of the atonement.

Now the full implications of these theories were not worked out by the early American Puritans. Their aim, as we have noticed earlier, was practical rather than theoretical. However, the main ideas occur again and again in their writings. They did have a profound realization of the necessity of covenant grace before man could fellowship with God.

However, in presenting their conception of the covenant they limited it quite exclusively to the elect and left little if any room for the exercise and development of human responsibility. Realizing that they could not determine absolutely who belonged to that class, they contented themselves at first with coming as closely to it as possible by demanding in addition to a sincere profession of faith and repentance and an exhibition of Christian conduct the relation of spiritual experiences as a requisite to church membership. Thus the covenant, in spite of their insistence to the contrary at times, became the concern of the individual in isolation. The group relation was not recognized at all. Experientialism, voluntarism and individualism went hand in hand in their construction of the Covenant of Grace. This strong tendency to stress the place of the elect individual obscured the organic aspect of the covenant relationship which integrated all of life as religiously bound to God.

When many lost sight of the absolute necessity of grace unto salvation, the doctrine of human depravity was modified. That this in turn caused the covenant idea to be forgotten is evident in several ways. The doctrine of human goodness gradually crept into the churches in spite of the preaching of the Edwardeans. The controversies of that period nearly all seemed to demand concessions in that direction. Chauncy pointed out that the old Calvinists virtually surrendered the whole of their position by refusing to admit that man's original sin alone was a sufficient ground for the condemnation of infants. The men of the New Divinity by stressing the moral relations in man's salvation at the expense of the legal virtually necessitated the rejection of the doctrines of original sin, substitutionary atonement, and total depravity. Thus in a sense they paved the way for the new theology of Bushnell, although they very likely would have disclaimed any affinity with his ideas.

With the gradual loss of the sense of sin[4] it was not necessary to conceive of God as first coming unto man with the revelation of His eternal covenant in Christ before the door unto fellowship with Him could be opened. Gradually salvation through Christ came to depend quite largely upon human reaction to the gospel message. Although the preachers insisted upon the need of divine grace in varying degrees, this was often construed as helping grace rather than as regenerating grace. Man at least somewhat had become independent of God. Therefore he did not owe his entire life to God either. Much of life seemed to fall outside of the scope of religion. When Bushnell in his own way sought to bring the organic relationships of life into the sphere of religion again, he no longer could or would make use of the traditional presentation of man's absolute helplessness and sinfulness apart from saving grace.

In connection with the loss of the covenant idea in New England theology the shift from the penal substitutionary to the governmental and moral theories of the atonement through Christ deserves mention.[4] It must not be forgotten that the Reformed conception of the covenant was intimately bound up with the idea that Christ satisfied the divine justice for His own, who were regarded as "in Him" by virtue of divine decree. The Savior was regarded as the Mediator of the new and everlasting covenant on the basis of Hebrews 8:6.

Under the influence of the new ideas advanced by Edwards and his successors the idea of the atonement was radically modified. Many rejected the position of the early Puritans, expressed also in the Westminster standards, on the basis of the argument that moral guilt requires personal atonement and therefore could not be assumed by another.[5] Although there is some weight to the argument, those who raised this objection to the Westminster construction forgot that it taught a definite, organic, covenantal relationship between Christ and His people. Losing sight of this, the substitutionary theory is robbed of its real meaning. It was therefore also the neglect of the covenant idea that contributed significantly to a reconstruction of the doctrine of Christ's work.

In the shift of emphasis away from the covenant idea we may further find in New England theology the development of a new idea concerning the church. From the beginning the church was regarded as the body of experiential believers who had been chosen by God unto eternal life. Thus they were bound together in covenant fellowship. This sprang from their voluntary acceptance of the will of God as determinative for their lives. The possibility of such a Christian experience necessary for entrance into this association lay in the work of God who alone could regenerate the heart. Thus although the idea of a voluntary covenant was prominent (as will become evident again when we consider the influence of this idea upon the development of Congregational church polity during the two centuries), this was not divorced from the special operation of God's Spirit.

Although children were regarded as members of the church by virtue of their parents' membership, this was in reality an anomaly in the Congregational churches as long as they desired to remain true to their view of the church as an association of experiential believers. Indeed, the earliest theologians definitely gave a place to the seed of believers. Cotton called them disciples of Jesus but insisted that the grace signified and sealed unto them was not sanctifying and internal grace but only federal grace. Here already we find the beginnings of the externalization of church membership. By such a construction Cotton opened the way for two types of church members: those who possessed saving grace and those who did not. This idea of a legitimate double standard of membership was in some measure due to the fact that Cotton and many with him stressed too much the eternal aspect of the Covenant of Grace and quite often seemed to identify this entirely with the decree of election. This led to a type of individualism in the churches which had little regard for the place of the seed of believers. For this reason the emphasis on experientialism and individualism became pronounced early in the history of American Congregationalism. Roger Williams demonstrated how the Separatistic ideal of a regenerate and elect church membership could easily lead to a denial of the covenant relationship of children to God and His church. The presence of many Anabaptists in the early years of the colony is further proof of the same thing. The Puritans tried to get around this difficulty inherent in their position by claiming that visible believers were proper material for the church. Children were thus supposed to be visible believers.

This brought up the vexing question how children might possibly be conceived of as such, when they could give no evidences of their faith in God and Christ. At first the issue was not clearly seen and defined. However, quite early the answer was given that the children were to be regarded as visible believers by virtue of their parents' covenant with God. That gave outward and visible expression which the Puritans sought. Of course, the danger here was that such a practice made the covenant depend upon the faith of the parents rather than upon the promises of God. It was almost universally held that if the parents did not explicitly covenant for their children, their seed should not receive the sacrament of baptism, because it did not belong to the Covenant of Grace. Davenport especially championed this position.

The expedient adopted by the Synod of 1662 aimed at upholding this position, while at the same time giving the majority of the colonists a place in the church. What the Synod really did was to externalize the requisites for church membership. The men of the opposition, willing to sacrifice the theocratic ideal for the sake of the pure church, also held that children were really only federally and outwardly holy. This may explain many things concerning the attitude of these men to the children who had been baptized. That they had but little if any real place in the fellowship of the church is evident from the fact that not the promises but the warnings of the covenant were constantly placed before them. They were generally re-garded as children of wrath, indeed in a more hopeful way of receiving the blessings of saving grace than the children of heathen countries because of their proximity to the means of grace, but none the less estranged from God and Christ. Not until the evidences of regeneration were present did the Puritan divines dare to assert that the children of the church were really in the Covenant of Grace.

It was especially this which worked havoc in the church. Neither Edwards nor his successors had any greater degree of hope for baptized children than did those who lived before them. However, with the toning down of the sterner qualities of God, the later theologians came to regard the children of the church in a more hopeful light. None, however, went back to the covenant promises. Their hopes were based rather upon a new view of God as a mild and merciful Father rather than as the Sovereign Covenant God who is faithful to His word.

Thus throughout the years the idea of obligation in religion was modified. Whereas the first preachers spoke constantly of duties enjoined, after the beginning of the eighteenth century a new emphasis arose. With the infiltration of Deistic ideas, from which the churches were by no means free during the decades immediately preceeding Edwards, man's happiness be-came the paramount question. This was continued by some of the New Divinity men, quite likely as their concession to the modified temper of the times. Although in the revivals the idea of "ought" was stressed, the motive which was adduced to urge man unto the fulfilment of his duty was that of personal enjoy-ment and happiness rather than the glory of God. This latter was no longer the dominant note in the life of the churches.

The ideal of the "pure church" was virtually surrendered in the days of the Synod of 1662. Since that time it was revived only for a brief period by Edwards and his disciples. These latter championed it but held that the relation of Christian experiences was unnecessary unto admittance into the Christian fellowship. With the neglect of discipline throughout a large part of the history of the churches, the ideal of a pure church was forced out of existence. Indeed, in the early years there was a most careful watch over the lives of individuals. This came to be restricted largely to morals after the decisions of 1662, since "graceless persons" were acknowledged as rightful members of the institution. This was, of course, greatly furthered by the Stoddardean expedient. Edwards' failure to win out in the struggle concerning the qualifications for membership in full communion in the Northampton church shows how far many had gone in repudiating the idea of careful watch over religion and morality among members of the church. The most flagrant sins were yet dragged out into the open. Public confession was demanded in such cases. However, the heart of the gospel was often forgotten in the legalistic emphasis which held sway.

That the place of children in the church fellowship went into eclipse during the period of the triumph of the revivals is very evident. Edwards in his eagerness to stress the old Puritan ideal of the necessity of Christian experience directed his attention almost exclusively to adults. In so far as he spoke about or to children, it was to those who because of age might be capable of some measure of response to the gospel call. Thus the covenant relationship of the children of believers to God was entirely obscured. This was further continued by the New Divinity. As this increased, the sacrament of infant baptism had to degenerate into a more or less formal ceremony. With the various theories held by these men the idea of children in covenant with God was incompatible. It is true that some of them insisted on religious training especially in the homes. They realized that one of the weaknesses in the religious life of the churches was the failure of parents to instruct their children in the fundamentals of the faith. However, none of them could attach any significance to the administration of the sacrament as a seal of the Covenant of Grace as long as the conscious and complete surrender of the individual to God after a pronounced conversion experience was stressed as the only legitimate manner of entrance into the Kingdom of heaven.

As a result Cyprian Strong and Nathaniel Emmons were only being consistent and logical in refusing to the children of believers status as covenant members. Their position was the necessary outcome of the individualism and experientialism of the revivals. Thus by the time of Bushnell the idea of the church had undergone a definite and radical transformation. Horace Bushnell tried to secure for the children a place in church fellowship. His criticism of the one-sidedness of the revival technique and ideal was to the point. It is only to be regretted that his reaction was somewhat extreme and led to a confusion of the operations of God in the realms of nature and grace. By basing his hopes of the salvation of children on Christian education in the home and the church, he was in danger of impinging on the necessity of regeneration by the Spirit of God. If this were no longer regarded as necessarily distinguishing God's people from the world, the church could not be regarded as a unique institution with a unique message of salvation for a unique people. It would then have to content itself with a position on the same level with various other institutions in society.

The influence of the covenant idea was nowhere more definitely shown than in the development of Congregational polity. It has been very significant in the development of the church both in its theoretical and practical aspects.

The Puritans who came to America desired in all things to be subservient to the will of God. Conscious and complete surrender to the divine pattern of life revealed in the Scriptures was their holy passion. Thus they also sought to develop a thoroughly Scriptural polity for their churches. In their zeal to retain the Biblical pattern they stressed very strongly the independence of each congregation. This was partly occasioned by the religious situation in the homeland. In England the Separatists had broken away from the State Church, because it was "Babylon" to them. In their endeavor to break away from a system which retained too many Romish customs to suit their taste, they developed the idea of the complete autonomy of the local church. Thus Robert Browne and others sought to justify their separation from the English Church. The Puritans following their brethren of Plymouth virtually became Separatists upon coming to this country, although they rejected the full implications of the position. It was their unwillingness to go as far as did the Pilgrims that accounts for the presence of Presbyterian sentiment in New England from time to time. However, the leaders, fearing the national church system as the root and cause of innumerable evils, developed the Congregational rather than the Presbyterian form of church government.

Having rejected the idea of the national church in which everyone could have a place, they had to substitute something else. This gave rise to the question concerning the proper organization of the church of Christ. The answer which seemed most logical to the colonists, who were not only three thousand miles or more from the churches across the sea but often far removed from each other in the American wilderness, was that all churches should be organized independently of each other under a specific covenant. No one would be considered a member of the congregation, unless he voluntarily entered into covenant with God and his Christian brethren and sisters.

This covenant basis for church organization has found its strictest and most consistent form of application among the Anabaptists. Some of this was taken over by the Congregationalists. There, too, the emphasis on the explicit covenant of the local church tended to break up the unity with other congregations. Furthermore, it did not do justice to the covenant position of the children, since it required a definite profession before signing the covenant. Wherever this went hand in hand with an insistence upon relating Christian experiences, which was the case in nearly all of the churches at the beginning and in some of them for many decades, there was a definite approximation to the Anabaptist conception of the church.

It is true that the theocratic ideal maintained by the first settlers was in harmony with the similar ideal of John Calvin for Geneva. He argued for the place of the "holy community" in which all of life was to be regulated by the Scriptural pattern. In consequence all of life was subordinated to the will of God. This conception was found among several of the early leaders. It is evident from their treatises that they desired all of life to be controlled by this comprehensive ideal. God was acknowledged as the ruler of the land. Thus the families were under His direct supervision and guidance. Also, every parish had the duty to instruct its people both old and young. In order that there might be an educated community, the law insisted that in every locality schools must be built for the children. The individual as a man dedicated to the service of God had to know his Maker and Redeemer before he could possibly serve Him. Even in the political order all things were to be done according to the Word of God. As long as the majority in the country were Christians who could lay claim to the Christian experience demanded upon entrance into church fellowship, these ideals were realizable. This had been the case with Geneva for some years, where the population was definitely recognized as Christian. As long as the New England Puritans made the same general affirmation of the colonists as a group, this ideal could be consistently upheld. Of course, by affirming this no one meant that every individual either in Geneva or New England was a devout Christian. The judgment was rather made of the group as a whole.

When now in New England the emphasis fell on explicit covenanting as the only means of entrance into the church, the danger was that the theocratic ideal which maintained that the population as a whole was committed to Christian ideals would be lost. On this basis only a few were given a voice in the rule of the colony, since only they could be considered true Christians. Those who held that implicit covenanting was sufficient unto church membership could uphold the ideal of the holy community much better. The longer the high experiential standard was maintained with the result that the majority could not enter the church fellowship, the easier it was for the Puritans to approach the Anabaptist ideal of a regenerate church.

In order to give the majority of the inhabitants of the land a place in the church, so that the theocratic ideal could be maintained, the leaders began to compromise with these standards of church membership. Because they felt the necessity of including as many as possible under the supervision of the local congregations, the men of 1662 adopted the double standard of membership. They admitted that there were unregenerate and graceless persons in the church anyway. All that was still to be done was to put official approval upon the situation, in the hope that those who were only half-way in church fellowship might some day take the step of covenanting explicitly for themselves and thus become members who attained to the proper standard of Christian experience. Baptism was made the sacrament for this first degree of church membership. Thus it was definitely admitted that children really had no complete standing in the church at all.

It was this conception of a double standard for membership which controlled much of the life of the church for the next century and a half. The question was bound to come up time and again, whether the baptized children and those who had been baptized in infancy and upon reaching maturity did not enter into full communion with the church should be considered members at all. The position upheld by many supporters of the decisions of 1662 and later on by Edwards and his successors was that they might not be viewed as members of the Covenant of Grace made by God with His own. Since they virtually identified the subjects of the Covenant of Grace with the elect, this was the only position which they could consistently adopt. This left no room for the historical aspect of the covenant which according to the Reformed position included the children of believers along with their parents, in such a way that all the promises of God were sealed unto them. Thus until the time of Edwards, who modified the Puritan conceptions in several directions, there was little if any room for a consistent emphasis upon covenant responsibility.

Stoddard and his followers maintained that all these people might conceivably belong to the Covenant of Grace in some sense or other. In attempting to define this his successors developed the idea of two covenants, the one gracious and the other graceless. Thus the double standard within the church was continued. And since the preacher never knew whether those in his audience were in the gracious or in the graceless covenant, he could not, as long as he maintained the doctrines of total depravity and the necessity of regeneration, preach responsibility.

Since the churches had no adequate conception of the Covenant of Grace and developed their church polity largely on the basis of the explicit voluntary covenant which was foreign to the Reformed idea of the church, the Congregationalists in their ecclesiastical life came to occupy a half-way house between the Calvinists and the Anabaptists. Very likely this accounts to a large extent for the ease with which many Congregationalists on the one hand entered the Presbyterian churches and on the other hand the Baptist fellowship.

The third direction in which the New England theologians developed the covenant idea was that of political theory. With the possible exception of Scotland under the national covenants, nowhere was this theocratic ideal of Calvin as attempted in Geneva more consistently developed than in the various Bible commonwealths of New England. It was the avowed aim of the colonists to establish in America a Christian country which should evoke the admiration of the whole world. Thus the men of the Mayflower realized that a Christian group undertaking a program of colonization should do so on the basis of Christian ideas and ideals. Therefore they gave to the world the Mayflower Compact. Although from the point of view of direct results this was the least influential of the three ways in which the covenant was applied, it did tend to pave the way for the ultimate triumph of democracy in New England.

This may seem strange at first glance, when we remember that the earliest settlers were definitely not committed to the democratic ideal in politics. The leadership of the various townships was in the hands of the church members. In the Massachusetts Bay colony the rule of this spiritual aristocracy went much farther than in Plymouth, although there too the franchise was severely limited. Only Connecticut formed somewhat of an exception to the general practice that the minority ought to rule the majority. This was made to harmonize with the theocratic ambitions according to which God was said to rule the world through His chosen people. Thus during the first century the smaller group, generally with the minister at the head, virtually ruled New England.

This should not be taken in any sense as a direct and derogatory criticism of the colonists. They were children of their own time and came from a social and political background saturated with the aristocratic ideal. It was indeed no spiritual aristocracy which ruled England in those days, but none the less it was the rule of the majority by the few. It was not surprising therefore that in New England a somewhat similar inequality should prevail.

However, in spite of the fact that among them only a small fraction of the population had any voice in the government, the seeds of democracy were latent in the theories which they held. The democratic conception was certainly applied to church government. All who could lay claim to an experiential understanding of the Christian way of life had a voice in the government of the congregation. Whether rich or poor, young or old, educated or illiterate, the same privileges were extended to all who met the requirements. In the rule of the church every male member could vote, and the majority ruled the minority. It was from this point of view a sad thing that the office of ruling elder in the churches soon merged with that of teaching elder. In this way the ministers came to control both the internal affairs of the church and especially the relations sustained by one church to another.

As soon as the theocratic ideal began to wane, New England was ripe for applying the democratic way to politics.

The earliest protest against the spiritual aristocracy was led by Thomas Hooker. He insisted that not only church members but also others resident in the New England communities had a right to take part in the government. This occasioned at least in part the exodus from Dorchester and other Massachusetts towns to Hartford. In 1638 the celebrated Fundamental Orders were drawn up. The most significant departure from the code of the Massachusetts colony was their omission of the religious test for citizenship.

A more consistent democracy was for a time adopted by various colonies in the Rhode Island area. Like the Pilgrims Roger Williams and others who settled Providence entered into a covenant by which they pledged obedience to all the rules and regulations which should be enacted by a majority of the house-holders. Once in a fortnight all the heads of the families met to settle anything which had come up. It was distinctly under-stood, however, that this pertained only to civil affairs.[6] Here we find, then, the first true separation between church and state among the commonwealths of New England. This form of the democratic ideal based on the explicit covenant was more in harmony with Anabaptist positions than with those of the Calvinists. After the death of Williams Rhode Island did not maintain his ideals in this respect. During the seventeenth century a law was passed requiring that all voters had to be pro-fessing Christians.[7] Likewise after the Revolution of 1688 the Catholics were disenfranchised, and until the middle of the nineteenth century there were laws withholding the ballot from the Jews.[8]

During this time there were also property tests for suffrage, by which those who owned no land could not enter the political covenant. Although this did restrict the number of voters, the results were never as far-reaching as in England, because in America land was always comparatively cheap.

Although the civil compact in New England did not make any direct contribution to the development of democracy as we understand it today, it did prepare the way. Its emphasis on the voluntary covenant could be made to harmonize with some of the political theories of such men as Rousseau and Montesquieu by secularizing the former ideal and carrying through consistently the principle of the separation of church and state.

Chapter 11.

The Weaknesses of the Covenant Idea in New England Theology

HAVING summarized the influence which the covenant conception exerted in several directions among the Congregationalists from the time of Cotton to Bushnell, we will also attempt to point out where they were weak in their construction.

The first apparent weakness in the covenant idea as current in the churches was that the Covenant of Grace and the church covenant were not sufficiently linked together. It is true that in the first years the church covenant was said to give form to the Covenant of Grace. Thus only those who were considered members of the latter were allowed a place in the former. In the main this harmonized well with the theories and practices of Reformed churches the world over. However, as soon as the leaders admitted not only that there were in the churches many who were destitute of grace but also that these had to be given official standing, the two could no longer be united. Thus there were many more in church covenant than in the Covenant of Grace. This especially demanded that the whole question of the nature of the church and the requirements for membership be studied. The revisions both in theory and practice occasioned by the various controversies led the Congregationalists far from the Calvinistic or Reformed position that the church consists properly only of believers and their children who are in covenant relationship with God.

Very intimately bound up with this is the fact that in the churches there was never a sufficient appreciation of the historical aspect of the Covenant of Grace. The Reformed had always linked up the Covenant of Grace with the Covenant of Redemp-

215

tion, but then in such a way that the two were readily distinguished. They held that in working out His plan of salvation God honored the relationships rooted in creation by giving the promises to the seed of believers with the result that the church and the covenant with man would be perpetuated through them as a group. Realizing that not every covenant child would in his later years give evidence of saving grace, the Reformed theologians usually distinguished between covenant members who belonged to the Covenant of Grace as a legal relationship and those who found in it a communion of life.[1] Since it was not revealed in the individual case whether the child possessed or was destined to possess saving grace, the Reformed asserted of the entire group that they were in the Covenant of Grace. This they maintained of the individuals by a judgment of charity until the contrary would become evident, whereupon ecclesiastical discipline was to be applied. In this way, though acknowledging that not all who were in the church belonged to the Covenant of Grace as a communion of life, an attempt was made by such discipline to keep only the living members within the church. The others were to be warned and their responsibilities pointed out to them. Because of the reality of God's promises none might use personal depravity as an excuse for negligence, indifference, or hostility to things spiritual.

The Congregationalists on the other hand virtually identified the Covenant of Grace with the Covenant of Redemption and the decree of election. In this they carried through the logic of Westminster relentlessly. Their aim was to emphasize the sovereignty of God, which, because they failed to balance the doctrine of total depravity with that of the covenant promises and blessings extended to the seed of believers, led them to neglect human responsibility within the covenant.

Still more tragic was their failure to apply church discipline and excommunication to those who were content with a partial membership in the church and openly admitted that they were graceless members. The leaders by giving these a place in the church completely divorced the church membership from membership in the Covenant of Grace. One of the sad results was the development of the theory of the presence of the real and living church within the church as an institution. Also, this led to the controversies about the external and internal covenants in the days of the men of the New Divinity. By granting that those who were not in the Covenant of Grace still had a right to church membership, the leaders broke down the wall of separation between the church and the world and virtually rejected the position that the members of the church as the people of God were a distinct and separate group.

It is true that among the men of the New Divinity there seemed to be a renewed appreciation of the covenant doctrine. However, because of their allegiance to the theory of revivalism, it was not the Covenant of Grace and the church conception which was characteristic of Calvinism in general.

The third weakness in the presentation of the theologians of New England is to be found in their stress on the subjective element in religion, also in the covenant relationship between God and man, at the expense of the objective. This is to be found at the very outset of the history of the churches. Even the first settlers spoke much more of man's acceptance of the covenant than of God's institution of the same. This was definitely in harmony with their experientialism and voluntarism.

This had already run a sad and riotous course in the extravagant theories of Anne Hutchinson. The type of individualism for which she stood completely repudiated all organic relations which believers sustained to one another, their children, and the church. In fact, she even rejected the validity of the objective means of grace by insisting upon the special indwelling of the Holy Spirit and repudiating the place of good works as evidences of saving grace. Here also an attempt was made to establish an "ecclesiola in ecclesia," a position much more in harmony with the Anabaptist type of piety than the Reformed. Although her positions on the covenant and church membership were condemned by the ministers, Cotton was inclined to move somewhat in the same direction.

The subjectivism in the covenant conception of the Congregationalists is seen much more clearly in the way in which children were regarded as members of the Covenant of Grace. The
basis upon which their place rested was the profession or explicit covenanting of the parents, who at the beginning of the
history of the churches had to be members in full communion.
Because of this one-sided appreciation of the subjective and
personal aspect, the doctrine of the Covenant of Grace as
historically developed in the Reformed circles was obscured and
all the emphasis fell instead on the voluntary church covenant
explicitly affirmed by the individual.

Another weakness in the position of the Puritans and their
successors was their virtual dualism between nature and grace.
This was inherent in many of their positions, in spite of the
fact that several early leaders never seemed to weary of stating
that all of life was in covenant relation with God. The very
fact that the churches insisted that besides a godly walk of life
according to the Lord's commandments a relation of spiritual
experiences was necessary shows that they did not appreciate the
position of the Calvinistic Reformation which maintained that
saving grace restores natural life.[2] This emphasis on experience
is much more in harmony with the Anabaptist idea that the
work of grace really constitutes a new creation.

It was this dualism, latent in many of the early leaders, which
was greatly developed with the rise and triumph of the revivals.
Edwards himself did not a little to divorce religion from natural
life in this way. We appreciate fully his opposition to the theory
that morality and Christianity could be synonymous. That had
been the tendency during the half century immediately preceding the Great Awakening. With the revivals, however, the place
of the religious affections seems to have been overemphasized.
In many cases this was accompanied by a false type of enthusiasm
which put its trust in extraordinary religious experiences. It is
true that Edwards very positively rejected many of the extreme
positions taken by the advocates of the revivals. However, the

affections retained their important place in his scheme. Wherever the emotional aspect of religious life was given priority over the intellectual, only discernible supernatural operations of the Holy Spirit upon the individual soul could be considered the marks of true religion. Such a position naturally led to a radical divorce between nature and grace. When Bushnell appeared on the scene, he sought to relate the two again. However, because of his construction of the relation between the natural and the supernatural the result removed the churches still further from their original Calvinism. In his construction the organic or natural relationships were in danger of superseding the supernatural operations of the Holy Spirit upon the soul of man and rendering these last superfluous. Therefore he repudiated the covenant idea in his interpretation of man's relation to God and substituted a position entirely foreign to the conceptions of the Calvinistic theologians.

The last weakness which must be mentioned is the great concern which the theologians definitely evidenced for the practical aspects of ecclesiastical life at the expense of the theoretical. It is quite evident that generally they first adopted a position and then argued it out on the basis of Scripture and experience. Because this rather pragmatic approach regarded only the immediate consequences, the underlying issues were often obscured. Thus solutions to certain problems relative to the welfare of the churches were adopted which proved very detrimental over a period of years. Closely associated with this practical interest was the lack of agreement on what constituted the Covenant of Grace. Because there was no reasonable uniformity and unanimity in their opinions on this important concept, dissension acutely disturbed the churches. Not until some of the more fundamental approaches were agreed upon could the churches possibly have escaped this evil. It was the lack of such uniform opinions as well as the pragmatic interest which made it possible for Bushnell to find a hearing for his new ideas among churches which at the beginning of their history pledged themselves to seek their glory in championing the Reformed faith.

Chapter 12.

New England Calvinism in the Light of the Covenant Idea

TO CLOSE this study with a discussion and enumeration of the weakness of the Congregationalist presentation would hardly do them full justice. In spite of the various shortcomings mentioned there are certain elements in their construction which can be appreciated and even admired.

The first of these is their strong antipathy to the national church idea. Very likely one of the greatest factors operative in driving the Separatists closer to the Anabaptist ideal of the pure church is to be found in the many abuses and evils found in other Reformed churches of that day. It is a known fact that many of the Calvinistic churches championed a form of the national church ideal in which every citizen was to have a place. Wherever this was done it was difficult, if not impossible, to develop and sustain a church possessing the three characteristics generally considered by Calvinists to be the marks of the true church of Christ: the pure preaching of the gospel, the proper administration of the sacraments, and the exercise of discipline.[1] It would be virtually impossible to excommunicate the unbelievers and indifferent on the basis of an all-embracing national church. Where discipline was not faithfully exercised, there could hardly be any careful watch over the administration of the sacraments. All children, by virtue of their birth in a so-called Christian country, would be entitled to baptism. To be assured of communicants the bars would have to be lowered in the case of the sacrament of the Lord's Supper. Where such practices were found, it was nothing short of the impossible to maintain the pure preaching of the gospel. At every turn of the road compromises would have to be made. In many instances this seems to have been the case with the national churches of Reformed origin. Pilgrims and Puritans complained bitterly about the careless administration of the sacraments in the English State Church. Furthermore, although appreciating many of the doctrinal positions of the Dutch churches, they felt that these too suffered woefully from a deficiency of spirituality because of lack of discipline and neglect of supervising the sacraments, especially baptism. John Davenport bewailed this in several of his works and letters. Many of the Pilgrims and Puritans felt the closest affinity with the French Reformed Churches, which like themselves constituted a minority group and thus did not have to meet the difficulties inherent in the national church ideal.

It would have been comparatively easy for the early Congregationalists to accept the national church idea with its parish system. When they first settled New England, they were by far and away the majority group. They outnumbered all dissenters. They controlled the government. They regulated much of social life by law. And yet they refused to sacrifice their emphasis on personal religion for the sake of possible greater prestige. Of course, the Congregationalists at that early date did not tolerate any other denomination next to their own. However, the free church ideal, developed later on in certain Calvinistic circles largely under the more or less indirect influence of certain Anabaptist positions, harmonized better with their position than the ideal of an all-inclusive national church.

Moreover, it is to the credit of these churches that they earnestly desired to maintain a high standard for church membership. They realized that not every one had a place in the church of Jesus Christ and the covenant with God. To let down the bars would be tantamount to ecclesiastical suicide, they contended. Therefore quite unanimously at the beginning of their history they insisted upon rigid examination by the church officers and even before the whole congregation before anyone was admitted unto church fellowship. An earnest and zealous desire to uphold this standard caused many to hesitate at first in adopting the Half-way Covenant and thereafter Stoddardeanism. In the former the double standard of membership still enabled the church to a certain extent to maintain the original ideal of an experiential membership, even though the doors of the instituted church were officially opened to many who would never attain unto full membership.

This same zeal for genuine piety moved Jonathan Edwards. His reaction against the dead orthodoxy of his day was due to his adherence to certain Puritan fundamentals concerning the necessity of personal experience. For this reason he opened the attack on the Half-way Covenant, which was carried to a successful conclusion by his disciples.

Finally, the zeal for the welfare of the church which characterized all the leaders from Cotton to Bushnell merits more than a passing word of commendation. In the lives of nearly all of them the church in its organized form occupied a prominent place. They realized full well its significance in the lives of the individuals and the community at large. Therefore they sought very earnestly and diligently, if not altogether wisely, to extend her scope and influence. Many of the arguments used in the various controversies reflect this attitude. The positions advocated by the Synods of 1646-1648 and 1662 were based upon this. Stoddard argued for his novel theory on the basis that it would promote the welfare of the churches. Edwards and the men of the New Divinity made much use of the same argument. The successors of Stoddard refused to relinquish their position, because they felt it would be detrimental to the church. And finally, Horace Bushnell likewise supported his contentions with the claim that they would greatly enhance the place of the church in the lives of men.

The reason for their great concern on this score can not be sought in the personal advantages which they might possibly have reaped from their position in the organization. Many of these leaders had enjoyed at best a precarious existence. Some were even banished from their parishes and pulpits. And yet the cause of the church meant everything to them. Realizing and believing that in and through it the glory of the God whom they served was being promoted, they were willing to suffer personal loss for the sake of its welfare. Such men are worthy of our deep respect and sincere admiration.

None of these three elements in Congregational ecclesiastical life made a permanent contribution to the development of the covenant idea as such. In the construction of this conception among them there is little that can be commended. The reason for this is to be found in the fact that although they wrote voluminously about the covenant, they never allowed the concept to control their theory. Their individualism and experientialism precluded any deep and lasting appreciation of this idea on the part of the leaders. Much of what they said and wrote about it was excellent. And yet because it did not become an integral part of their theology, it was easily obscured and finally forgotten.

That these churches in New England have departed definitely from the Calvinism which controlled them at the beginning of their history is a recognized fact. The short and simple "Statement of Doctrine" of 1883 contains no single distinctively Calvinistic doctrine.[2] Rather, it prides itself on being less scholastic and more catholic than the standards of the early Puritans.

The reasons for the final collapse of Calvinism in the churches are numerous. No single one explains the historical development through which they passed. But surely the lack of a consistent and thorough understanding of the covenant concept contributed significantly to this process. Because they did not grasp this as one of the pivotal teachings of the Reformed faith, it became necessary for them to make concessions and changes in the faith and practice of their churches from time to time.

New England Congregationalism during the two centuries here considered has had in many ways an illuminating and inspiring history. Indeed, there were obvious shortcomings and painful mistakes. Yet there was always a sincere and conscientious grappling with the various problems which have arisen at different times within the Christian church. For these questions the leaders found answers. Profound thought mingled with an abiding love for the church and the spiritual heritage of the fathers and an insistence upon vital personal religion characterized the outstanding theologians during these times. Each group of them in its own way sought to make a permanent and positive contribution to the development of the churches.

This development is thus very instructive. The treatises which were written touched nearly every phase of the faith and practice of the group. The development of Christian doctrine can almost be found in microcosmic form within American Congregationalism. Its weaknesses and failures, some of which we have attempted to point out, are warnings to those who are still wrestling with these questions. Its triumphs are a source of constant inspiration.

In several respects the passing of Calvinism in the churches may well be lamented. This is said in spite of a definite recognition of the obvious and painful fact that some who prided themselves on their Calvinism failed to meet the religious and spiritual challenges of the environment in which they lived. Much of this, however, should be attributed to an ofttimes distorted and unbalanced representation of Calvinistic doctrine rather than to the genius of Calvinism itself.

While the Reformed faith flourished, it gave to those who accepted it a profound recognition of the sovereignty of God in human life. Surely our modern world, vacillating between a superficial and shortsighted optimism and a morbid and unchristian pessimism, needs to catch again something of the Puritan faith in God who has ordained all things according to the counsel of His unchangeable will.

The Calvinism conception furthered the belief in the true dignity of man. Indeed, it insisted that man was a sinner who apart from the special grace of God was destitute of saving good. It did not leave that picture unrelieved, however. It also held that this same man was created in the image of God and thus occupied a unique and exalted position in the world. He was capable of being restored to his original position of honor and worth through the sure mercies of Jesus Christ, in whom and through whom God had made an immutable covenant with the race. Today with the almost total disregard for the dignity of man on the one hand and the fairly unbounded insistence upon individual worth and rights apart from God on the other hand something of the Calvinistic appreciation of man in covenant relationship to the Sovereign God would be a wholesome antidote.

Although holding fast to the sovereignty of God the Reformed faith of the first settlers by no means excluded the gospel of His love and mercy in Christ. Few systems of Christian thought give such an exalted position to the Savior-King whose name is above every name and before whom every knee must bow. He is the Lord of the cosmos, the created order. Not only certain elect individuals but rather the whole creation has been redeemed unto God by Him as the second Adam, the Mediator of that new and everlasting covenant. This conception taught the Calvinists that Christ's Kingdom embraced not only the hearts of the believers but their entire lives. In this present world of sin and strife we as disciples of the Lord need as never before the wholehearted recognition of His Kingship over all of life. The Calvinists traced this back as far as they could, rooting it not merely in creation ordinances but rather in the eternal counsel and purpose of God.

Finally, the covenant conception among them gave a place of honor and importance to the instituted church. It was viewed as a divine organization, ruled by the divine King, and quickened and guided by the divine Spirit. God alone determined who could rightly belong unto the institution. In our days the place of the church is hardly an enviable one. Indeed, many are still affiliated with her. However, her divine origin, constitution and purpose are altogether too often forgotten. The emphasis has fallen too much on the human aspect. Thus the individual and he alone quite generally determines in our day whether or not he shall belong. May it not be the catering to personal preferences which has cost the church in several quarters her prestige and power? The Calvinists did not reject the human aspect of the church. They recognized it by virtue of their acceptance of the covenant concept that the individual has his responsibility. Yet to them the church was primarily that divine institution into whose fellowship God called His own.

There were obvious weaknesses in the Calvinism of both the first settlers and Edwards and his disciples. In some instances these weaknesses gave birth to glaring inconsistencies. Contradictory elements from time to time marred the positions which were championed. It was therefore necessary that those who followed would in some way seek to remedy the situation.

We can not but admire the zeal with which many sought to save the churches from too great inconsistency.

We must regret that the solutions which were advocated and adopted from time to time did not more closely approximate the first principles of the fathers, which gave a large place to the covenant idea.

All in all, we are humbly aware that behind their efforts stood the Holy Spirit, Christ's glorious and indispensable gift to His church upon earth. He has led and still leads the church called unto everlasting life into all truth. May He then teach the church of the twentieth century to profit by the efforts and experiences of those who have already been translated out of the kingdom of grace into the kingdom of glory.

NOTES AND REFERENCES

INTRODUCTION

1. Herbert Wallace Schneider: *The Puritan Mind*. New York: Henry Holt and Co., 1930.
2. Haroutunian, Joseph: *Piety versus Moralism*. New York: Henry Holt and Co., 1932.
3. School of theology which flourished especially in the Netherlands during the last half of the seventeenth and the first quarter of the eighteenth century. Its greatest leader was Cocceius (Johannes Koch). Cf. Otto Ritschl: *Dogmengeschichte des Protestantismus*, III Band "Die reformierte Theologie des 16. und des 17 Jahrhunderts in ihrer Entstehung und Entwicklung."
4. Lewis Bevens Schenck: *The Presbyterian Doctrine of Children in the Covenant*. (An Historical Study of the Significance of Infant Baptism in the Presbyterian Church in America) New Haven: Yale University Press, 1940.

PART ONE

Chapter 1

1. *Ante-Nicene Fathers*, vol. I, p. 139, 145-146.
2. *Ibid*, p. 472-475.
3. Ibid, vol. II, p. 452 and note iii on p. 476-477.
4. *Nicene and Post-Nicene Fathers*, vol. IV, p. 421-422.
5. *Ibid*, vol. V, p. 24.
6. On the place of the covenant idea in Lutheran theology cf. Vos: *De Verbondsleer in de Gereformeerde Theologie*, p. 1, and note 1 on p. 63.

"De Luthersche theologen, die het verbondsbegrip eene plaats gunden in hun stelsel, worden opgegeven door Diestel: *Jahrb, f. Deuteche Theol.*, X, pag. 266. Het zijn Calixtus, Wolfgang Jäger van Tübingen, Caspar Exner, Reuter, e.a. Coccejus stond, vooral als exegeet bij de Duitschers in groot aanzien, zelfs bij de Lutherschen. Op het werkverbond werd veel nadruk gelegd, wat te meer bevreemdt, dewijl in het consequent Luthersch stelsel voor een werkverbond geene plaats is. Men stelde in het werkverbond de foederale en de natuurlijke eenheid naast elkaar, zonder de eene adn de andere ondergschikt te maken. In het genadeverbond komt het eigenaardig-Luthersche daarin uit, dat men niet iets anders dan geloof als stipulatio-foederis weten wilde. De Gereformeerden rekenen hiertoe zonder bedenken ook de nieuwe gehoorzaamheid, en zeggen, dat het bij de rechtvaardiging door het geloof alleen gaat, maar dat het verbond veel wijder is."

7. Calvin: *Institutes of the Christian Religion*, first published in 1536. Edition used here is Allen's *Translation*, 7th American edition, revised and corrected, 1936.
9. *Ibid*, IV, 14, 1. (II, 555)
8. *Ibid*, Book IV, chapter 1, section 23. (Allen, vol. II, p. 296.)
10. *Ibid*, IV, 14, 6. (II, 559)
11. *Ibid*, IV, 15, 1. (II, 583)
12. *Ibid*, IV, 15, 22. (II, 602)
13. *Ibid*, IV, 16, 17. (II, 620)
14. *Ibid*, IV, 17, 1. (II, 642)
15. Calvin: *Articuli A Facultate Sacrae Theologiae Pariscensi Determinati . . cum Antidote. Corpus Reformatorum*, XXXV, 8. quoted by Schenck, *op. cit.*, p. 11-12.
16. Calvin: *Institutes of the Christian Religion*. IV, 14, 7. (II, 561)
17. *Ibid*, IV, 16, 29. (II, 633)
18. *Ibid*, IV, 16, 32. (II, 641)
19. Calvin: *Interim Adultero * Germanum; cui adiecto est vere Christianae Pacificationis et Ecclesiae Reformandae Ratio. Corpus Reformatorum*, XXXV, 619. quoted by Schenck, *op. cit.*, p. 13.
20. Calvin: *Institutes of the Christian Religion*, IV, 1, 13. (II, 284)
21. *Ibid*, In this connection he mentioned the Cathari, Donatists, and Anabaptists. (II, 285)
22. *Ibid*. Cf. the chapter on "The True and the False Church Compared." IV, 2. (II, 302)
23. *Ibid*, II, 10, 2.
24. *Ibid*, II, 11.
25. *Ibid*, II, 8, 13-50.
26. Zwingli: *Sämtliche Werke* (Egli-Finsler edit.) Band IV, p. 188-337.
27. Schenck, *op. cit.*, p. 26-27.
28. Bullinger: *Compendium Religionis Christianae*. Quoted by Kuyper: *Dictaten Dogmatiek*, vol. III "Locus de Foedere," p. 69.
29. Schenck, *op cit.*, p. 77.
30. Ursinus: *Commentary on the Heidelberg Catechism*, First American Edition. On Infant Baptism, p. 365-373. On Circumcision, p. 373-376. His tenth thesis on Baptism reads as follows: "Since the infant children of Christians are also included in the church, in which Christ will have all those who belong to him to be received, and enrolled by baptism; and as baptism has been substituted in the place of circumcision, by which (as well to the infants as to the adults belonging to the seed of Abraham) justification, regeneration and reception into the church were sealed by and for the sake of Christ; and as no one can forbid water that those should not be baptized who have received the Holy Spirit purifying their hearts, it follows that those infants should be baptized, who are either born in the church, or come into it from the world with their parents." P. 373.
31. Vos, *op cit.*, p. 46.
32. *Ibid*, p. 46.
33. *Ibid*, p. 27-28.

34. On Junius cf. Otto Ritschl, *op cit.*, p. 420-423. His ideas are developed in Theses Theologicae Nr. 25: "De foederibus et testamentis divinis" in *Opuscula*, ed. Kuyper 1882, p. 183 f. It is interesting to note that Junius was in correspondence with the Brownists at Amsterdam. Cf. De Hoop Scheffer: *History of the Free Churchmen*, p. 62-63.
35. *Ibid*, p. 423.
36. Vos, *op. cit.*, p. 8.
37. Ritschl, *op. cit.*, p. 427-428.
38. Vos, *op. cit.*, p. 7.
39. *Ibid*, p. 31.
40. Berkhof: *Reformed Dogmatics*, p. 212.
41. Berkhof: *Reformed Dogmatics*, "Introductory Volumes," p. 69.
42. Vos, *op. cit.*, p. 9.
43. *Ibid*, p. 11.
44. Dexter: *Congregationalism as Seen in Its Literature*, p. 400-403.
45. *Op. cit.*, Locus de Foedere, p. 7.
46. Müller: *Bekenntnisschriften der Reformierten Kirche*, p. xvii.
47. *Ibid*, p. 2, lines 21-24.
48. *Ibid*, p. 2, lines 30-36.
49. *Ibid*, p. 8, lines 2-4.
50. *Ibid*, p. 8, line 20.
51. *Ibid*, p. 12, lines 25-28.
52. *Ibid*, p. 28, lines 41-44.
53. *Ibid*, p. 95, lines 22-25.
54. *Ibid*, "Einleitung."
55. *Ibid*, ———
56. *Ibid*, p. 83, line 8.
57. *Ibid*, p. 83, lines 25-26.
58. *Ibid*, p. 83, lines 30-32.
59. *Ibid*, p. 83, lines 35-36.
60. *Ibid*, p. 84, lines 2-4.
61. *Ibid*, p. 85, lines 46-47.
62. *Ibid*, p. 35, lines 38-40.
63. *Ibid*, p. 45, lines 24-25.
64. *Ibid*, p. 45, lines 28-30.
65. *Ibid*, p. 45, lines 39-41.
66. *Ibid*, p. 46, lines 10-11.
67. *Ibid*, "Confessio Helvetica Prior." Cf. also Schaff: *Creeds of Christendom*, vol. III, p. 217.
68. *Ibid*, p. 103, lines 34-35.
69. Schaff, *op. cit.*, vol. III, p. 217.
70. Muller, *op cit.*, p. 106, lines 36-38.
71. Schaff, *op cit.*, vol. III, p. 224. Article XXII in the Latin edition corresponds with Article XXI in the Swiss.
72. *Ibid*, vol. III, p. 247.
73. *Ibid*, p. 266-267.
74. *Ibid*, p. 290.

75. *Ibid*, p. 290.
76. *Ibid*, p. 291.
77. *Ibid*, p. 291.
78. Müller, *op. cit.*, p. 930, line 11.
79. *Ibid*, p. 930, lines 26-27.
80. *Ibid*, p. 931, lines 10-11.
81. *Ibid*, p. 931, lines 24-27.
82. *Ibid*, p. 931, lines 34-35.
83. *Ibid*, p. 274, lines 7-9.
84. *Ibid*, p. 274, line 11.
85. *Ibid*, p. 274, lines 15-16.
86. *Ibid*, p. 353, line 44.
87. *Ibid*, p. 353, line 45 through p. 354, line 1.
88. *Ibid*, p. 354, lines 14-15.
89. *Ibid*, p. 268, lines 6-8.
90. *Ibid*, p. 380, lines 38-40.
91. *Ibid*, p. 421, line 41.
92. *Ibid*, p. 422, lines 15-17.
93. *Ibid*, p. 112, lines 13-15. Genfer Bekenntnis: "Mais au contraire, s'il est delaisse de Dieu en sa propre natur, il ne peult synon demourer en ignorance et estre abandonne a toute iniquite."
94. *Ibid*, p. 114, line 17.
95. *Ibid*, p. 114, lines 24-25.
96. *Ibid*, p. 114, lines 28-30.
97. *Ibid*, p. 164, lines 35-37.
98. *Ibid*, p. 224, line 14.
99. *Ibid*, p. 224, lines 23-25.
100. *Ibid*, p. 230, lines 20-22.
101. *Ibid*, p. 238, lines 31-32.
102. Schaff, *op. cit.*, p. 530.
103. *Ibid*, p. 531.
104. *Ibid*, p. 532.
105. *Ibid*, p. 505.
106. Müller, *op. cit.*, p. 705, lines 20-21.
107. *Ibid*, p. 702, lines 1-7.
108. *Ibid*, p. 685, lines 8-9. "beyder über angeborne und würckliche sünden."
109. *Ibid*, p. 851, line 40.
110. *Ibid*, p. 849, lines 6-7.
111. Schaff, *op. cit.*, p. 615, Chapter VI, 3.
112. *Ibid*, p. 616, VII, 1.
113. *Ibid*, p. 617, VII, 4.
114. *Ibid*, p. 617, VII, 3.
115. *Ibid*, p. 618, VII, 6.
116. *Ibid*, p. 660, XXVII, 1.
117. *Ibid*, p. 661, XXVII, 3.
118. *Ibid*, p. 661-662, XXVII.
119. *Ibid*, p. 662-663, XXVII, 4. note 1, p. 663.

120. *Ibid*, p. 666, XXIX, 7.

121. Müller, *op. cit.*, p. xlviii.

122. *Ibid*, p. 614, line 49.

123. *Ibid*, p. 615, line 14.

VBD. Ibid, p. 615, line 22.

125. *Ibid*, p. 864, lines 41-43.

126. *Ibid*, p. 868, line 34.

127. Berkhof, *op. cit.*, p. 215.

128. It should be borne in mind that the Reformed did not teach that saving grace simply restored nature, that is, that it restored unto the redeemed humanity the same position and blessings enjoyed in the state of rectitude. Vos ascribes this limited view to the Lutherans (*op. cit.*, p. 16.). The Reformed went beyond this and claimed that Christ had as the second Adam perfected in Himself the human race, so that it could not again fall away from God but on the contrary would certainly inherit eternal life. Thus the doctrine of redemption through the active and passive obedience of Christ for the elect necessarily implied the doctrine of the perseverance of the saints.

129. Kramer: *Het Verband van Doop en Wedergeboorte*, p. 122 f. (Transl. given by Berkhof, *op. cit.*, p. 640.)

130. Ernst Troeltsch in attempting to work out some of the fundamental Calvinistic positions holds that there was indeed a type of individualism among the Calvinists but of an altogether different type than among the Roman Catholics and Lutherans. It was directed not towards the emotional side of religion but rather towards the volitional, that is, "from all sides the individualism of the Reformed Church was impelled towards activity."—*The Social Teaching of the Christian Church*. To demonstrate that this individualism found expression within the group he discusses further the "Holy Community" and shows how this differed again from the teachings of the Anabaptists. *Op. cit.*, p. 587-602.

131. In discussing the various theories which arose in an attempt to answer the question when the covenant promises were realized in the lives of the children of believers, Vos distinguishes three lines:
   1—those who held that the elect seed within the group was regenerated from early infancy. Those who championed this position were Ursinus, Polanus, Junius, Walaeus, Cloppenburg, Voetius, and Witsius.
   2—those who refused to specify any time and held that regeneration could occur at any time, either before, during, or after baptism. This view was held by Zanchius, Amesius, and Fr. Spanheim the elder.
   3—those who maintained that the Word of God in the preaching of the gospel was generally employed by the Holy Spirit as a means in connection with which regeneration occurred. Beza and Ussher are mentioned as holding this position. Cf. Vos, *op. cit.*, p. 55-60.

132. In connection with the sacraments the Lutherans, Berkhof claims, did not always steer clear of the idea that they function ex opere operato. Cf. Berkhof, *op. cit.*, p. 607.

Chapter 2

1. Troeltsch: *The Social Teaching of the Christian Church*, p. 664. "But whichever line it took, Congregationalism stood midway between the Calvinistic church-type and the sect-type; to some extent this was involved in the fact that Calvinism itself had many affinities with the sect-type; in reality, however, Congregationalism only arose under Anabaptist influences . . ."

2. *Ibid*, p. 707.

3. Champlin Burrage: *The Church Covenant Idea*, p. 13.

4. Williston Walker: *A History of the Christian Church*, p. 367-368. Also Burrage, *op. cit.*, p. 15-16.

5. Burrage, *op. cit.*, p. 17 where the quotation from the original is given as follows: "Ir Tauf sey ain zaichen ainer verpundtnuss unnd verwilligung gegen got unnd der christenlichen gemaindt."

6. *Ibid*, p. 19.

7. *Ibid*, p. 20.

8. Zur Linden: *Melchior Hoffman, ein Prophet der Wiedertäufer*, p. 252.

9. Burrage, *op. cit.*, p. 24.

10. Douglas Campbell: *The Puritans in Netherlands, England, and America*, vol. I, p. 487.

11. *Ibid*, p. 489-490. Cf. also note * on p. 490.

12. Henry E. Dosker: *The Dutch Anabaptists*, p. 116.

13. *Ibid*.

14. On Browne, cf. Walker: *Creeds and Platforms of Congregationalism*, p. 8-27. Also Dexter: *Congregationalism as Seen In Its Literature*, chapter on "Robert Browne and His Co-workers," p. 59-128.

15. *A True and Short Declaration, both of the Gathering and Ioyning Together of Certaine Persons: and also of the Lamentable Breach and Divisions which fell Amongst Them*. p. 6. Dexter, *op. cit.*, p. 62, claims that this is the spiritual autobiography of Browne during the ten most significant years of his life. The quotation itself is found in Dexter, *op. cit.*, p. 67.

16. De Hoop Scheffer: *History of the Free Churchmen*, p. 8.

17. Walker: *Creeds and Platforms of Congregationalism*, p. 18. Question and Answer 2.

18. *Ibid*, p. 18-20.

19. De Hoop Scheffer, *op. cit.*, p. 8.

20. *Ibid*, p. 56-59.

21. Quoted from Walker, *op. cit.*, p. 33-40.

22. *Ibid*, p. 37.

23. *Ibid*, p. 70.

24. De Hoop Scheffer, *op. cit.*, p. 111.

25. These "Seven Articles" can be found in Walker, *op. cit.*, p. 89-91.

26. *Ibid*, p. 91.

27. *Ibid*, p. 89.

PART TWO

Chapter 3

1. Smith: *History of the Christian Church*, p. 74.
2. Bradford: *History of Plimouth Plantation* (Everyman's Library) quoted from the original edition by Burrage: *The Church Covenant Idea*, p. 86. Also found in Walker: *Creeds and Platforms of Congregationalism*, p. 92.
3. On John Calvin's political theory and related subjects, cf. E. Choisy: *La Theocratie a Geneve au temps de Calvin.* (1897)
4. Burrage, *op. cit.*, p. 180.
5. Walker, *op. cit.*, p. 236.
6. *Ibid*, p. 236.
7. Felt: *Ecclesiastical History of New England*, vol. I, p. 58 f.
8. Uhden: *The New England Theocracy*, p. 71.
9. *Ibid*, p. 79.
10. Dexter: *Congregationalism as seen in its Literature*, p. 393.
11. Uhden, *op. cit.*, p. 54-55.
12. Cotton Mather: *Magnalia Christiana Americana*, vol. I, p. 362.
13. Burrage, *op. cit.*, p. 88. Cf. notes in Walker, *op. cit.*, p. 95-96 as to the contents of the Covenant of 1629.
14. Walker, *op. cit.*, p. 106.
15. *Ibid*, p. 116-117.
16. *Ibid*, p. 113. The Anti-Quaker article is recorded on p. 118.
17. Recorded by Walker, *op. cit.*, p. 119-120.
18. *Ibid*, p. 117.
19. Felt, *op. cit.*, p. 115 f.
20. *Ibid*, p. 278-282 for the Questions. The Answers are summarized on p. 380-386.
21. John Cotton: *The Covenant of God's Free Grace, Most Sweetly Unfolded*, p. 2.
22. *Ibid*, p. 21.
23. John Cotton: *The Grounds and Ends of the Baptisme of the Children of the Faithfull*, p. 43.
24. *Ibid*, p. 44.
25. *Ibid*, p. 45.
26. *Ibid*, p. 125.
27. *Spiritual Milk for Babes* was widely used by the New England churches. It was only one of many such catechisms, however, all of which reflected basically the same attitude towards the children of believing parents.
28. Quoted from Adams: *Three Episodes of Massachusetts History*, vol. I.
29. John Cotton: *The Covenant of Grace*, p. 9. That the Covenant of Grace included all of life Cotton made plain in his discussion of Jacob's attitude reflected in his words, "These are the children which God of his grace hath given me." Gen. 33:5. "So he looked at them," Cotton wrote, "as God's wives, and children and servants, and cattel; and this is the very life of

the Covenant of Grace, when as the Lord is wrapped up in all his blessings." p. 10-11.

30. *Ibid*, p. 25.
31. *Ibid*, p. 26.
32. *Ibid*, p. 37-38.
33. *Ibid*, p. 92.
34. *Ibid*, p. 229.

Chapter 4

1. William Warren Sweet: *The Story of Religions in America*, p. 76.
2. Cotton Mather: *Magnalia Christiana Americana*, vol. I. Also, Felt: *Ecclesiastical History of New England*, vol. I, p. 313-319.
3. Armitage: *History of the Baptists*, p. 625.
4. Massachusetts Historical Collection, vol. XXXVIII, p. 291, quoted by Horr: *Religious History of New England*, p. 147.
5. Mather, *op. cit.*, vol. II, p. 498.
6. *Ibid*, p. 508-522.
7. John Cotton: *The Way of the Congregational Churches Cleared.* (1645) These views were opposed by Prof. Samuel Rutherford in his Due Right of Presbyteries. Cf. Walker: *Creeds and Platforms of Congregationalism*, p. 139.
8. *American Church History Series*, vol. II, p. 124.
9. *Ibid*, p. 127.
10. Foster: *Genetic History of New England Theology*, p. 18.
11. Mather, *op. cit.*, vol. I, p. 292.
12. *Ibid*, p. 293.
13. *Ibid*, p. 473.
14. Increase Mather: *First Principles of New England*, p. 2-4.
15. *Ibid*, p. 3-4.
16. *Ibid*, p. 10.
17. Walker, *op. cit.*, p. 160.
18. Walker, *op. cit.*, p. 143.
19. Thomas Hooker: *A Survey of the Summe of Church Discipline*, part III. Hooker perhaps expressed himself more cautiously on the whole question than the others. He was inclined to disagree with the wider administration of baptism at first. (Cf. Walker, *op. cit.*, p. 251). His system, however, would allow for it by including baptized but non-professing adults in the church as "visible saints". It was precisely in this direction that nearly all the leaders moved, including Richard Mather who at first protested vigorously against the new way. Had Hooker lived beyond 1647, it is likely that he would have sided with the majority against John Davenport, Charles Chauncy and others who fought the decisions of the Synod of 1662. Cf. his Survey, pt. III, p. 9-27; Increase Mather: *The First Principles of New England*, p. 7-8; also the Preface to the *Propositions Concerning the Subject of Baptism* (Synod of 1662), p. 307, 310.
20. Concerning the limits of the franchise Walker tells us that before 1643 only 1708 persons out of a population of more than 15,000 had become

citizens of Massachusetts Bay colony. Of these 1708 a number had removed to Connecticut. In Plymouth the situation was even worse, where only 230 out of 3,000 were enfranchised.

21. Walker, *op. cit.*, p. 169.
22. *Ibid*, p. 179-180.
23. Walker, *op. cit.*, p. 185.
24. All quotations from the Platform are taken from Mather's *Magnalia*, vol. II, p. 211-236. Ch. III, 2, p. 213.
25. IV, 6, p. 216.
26. XXI, 7, p. 227.
27. Walker, *op. cit.*, p. 247.
28. Lechford: *Plain Dealing*, p. 21-22. (Trumbull's print, p. 56)
29. Richard Mather: *A Plea for the Churches of Christ in New England*, quoted by Increase Mather, *op. cit.*, p. 10-11.
30. Richard Mather, pastor of Dorchester was one of the first to adopt the new expedient and argue for it. He was also very influential in developing the polity of the churches.
31. Increase Mather, op. cit., p. 10-11.
32. Shepard: *Works*, vol. III, p. 517-518.
33. Quoted by Cotton Mather, *op. cit.*, vol. II, p. 402.
34. *Ibid*, p. 549.
35. Norton: *The Orthodox Evangelist*, p. 142-143.
36. *Ibid*, p. 314.
37. *Ibid*, p. 227.
38. Shepard, *op. cit.*, p. 518.
39. Hooker: *Survey*, part I, p. 48. Quoted in *Preface to the Propositions of 1662.*
40. Hooker: *The Poor Doubting Christian Drawn to Christ*, p. 77.
41. Mather. *op. cit.*, vol. II, p. 311-312.

Chapter 5

1. Quoted by Walker: *Creeds and Platforms of Congregationalism*, p. 164-165, note 5.
2. Extracts from the Result of 1657; Question 6, answer 2. Walker, *op. cit.*, p. 294.
3. *Ibid*, p. 286.
4. *Ibid*, p. 279, note 3.
5. *Ibid*, p. 264.
6. Chauncy: *AntiSynodalia Scripta Americana*, p. 28.
7. Mitchell: *Preface to the Result of the Synod of 1662*, p. vi.
8. *The Answer of the Elders and Other Messengers of the Churches*, etc., p. 1-2.
9. *Ibid*, p. 4.
10. *Ibid*, p. 4.

11. *Ibid*, p. 12.
12. *Ibid*, p. 18.
13. *Ibid*, p. 25.
14. Chauncy was born in England, educated at Cambridge, and entered the ministry of the Established Church. Because of Puritan sympathies he found himself in trouble. Laud served him a license for sports on the Lord's Day. (Cotton Mather: *Magnalia*, vol. I, p. 465). He removed to New England in 1637 and became pastor of the church of Scituate. In 1654 he became president of Harvard in the place of Henry Dunster.
15. Chauncy: *The plain doctrine of the justification of a sinner in the sight of God*, p. 28.
16. *Ibid*, p. 32.
17. Chauncy: *Anti-synodalia Scripta Americana*, p. 28.
18. *Ibid*, p. 24.
19. *Ibid*, p. 32.
20. *Ibid*, p. 34.
21. Quoted by Cotton Mather, *op. cit.*, vol. I, p. 324.
22. Davenport was born at Coventry in England. He entered Oxford at the age of thirteen or fourteen and at nineteen was called "unto publick and constant preaching in the city of London". In 1633 he was called to become the associate of the Rev. Paget of the English church at Amsterdam.
23. Letter of Davenport to the Classis of Amsterdam is recorded by Calder: *Letters of John Davenport*, p. 44.
24. Street was another who was forced to migrate to New England because of the persecutions. He served Taunton from 1638 to 1659, when he removed to New Haven.
25. Increase Mather was one of the first American-born ministers of the Congregational churches. He was born at Dorchester in 1639. After graduating from Harvard. he went to England for some time. In 1661 he settled in Boston as the pastor of the famous Second Church. Walker describes him as essentially conservative and adds that "no man in New England equalled him in influence in his lifetime".
26. Quoted by Increase Mather from Cotton: *Way of the Churches Measured by the Golden Reed of the Sanctuary*, p. 51.
27. Increase Mather: *Preface*.
28. Allin: *Animadversions upon the Antisynodalia Americana* etc., p. 2.
29. *Ibid*, p. 18-19.
30. *Ibid*, p. 25.
31. Increase Mather: *The First Principles of New England*, p. 5. Postscript.
32. By this time the debate concerned itself more with personal sentiment and opinion than with objective principle. In this way Mather also tried to appeal both to the dissenting brethren of the synod and the opponents to the new way in the various congregations. In his Discourse he wrote:

"There are many godly Souls in New England, that the great motive which prevailed with them to come into this wilderness, was that so they might leave their Children under the Government of Christ in his Church. . . . Have we for our poor children's sake in special, left a dear and pleasant Land, and ventured our Lives upon the great waters, and encountered with the difficulties and miseries of a wilderness, and doth it at last come to this, that they have no more Advantages as to any *Church* care about them, than the *Indians* and *Infidels* amongst whom we live? O this is sad!" p. 30-31.

33. Walker, *op. cit.*, p. 270, note 3.
34. Cf. histories of the various churches at Hartford noted in the bibliography.
35. Quoted by Walker, *op. cit.*, A Direction for a Publick Profession in the Church Assembly. after private Examination by the Elders, p. 121.
36. Dexter: *Congregationalism as seen in its Literature*, p. 476 note.

Chapter 6

1. Thomas Prince: *The Christian History, containing Account of Revival, and Propagation of Religion in Great Britain, America*, etc. vol. I, p. 84.
2. Byington: *The Puritan in England and New England*, p. 313.
3. Walker: *Some Aspects of Religious Life in New England*, p. 49.
4. Cotton Mather: *Magnalia Christiana Americana*, vol. II, p. 327.
5. Byington: *The Puritan as Colonist and Reformer*, p. 278.
6. Famous sermons of this period include William Stoughton's of 1668 before the legislature of Massachusetts, that of Thomas Walley in Plymouth in 1669, and several of the Mathers.
7. Increase Mather: *The Order of the Gospel*, p. 12.
8. Cotton Mather, *op. cit.*, vol. II, p. 316-338.
9. *Ibid*, p. 326-327.
10. *The Necessity of Reformation with the Expedients subservient thereunto asserted. (The Result of* 1679) Quest. I, answer I. Walker: *Creeds and Platforms of Congregationalism*, p. 427.
11. Cotton Mather, *op. cit.*, p. 327.
12. Cotton Mather, *op. cit.*, p. 333.
13. Schneider: *The Puritan Mind*, p.
14. Cotton Mather, *op. cit.*,
15. Stoddard was born at Boston in 1643 and educated at Harvard, from which college he was graduated in 1662. After serving there as tutor for some time, he went to preach in Northampton. Three years later he was formally called to the church and remained until his death in 1729.
16. MacGiffert: *Jonathan Edwards*, p. 112-113.
17. Quoted by Walker, *op. cit.*, p. 280-281, note 3.
18. The story of Stoddard's revision of the early draft of one of the conclusions of the Reforming Synod according to his own words is told by Walker, *op. cit.*, p. 280, note 2.
19. Cotton Mather, *op. cit.*,
20. Walker, *op. cit.*, p. 278. Schneider, *op. cit.*, p. 94-95.
21. Walker, *op. cit.*, p. 483-484.

22. Schneider, *op. cit.*, p. 97-98. John Wise justified the existence of the churches on the grounds that they tended to "cultivate humanity and promote the happiness of all and the good of every man in all his rights." The significant element in his contention was not the democratic emphasis of his theory. Rather, as Schneider points out, there is to be found here a beginning of the secularization of the ideals of the early Puritans.

23. Stoddard: *Doctrine of the Instituted Churches*, p. 21.

24. *Ibid.*

25. *Ibid.*

26. Increase Mather, *op. cit.*, p. 8.

27. Quoted by Dexter, *op. cit.*, p. 483.

28. Increase Mather: *A Dissertation, Wherein the Strange Doctrine, ... is examined and confuted*, p. 18-19.

29. Stoddard did not believe that all unregenerate might partake of the Lord's Supper. According to his writings he allowed only such as were church members, i.e., those who "owned the covenant" and led respectable lives, to come to the table.

30. Increase Mather, *op. cit.*, p. 32.

31. *Ibid*, p. 33.

32. Stoddard: *Appeal to the Learned*, p. 25.

33. Churches in the days of Edwards were divided on the issue as follows: In the old Hampshire Association the following held with the new way: Amherst, Brimfield, Deerfield, East Granville, Great Barrington, Greenwich, Hadley, South Hadley, Longmeadow, New Marlborough, Northfield, Northampton, Sheffield, Shutesbury, Southampton, Springfield, West Springfield, Sunderland, Westfield, Wilbraham, Somers in Conn., and Suffield in Conn. The Anti-Stoddardean churches were Belchertown, Enfield in Conn., and Pelham. Hatfield was doubtful on the issue.

34. Schneider, *op. cit.*, p. 97-98.

35. Walker, *op. cit.*, p. 282, note 3.

36. Arminianism as a term used in those days and afterward has been defined by Walker thus: By it "increasing weight was laid upon the cultivation of morality as a means to a Christian life, rather than upon an insistence on the prime necessity of a divinely wrought change in man's nature, a change of which morality should not be the means, but the fruit." *Creeds and Platforms of Congregationalism*, p. 284.

     Francis Albert Christie in an article on "The Beginnings of Arminianism in New England" has attacked the general opinion that Arminianism was wide-spread before the Great Awakening. Says he, "The myth of Arminianism among the Congregational clergy began with Whitefield's rash and unwarranted aspersions. In 1740 he brought with him suspicions of Harvard College based on his knowledge of English seats of learning. 'Tillotson and Clarke are read instead of Shepard and Stoddard . . . therefore I chose to preach on these words: We are not as many who corrupt the word of God'. The censure rankled and was repeated." *Papers of the American Society of Church History*, vol. III, p. 159. Christie claims that this was really the first reference to that doctrine. Further, he contends that what Edwards feared was Episcopalianism and its parish system, which he called Arminianism.

Christie's claims cannot be substantiated. There is too much evidence for the traditional view that in the churches there was Arminianism in the sense in which Walker defined it, resulting from an over-emphasis on the use of means and morality as stepping-stones to spiritual experience. The testimony of Edwards the Younger (*Works*, vol. I, p. 480-481) militates against the theory of Christie. Also the fact that as early as 1734 John White in his *Lamentations* specifically mentions the presence of theories which he calls "Arminian principles". Further, there is the case of the Rev. Robert Breck of Springfield, who in 1736 was charged with being an Arminian. Cf. Byington: *The Puritan in England and New England*, p. 345. Thus Whitefield cannot be said to have levelled a new charge against the clergy of New England. He was merely repeating what others had been saying for some time.

37. Trumbull, B.: *A Complete History of Connecticut* (New Haven, 1818), vol. II, p. 176.
38. Foster, *Genetic History of New England Theology*, p. 43.

Chapter 7

1. This criticism seems to be quite general. Among others Bates gives it, in these words, "He moved back and forth between the two poles of the individual and the universal, and in neglecting the intermediate stages of social activity, he facilitated the withdrawal of religion into the limited field of individual conduct to concern itself above all with the subjective conscience." *The American Faith*, p. 208.
2. Alexander V. G. Allen: *Jonathan Edwards*, p. 2-3.
3. *Ibid*, p. 36.
4. Published in 1754 while he was laboring among the Housatonic Indians at Stockbridge, Mass.
5. For a discussion of the differences between Edwards and certain other Reformed theologians, e.g. B. De Moor, cf. Ridderbos: *Jonathan Edwards*, p. 115-116. Whereas Edwards held that the decision or choice of the will was determined by the motives De Moor maintained that the will followed the intellect indeed, but even in this was essentially self-determinative. De Moor thus guarded the specific activity of the will better than Edwards. Edwards was in no sense a determinist according to Ridderbos. Cf. *Ibid*, p. 118.
6. Ridderbos, *op. cit.*, p. 170 f.
7. Foster: *A Genetic History of New England Theology*, p. 87-88.
8. Dunning: *Congregationalists in America*, p. 238-239.
9. Edwards: "God Glorified in Man's Dependence" from *Selected Sermons of Jonathan Edwards*, edited by H. Norman Gardiner, p. 19.
10. Schneider: *The Puritan Mind*, p. 105.
11. Edwards: *Narrative of the Surprising Work of God* (1735), p. 35-37.

12. *Ibid,* p. 39.

13. *Ibid,* p. 46.

14. *Ibid,* p. 46-47.

15. *Ibid,* p. 69.

16. *Ibid,* p. 105.

17. In this book he speaks of children who were powerfully converted, on p. 46, 47. He especially mentioned the case of Phebe Bartlett, age four, p. 97 f.

18. Edwards: "Sinners in the Hands of an Angry God" from *Selected Sermons,* p. 96.

19. Edwards: *Treatise concerning Religious Affections,* p. 409-410.

20. Platner: *Religious History of New England,* p. 47.

21. One of the greatest causes of difficulty in connection with the revivals was the censorious spirit which it bred. In those days the ministers were often criticized unmercifully and charged with being in an unconverted state. The one who did much to bring this about was Whitefield. In his days in England it was customary to regard many of the ministers as unconverted. There were those who took up the ministry merely as a profession, even from mercenary motives. Thus it was natural for Whitefield to denounce many as unregenerate. Bacon in his Thirteen Historical Discourses claims that in so doing he was committing a grave injustice to the New England ministry, for there "every minister was both by the most solemn profession on his own part, and by the most solemn recognition on the part of the churches, a man renewed by the Spirit of God". p. 211. But especially the itinerant ministers who followed Whitefield denounced the ordained clergy. James Davenport was the most infamous of these in Connecticut at that time. His entire record was unsavory, largely because he was sensational to the extreme. Cf. Chauncy: *Seasonable Thoughts,* p. 99, and Bacon, *op. cit.,* p. 213.

    The question, however, arises whether Bacon was not claiming too much by affirming that New England was not in danger of harboring an unconverted ministry? Stoddard at the beginning of the century had openly championed the view, largely in connection with his personal experience, "If a man do know himself to be unregenerate, yet it is lawful for him to administer baptism and the Lord's Supper. The blessing of this ordinance doth not depend upon the piety of him that doth administer it. . . . Men that are destitute of grace are not prohibited in the word of God to administer the ordinances of God." Sermon, p. 14. On p. 6. of the same he even urged as a ground for his position the fact that Christ commissioned Judas Iscariot to preach the gospel. In view of the sad decline between 1700 and 1740 it is not unreasonable to suppose that all of New England's ministers were by no means converted.

22. Walker: *Some Aspects of Religious Life in New England,* p. 113-114.

23. *American Church History Series,* vol. II, p. 243.

24. *Ibid,* p. 245.

25. Walker: *A History of the Christian Church,* p. 570. In further support of this contention cf. also Schenck: *The Presbyterian Doctrine of Children in the Covenant.* What he says in connection with the Presbyterians of the

revival times and their emphasis holds to a large degree for the Congregationalists in New England also.

"It was unfortunate that the Great Awakening made an emotional experience, involving terror, misery and depression, the only approach to God. A conscious conversion from enmity to friendship with God was looked upon as the only way of entrance into the kingdom. Sometimes it came suddenly, sometimes it was a prolonged and painful process. But it was believed to be a clearly discernible emotional upheaval, necessarily 'distinct to the consciousness of its subject and apparent to those around'. Preceding the experience of God's love and peace, it was believed necessary to have an awful sense of one's lost and terrifying position. Since these were not the experiences of infancy and early childhood, it was taken for granted children must, or in all ordinary circumstances would, grow up unconverted. Infants, it was thought, needed the new birth as well as adults. They could not be saved without it. But the only channel of the new birth which was recognized was a conscious experience of conviction and conversion. Anything else, according to Gilbert Tennent, was a fiction of the brain, a delusion of the Devil. In fact, he ridiculed the idea that one could be a Christian without knowing the time when he was otherwise." p. 71.

27. Edwards: *Works*, vol. IV, p. 286.
28. *Ibid*, p. 292.
29. *Ibid*, p. 294.
30. *Ibid*, p. 311.
31. *Ibid*, p. 320.
32. *Ibid*, p. 321.
33. *Ibid*, p. 321-322.
34. *Ibid*, p. 335.
35. *Ibid*, p. 351.
36. *Ibid*, p. 367.
37. *Ibid*, p. 367.
38. *Ibid*, p. 381.
39. *Ibid*, p. 413.
40. *Ibid*, p. 414.
41. *Ibid*, p. 423.
42. *Ibid*, p. 427.
43. *Ibid*, p. 434.
44. *Ibid*, p. 435-442.
45. *Ibid*. p. 442.
46. *Ibid*, p. 445.
47. *Ibid*, p. 449.
48. Solomon Williams, pastor at Lebanon, Conn., was an ardent defender of the Stoddardean position.
49. Williams: *The True State of the Question concerning the Qualifications Necessary to Communion*, p. 128.
50. Concerning Hemmenway, Moses Mather and others, cf. discussion of their views in the next chapter.
51. Williams, *op. cit.*, p. 132.

52. *Ibid*, p. 3.
53. Edwards: *Works*, vol. IV, p. 490.
54. Edwards, *op. cit.*, p. 529 f.
55. *Ibid*, p. 529.
56. *Ibid*, p. 592-594.
57. MacGiffert: *Jonathan Edwards*, p. 59.
58. Edwards: *A History of the Work of Redemption*, p. 20.
59. *Ibid*, p. 43, 56, 77.
60. *Ibid*, p. 113.
61. *Ibid*, p. 212-213.
62. *Ibid*, p. 261.
63. Ridderbos, *op. cit.*, p. 315-316.
64. Hodge: *Systematic Theology*, vol. III, p. 545.
65. Bronkema: *The Essence of Puritanism*, p. 98-99. Ridderbos, *op. cit.*, p. 315.

Chapter 8

1. Bates: *The American Faith*, p. 214.
2. Foster: *A Genetic History of New England Theology*, p. 85.
3. Edwards: "The Great Christian Doctrine of Original Sin Defended," in *Works*, vol. II, p. 301-583.
4. Edwards' theory of the identity of all men with Adam in his first sin rests upon a novel conception of the relation of all men to him. He fights against what he conceives to be the false conception of this relationship. His idea rests upon the theory of creatio continua, i.e., that all created substance is upheld in its existence by an immediate operation of God, a position closely related to his Idealistic emphasis. This leaves virtually no room for the operation of natural law and thus stands in opposition to the traditional Reformed conception of Divine providence. Ridderbos: *De Theologie van Jonathan Edwards*, p. 165-167.
5. On the difference between Edwards and the school of Saumur, cf. Ridderbos, op. cit., p. 169-170.
6. A Winter Evening's Discussion upon the Doctrine of Original Sin. p. 5.
7. *Ibid*, p. 6.
8. *Ibid*, p. 5-6.
9. *Ibid*. He adds ". . . a sin which, if it comes upon them at all, certainly is without any fault or blame on their part."
10. *Ibid*, p. 8.
11. *Ibid*, p. 8.
12. *Ibid*, p. 25.
13. *Ibid*, p. 25.
14. Peter Clark: *The Scriptural Doctrine of Original Sin, Stated and Defended*, p. 2.
15. *Ibid*, p. 3.
16. *Ibid*, p. 42.

17. *Ibid*, p. 22 and appendix.
18. *Ibid*, p. 7, 8.
19. Hopkins aimed to deal definitely with the great problem of the permission of sin. Although sin was not the occasion of good because of any inherent tendency, it was the necessary means of the greatest good, he claimed. Foster, *op. cit.*, p. 130-131. In these pages Foster also deals with the difference between Bellamy and Hopkins on this score. Cf. also p. 118-124.
20. Hopkins is named as one of the first Edwardean writers to devote considerable attention to the question of personal eschatology. In 1783 he published *An Inquiry concerning the Future State of Those Who Die in Their Sins*. It was strictly impersonal as well as thorough in its reply to the charges against the orthodox levelled by such Universalists as John Murray and Jeremiah White. Cf. Foster, *op. cit.*, p. 193-194.
21. Bellamy: *Works*, vol. III, p. 125.
22. Mather: *The Visible Church in Covenant with God*, p. 9.
23. *Ibid*, p. 36-37.
24. Quoted by Bellamy: *Works*, vol. III, p. 127.
25. Increase Mather: *Discourses concerning the subject of Baptism*, p. 52. Bellamy quotes this, *op. cit.*, p. 129.
26. Bellamy: *Works*, vol. I, p. 100.
27. *Ibid*, vol. III, p. 203.
28. *Ibid*, p. 211-212.
29. *Ibid*, p. 205.
30. Bellamy taught that in the sacraments man sealed his covenant with God. The idea of God sealing the covenant with man was largely obscured by the other emphasis. *Ibid*, p. 148.
31. *Ibid*, p. 205.
32. Bellamy, *op. cit.*, vol. III, p. 203.
33. This seems to be evident from the fact that Bellamy could write as he did about the opinion of the majority of the ministers in his day. Cf. note 34. Furthermore, Walker informs us in his Creeds and Platforms of Congregationalism that at the beginning of the nineteenth century, when New Divinity principles triumphed in nearly all Trinitarian Congregational churches, it was the general understanding among the clergy in central Connecticut not to introduce the system in families where it was not already in practice. p. 287, note 3.
34. Increase Mather, *op. cit.*, p. 54. Also quoted by Bellamy, *Works*, vol. III. p. 397.
35. *Ibid*, p. 397.
36. *Ibid*, p. 398.
37. *Ibid*, p. 401.
38. *Ibid*, p. 402.
39. *Ibid*, p. 406.
40. *Ibid*, p. 406.
41. *Ibid*, p. 407.
42. *Ibid*, p. 411.
43. *Ibid*, p. 430.
44. *Ibid*, p. 434.

45. *Ibid*, p. 436.
46. Bellamy makes the statement that only those who can pray the Lord's Prayer in sincerity are "entitled to pardon and eternal life." *Ibid*, p. 440.
47. *Ibid*, p. 338.
48. Jacob Green was pastor of a church at Hanover, N. J., and stood closely related to the men of the New Divinity in sympathies.
49. Green: *An Inquiry into the Constitution and Discipline of the Jewish Church*, p. 7.
50. *Ibid*, p. 16.
51. The Question is posited in the title of the book.
52. *Ibid*, p. 1.
53. *Ibid*, p. 3.
54. *Ibid*, p. 3.
55. Letter of Chandler Robbins to Cotton. dated at Plymouth, April 3, 1772. In his work *The General Practice* etc., p. 34.
56. Chandler Robbins: *A Reply to Some Essays lately published by John Cotton Esq.*, p. 12.
57. *Ibid*, p. 22.
58. *Ibid*, p. 48.
59. For the difference between the Lutherans and Reformed on this point see Berkhof: *Reformed Dogmatics*, p. 473-476.
60. Jedidiah Mills: *Inquiry concerning the State of the Unregenerate under the Gospel*. New Haven, 124 p.
61. Hopkins especially took up this question. Foster, *op. cit.*, p. 143.
62. Jonathan Mayhew: *Striving to Enter in at the Strait Gate. . . . and the Connection of Salvation Therewith*, (1761)
63. *Ibid*, p. 45.
64. Foster even calls it a "substantial Pelagianism, ascribing the gift of converting grace to the divine response to the efforts of the sinner." *Op. cit.*, p. 132.
65. Haroutunian: *Piety versus Moralism*, p. 58.
66. Hopkins: *Works*, vol. I, p. 233 f.
67. *Ibid*, p. 224.
68. *Ibid*, p. 235 f.
69. *Ibid*, p. 371. Also Foster, op. cit., p. 182.
70. It seems from Hopkins' writings, that he could not conceive of the possibility that some time might possibly elapse between regeneration and conversion. These would appear to be contemporaneous in every sense according to him. Cf. Foster, op. cit., p. 183-184.
71. Hopkins, *op. cit.*, p. 288-289.
72. Foster, *op. cit.*, p. 140.
73. Hemmenway: *Vindication of the power, obligation, and encouragement of the unregenerate to attend the means of grace*, p. 104.
74. Foster, *op. cit.*, p. 147.
75. Hopkins: *Works*, vol. III, p. 309 f.
76. Boardman, *op. cit.*, p. 162.
77. On the Taste scheme cf. Foster's discussion of Asa Burton and Nathaniel Taylor, *op. cit.*, p. 243-250.

78. Whittelsey's *Diary*, vol. I, p. 40 f. Quoted by Platner: *Religious History of New England*, p. 49.
79. Both the Presbyterians and the Dutch Reformed at that time quite generally opposed the Hopkinsian position. That the New Divinity was viewed with suspicion among the Presbyterians is evident from Schenck: *The Presbyterian Doctrine of Children in the Covenant*, p. 107-111. The Dutch Reformed were still less inclined to the new positions, if we may believe Ten Eyck's discussion in *Landmarks of the Reformed Fathers*, p. 215-216. In fact, he claims that two outstanding Reformed preachers in the early decades of the nineteenth century, Dr. Ferris and Milledoler, left the Presbyterian communion for that of the Reformed because they feared that Hopkinsianism was making serious inroads in their church. The position of the leaders in these two denominations is illuminating, when we remember that they repudiated the positions of the New Divinity on the grounds that they undermine the Calvinistic faith.
80. William W. Fenn: *Unitarianism, in Religious History of New England*, p. 129.
81. Hopkins: *Works*, vol. II, p. 291.
82. *Ibid*, p. 319.
83. *Ibid*, p. 334-335.
84. Cyprian Strong: *An Inquiry, wherein, the End and Design of Baptism*, etc., p. 9, 16.
85. *Ibid*, p. 61.
86. *Ibid*, p. 63.
87. *Ibid*, p. 64.
88. *Ibid*, p. 74.
89. *Ibid*, p. 80-81. However, he repudiated the idea that "if the parents dedicate their children to God in truth and sincerity, ... God will accept and reward them as faithful and obedient servants." p. 80.
90. *Ibid*, p. 87.
91. *Ibid*, p. 89.
92. *Ibid*, p. 91.
93. *Ibid*, p. 93.
94. The present struggle can only be discussed properly, when bearing in mind that several of the questions had been busily debated by Edwards and Williams and those of the early New Divinity men and old school Calvinists who succeeded them.
95. Emmons: *A Dissertation on the Scripture Qualifications for Admission and Access to the Christian Sacraments*, p. 14.
96. *Ibid*, p. 14.
97. *Ibid*, p. 21.
98. *Ibid*, p. 77.
99. *Ibid*, p. 81-132.
100. *Ibid*, p. 118.
101. *Ibid*, p. 119.
102. *Ibid*, p. 119.
103. *Ibid*, p. 119.
104. *Ibid*, p. 120.

Chapter 9

1. The Universalist controversy shows a tendency present in N. E. Congregationalism of this period to obscure the antithesis between the "saved" and the "unsaved". As has been shown in an earlier chapter, it touched the fringes of the covenant controversy in so far as this latter concerned itself with the salvation of infants. At that time the difference between those infants who had received the promise of God in baptism and those who have not was forgotten. One of the reasons why the Universalists could make their appeal to the people of the churches was because they were no longer convinced that God's covenant people were separate and distinct from the world.

2. Unitarianism appealed largely to those who were out of sympathy with the revivalistic movement. Its center of influence was Boston, far removed from the Connecticut valley, where the New Divinity men as champions of the revivals were influential. The emphasis of the Unitarians was on character education instead of a radical change of the will as the means of becoming a Christian. For this very reason Bushnell some time later found himself quite in sympathy with this aspect of their teaching, although he rejected many of their theological positions.

3. William Warren Sweet: *The Story of Religions in America,* p. 323.

4. *Ibid,* p. 323-324.

5. For statistics on the rapid growth of the Baptists in New England see Horr's article on Baptists in *Religious History of New England,* p. 164 f. Also *American Church History Series,* vol. II, p. 271.

6. Some very interesting sidelights are shed on the life of the churches during this period by the records of baptisms in the Second Church of Hartford. Often baptism seemed to be delayed in the case of children, until they were on the verge of death, Some of the cases recorded during the pastorate of Dr. Flint include the following:
   1791, Aug. 13—Sarah, Daughter of Wm. Andrus Jr., baptized at home, on account of sickness. Parents not in covenant. Died Aug. 14.
   1792, March 10—Phinehas, son of Phinehas Shepard. Died the same day.
   Febr. 20—Wealthy, Daughter of Jas. Taylor. Also baptized at home. Parents not in covenant. Died Sept. 15, 1793.
   April 20—Chauncey, son of Doras (Dorris) Clark. Died April 21. Age 4½ yrs.
   June 23—Lucy, daughter of Joseph Woodbridge. Died the same day. 1 day old.
   July 22—Nabby, daughter of Thomas Clapp. Died July 29. 12 yrs. old.
   Edw. Pond Parker: *History of the Second Church of Christ in Hartford.* 1670-1892, p. 377-378.

   Such records continued throughout the early years of his pastorate. The parents were often not in covenant with the church. It would seem that infant baptism did not possess great value except in the case of imminent death. Very likely under the influence of the Baptists and the revivals many delayed having baptism administered unto their children. Thus they would not receive the sacrament until they came to full membership after conversion.

7. Walker: *Creeds and Platforms of Congregationalism*, p. 287.
8. Leonard Woods: *Infant Baptism*, p. 30. Quoted by Bushnell: *Arguments for Discourse on Christian Nurture*, p. 78.
9. *Ibid*, p. 77.
10. Foster: *A Genetic History of New England Theology*, p. 357, 309.
11. Timothy Dwight, president of Yale for some years, handed down his theology in a series of sermons preached before the college audience each Sunday during the academic year. They were written in 1809 and finally published in 1818.
12. Dwight: *Theology Explained and Defended in a Series of Sermons*, vol. V, p. 140-141.
13. *Ibid*, p. 131.
14. *Ibid*, p. 145.
15. Austin was one of the prominent New Divinity preachers in his day. For twenty five years he served the church at Worcester, Mass. As a theologian he combatted especially the views of the Baptists and Unitarians.
16. Austin: *A View of the Economy of the Church of God*, p. i.
17. *Ibid*, p. 22.
18. *Ibid*, p. 39.
19. *Ibid*, p. 43.
20. *Ibid*, p. 64 f.
21. *Ibid*, p. 68.
22. *Ibid*, p. 72-73.
23. *Ibid*, p. 87.
24. *Ibid*, p. 87.
25. *Ibid*, p. 91.
26. *Ibid*, p. 91.
27. *Ibid*, p. 92.
28. *Ibid*, p. 268-269.
29. *Ibid*, p. 271.
30. *Ibid*, p. 272.
31. *Ibid*, p. 317.
32. *Ibid*, p. 317.
33. *Ibid*, p. 317.
34. *Ibid*, p. 319.
35. William W. Sweet, *op. cit.*, p. 325, 326.
36. Bushnell was born on April 14, 1802, at Litchfield, Conn. For years he served the North Church in Hartford, until ill health forced him to resign in 1859. The remaining years of his life, until his death in 1876, were spent in preaching occasionally and writing voluminously on theological subjects.
37. John W. Buckram: *Progressive Religious Thought in America*, p. 6. Some of the leading contributions of Bushnell which he mentions include:
   1—He is said to have delivered the New England churches from the bondage of inflexibility in connection with Christian experience by his work on Christian Nurture.

2—He delivered them from extreme rationalism in their construction of theology by insisting upon "a perceptive Power in Spiritual Life". *God in Christ*, p. 93. In such works as *Dissertation on Language, Christ in Theology, Dogma and Spirit, The Gospel a Gift to the Imagination*, he emphasized intuition and inner unity and experience at the expense of dogma in religion.

3—He delivered them from a refusal to criticize themselves. This he did by asking the question: Is it possible that theology . . . can ever become a science or attain to a fixed and properly authoritative statement? *Christ in Theology*, p. 86.

4—He recovered for the consciousness of the churches Christ as the central light and power of Christianity. New England theology had let the real Christ fade. His interpretation of Christ may be found in *Nature and the Supernatural*, chapter X. Buckram, *op. cit.*, p. 19-22.

38. Special attention should be devoted to Bushnell's new emphasis on the distinction between nature and the supernatural. Cf. his work on this subject. Buckram claims that this is the true sequel to Christian Nurture, *op. cit.*, p. 4. It is evident that Bushnell took sharp issue with the prevailing contention of New England theology which sharply divided life into two separate realms, the natural and the supernatural. Because this dualism was so strongly presented, religion was separated from daily life. Bushnell contended that "man himself belongs primarily and chiefly to the supernatural realm". *Nature and the Supernatural*, p. 43. He thus repudiated the old distinction entirely. His conception harmonizes much more with the Greek distinction between matter and spirit, dominant in Idealistic and Romantic types of philosophy, than with the Christian theory. On his basis the distinction between the "saved" and the "unsaved" had absolutely no validity.

39. Mac Giffert: *The Rise of Modern Religious Ideas*, p. 277, note.

40. Bushnell: *Discourses on Christian Nurture*, p. 25-26 (1st. edit.)

41. Title of the fourth chapter in the revised edition of 1876. Also the title of a sermon contained in the first edition (1846 , p. 183-209.

42. *Argument for the Discourse on Christian Nurture*, p. 110.

43. *Growth, not Conquest, the True Method of Christian Progress* (1st. edition, p. 147-181)

44. *Discourse on Christian Nurture*, p. 14.

45. *Ibid*, p. 14.

46. *Ibid*, p. 14.

47. *Ibid*, p. 14.

48. *Growth, not Conquest*, etc., p. 150.

49. *Ibid*, p. 166.

50. *Argument for Discourse*, etc., p. 99-100.

51. *Ibid*, p. 89.

52. *Discourse on Christian Nurture*, p. 15.

53. *Ibid*, p. 16.

54. *Ibid*, p. 40 f.

55. *The Organic Unity of the Family*, sermon in 1st. edition, p. 186.

56. *Ibid*, p. 205.
57. *Ibid*, p. 205.
58. Charles Hodge: "Discourse on Christian Nurture," in *The Biblical Repertory* and *Princeton Review* (Oct. 1847, vol. XIX, no. 4, p. 502 f.), p. 504.
59. *Ibid*, p. 509.
60. *Ibid*, p. 522.
61. *Ibid*, p. 524.
62. *Ibid*, p. 526.
63. *Discourse on Christian Nurture*, p. 14.
64. B. Tyler: *Letters to the Rev. Horace Bushnell, D.D.*, p. 62, 63.
65. *Ibid*, p. 63.
66. *Ibid*, p. 63.
67. *Ibid*, p. 63.
68. This is apparent from Bushnell's own statement, "So the Christian parent has, in his character, a germ which has power, presumptively, to produce its like in his children, though by reason of some bad fault in itself, or possibly some outward hindrance in the Church, or some providence of death, it may fail to do so." *Christian Nurture*, edition 1876, p. 40. Here we find the final obliteration of the Reformed conception of the covenant. There is no emphasis on the supernatural operation of the Holy Spirit in connection with the training of children. It has been made purely a matter of education. The basis of hope for the child's growth as a Christian is no longer found in the sure promises of God but altogether in the character of the parents.

PART THREE

Chapter 10

1. Cotton: *The Grounds and Ends of the Baptisme of the Children of the Faithful*, p. 47.
2. This expression is taken over from Cotton Mather: *Magnalia Christiana Americana*.
3. On the relation between the Covenant of Grace and the Covenant of Redemption among the Reformed see Vos: *De Verbondsleer in de Gereformeerde Theologie*, p. 33-34. The relation between the Covenant of Grace and the theory of election is discussed on p. 41-47.
4. The loss of the sense of sin in the churches and communities is discussed by Haroutunian in his *Piety versus Moralism*. He claims that the Half-way Covenant was the cause of much legalism and externalism which characterized the churches before the Great Awakening.
5. De Jong: *De Leer der Verzoening in de Amerikaansche Theologie*. The rise of the governmental and moral theories of the atonement through Christ was occasioned by the adoption of the position that benevolentia Dei was

the chief cause of all events in the universe. By obscuring the righteousness and justice of God the leaders necessarily overthrew the theory of vicarious sacrifice. p. 273 f. Edwards never taught the governmental theory, but some of the positions adopted by him prepared the way for its triumph. p. 24-25.

6. Chitwood: *History of Colonial America*, p. 160.
7. *Ibid*, p. 193.
8. *Ibid*, p. 193.

Chapter 11

1. The question of the two aspects of the Covenant of Grace has occasioned much discussion in the Reformed churches. Various terms have been employed to designate these two. Berkhof follows Vos and chooses for this terminology. Cf. his discussion in *Reformed Dogmatics*, p. 284-289. Concerning the unregenerate Dr. Bavinck says they are "in foedere" but not "de foedere". Berkholf explains this further by saying of them:
   "a. They are in the covenant as far as their responsibility is concerned...
    b. They are in the covenant in the sense that they may lay claim to the promises which God gave when He established His covenant with believers and their seed, ...
    c. They are in the covenant in the sense that they are subject to the ministrations of the covenant ...
    d. They are in the covenant also as far as the common blessings are concerned ..." p. 289.
   Kuyper discusses the same question in *Dictaten Dogmatiek*, vol. III, "Locus de Foedere", p. 153-154. He maintains that early in the history of the Reformed churches the theologians did not make this distinction. Only with the rise of the State Church did it become necessary to make some such distinction.

2. Karl Barth, quite generally considered a Neo-Calvinist, repudiates this position definitely. Brunner is on this score much more in harmony with the traditional views of Calvinism. Cf. his *The Divine Imperative*, notes, p. 615-616, 618.

Chapter 12

1. On the "marks" of the true church see Berkhof: *Reformed Dogmatics*, p. 576-578.

2. The "Commission" Creed of 1883 is given by Walker: *Creeds and Platforms of Congregationalism*, p. 580-582.

BIBLIOGRAPHY

General Reference Works

Dexter, Henry Martyn: *Congregationalism as Seen in Its Literature.* New York: Harper and Bros., 1880.

Hastings, Selbie, et al.: *Encyclopedia of Religion and Ethics.* New York: C. Scribner's Sons, 1927.

Jackson, Samuel Macauley, et al.: *The New Schaff-Herzog Encyclopedia of Religious Knowledge.* New York: Funk and Wagnalls Co., 1908.

Johnson, Allen: *Dictionary of American Biography.* New York: Charles Scribner's Sons, 1928.

Müller, E. F. Karl: *Die Bekenntnisschriften der reformierten Kirche.* Leipzig: A. Deichert, 1903.

Roberts, Donaldson, et al.: *The Ante-Nicene Fathers.* Buffalo: The Christian Literature Publishing Co., 1887.

Schaff, Potter, et al.: *The American Church History Series.* New York: 1893-1897.

Schaff, Philip: *A Select Library of the Nicene and Post-Nicene Fathers of the Christian Church.* New York: Charles Scribner's Sons, 1908.

Schaff, Philip: *The Creeds of Christendom.* New York: Harper and Brothers, 1919.

Walker, Williston: *The Creeds and Platforms of Congregationalism.* New York: Charles Scribner's Sons, 1893.

Primary Sources

Allin, John: *Animadversions on the Antisynodalia Americana.* Cambridge: S.G. and M.J. for Hezekiah Usher, 1664.

Anonymous (attributed to Richard Mather by Holmes): *A Disputation concerning Church-Members and their Children in Answer to XXI Questions: Wherein the State of such Children when Adult, together with their Duty towards the Church, and the Churches Duty towards them is discussed.* London: J. Hayes for Samuel Thomson, 1659.

Austin, Samuel: *A View of the Economy of the Church of God . . .* as it existed primitively under the Abrahamic Dispensation and the Sinai Law; and as it is perpetuated under the more luminous Dispensation of the Gospel; particularly in regard to the Covenants. Worcester: Thomas and Sturtevant, 1807.

Bellamy, Joseph: *The Works of Joseph Bellamy* (3 vol.). New York: S. Dodge, 1811-1812.

Bellamy, Joseph: *The Works of J. Bellamy D.D. With a Memoir of his life and character.* Boston: Doctrinal Tract and Book Society, 1853.

Bellamy, Joseph: *That there is but one covenant, whereof baptism and the Lord's supper are seals, viz. the covenant of grace;* (proved from the word of God) and, the doctrine of the external, graceless covenant, lately advanced, by the Rev. Moses Mather: in a pamphlet, entituled, *The visible church in covenant with God, &c., shewn to be unscriptural doctrine.* New Haven: Printed by T. and S. Green, 1769.

Bushnell, Horace: *Views of Christian Nurture and of Subjects Adjacent Thereto.* Hartford: Edwin Hunt, 1847.

Bushnell, Horace: *Nature and the Supernatural.* New York: Charles Scribner, 1858.

Bushnell, Horace: *Christian Nurture.* New York: Charles Scribner's Sons, 1888.

Bushnell, Horace: *God in Christ.* New York: Scribner, Armstrong and Co., 1877.

Chauncy, Charles: *The plain doctrine of the justication of a sinner in the sight of God, justified by the God of truth in His holy word, and the cloud of witnesses in all ages.* London: Printed by R.I. for A. Byfield, 1659.

Chauncy, Charles: *Antisynodalia scripta Americana.* Propositions concerning the subject of baptism and consociation of churches, collected and confirmed out of the word of God, by a synod of elders and messengers of the churches in the Massachusetts-colony in New-England. Assembled at Boston, according to the appointment of the honoured Court, in the year, 1662. . . . Whereto is annext the answer of the dissenting brethren and messengers of the churches of New-England, &c. London, 1662.

Chauncy, Charles: *Seasonable Thoughts on the state of religion in New England,* a treatise in five parts. Boston: Printed by Rogers and Foule for S. Eliot, 1743.

Chauncy, Charles: *Conversation, concerning original sin, wrote by the Rev. Mr. Peter Clark.* Boston: Green and Russell, 1758.

Calvin, John: *Joannis Calvini opera quae supersunt omnia. Ediderunt G. Baum, E. Cunitz, v. Reuss. Brunsvigae: C. A. Schwetschke et filium,* 1863-1900. *Corpus Reformatorum.*

Calvin, John: *Institutes of the Christian Religion* (2 vol.). Philadelphia: Presbyterian Board of Publication.

Clark, Peter: *The Scripture-Doctrine of Original Sin,* Stated and Defended, In a Summer Morning's Conversation, between a minister and a neighbour. Boston: S. Kneeland, 1758.

Cotton, John: *The Keyes of the Kingdom of Heaven and Power Thereof, According to the Word of God.* (first published by Tho. Goodwin and Philip Nye in London, 1644) Boston: Tappan and Dennet, 1843.

Cotton, John: *The Covenant of God's Free Grace,* Most sweetly unfolded and comfortably applied to a disquieted soul, from that text of 2 Sam. 23, vs. 5. London: Matthew Simons, 1645.

Cotton, John: *The Grounds and Ends of Baptisme of the Children of the*

Faithfull, Opened in a familiar discourse by way of a dialogue or brotherly conference. London: Andrew Crooke, 1647.

Cotton, John: *The Covenant of Grace*: discovering a great work of a sinner's reconciliation to God. London: Printed by Matthew Simons for John Allen, 1655.

Cotton, John: *Spiritual Milk for Boston Babes In Either England,* Drawn out of the Breasts of both Testaments for their souls nourishment. But may be of like use to any Children. Boston: Printed by Samuel Green for Hezekiah Usher, 1656.

Cotton, John: *The New Covenant,* or a Treatise unfolding the order and manner of giving and receiving the Covenant of Grace. As also: shewing the difference between the law and the Gospel. Being the substance of sundry sermons preached by Mr. Cotton at Boston in New-England. London: Printed by Matthew Simons for Francis Eglesfield and John Allen, 1654.

Cotton, John (of Plymouth): *The General Practice of the Churches of New-England* relating to Baptism vindicated containing an answer to the Rev. Chandler Robbins' reply relative to the question whether the practice of persons owning or renewing the covenant, and having baptism for their children, without coming immediately into full communion, be warrantable? Boston: Ezekiel Russell, 1772.

Davenport, John: *Another Essay for the Investigation of the Truth,* In Answer to Two Questions. Concerning I The Subject of Baptism, II The Consociation of Churches. Cambridge: Printed by Samuel Green and Marmaduke Johnson, 1663.

Davenport, John: *Letters* (edited by Elizabeth M. Calder). New Haven: Yale University Press, 1937.

Davenport, John: *A Profession of Faith and the New Haven Catechism* (edited by the Rev. Leonard Bacon). New Haven: B. L. Hamlin, 1853.

Doddridge, Philip: *Sermons on the Religious Education of Children.* London: C. Hitch and L. Dawes, 1760.

Dwight, Timothy: *Sermons* (2 vol.) New Haven: H. Howe and Dunnie & Peck, 1822.

Dwight, Timothy: *An Address to the Emigrants from Connecticut, and from New England Generally, in the New Settlements in the United States.* Hartford: Peter B. Gleason & Co., 1817.

Edwards, Jonathan: *The Works of President Edwards* (8 vol.) Worcester: I Thomas, I Sturtevant (printer), 1808-1809.

Edwards, Jonathan: *A Treatise Concerning Religious Affections,* in three parts. Boston: S. Kneeland and T. Green, 1746.

Edwards, Jonathan: *A History of the Work of Redemption.* Containing the outlines of a body of divinity, in a method entirely new. Worcester: Isaiah Thomas and Leonard Worcester, for Isaiah Thomas, 1792.

Emmons, Nathaniel: *Works of Nathaniel Emmons.* Boston: Congregational Board of Publication, 1860.

Emmons, Nathaniel: *A Dissertation on the Scriptural Qualifications for Admission and Access to the Christian Sacraments*, comprising some strictures on Dr. Hemmenway's Discourse concerning the Church. Worcester: Leonard Worcester, 1793.

Emmons, Nathaniel: *A Discourse on the Proper Mode and Proper Subjects of Christian Baptism*. Boston, 182—.

Green, Jacob: *An Inquiry into the Constitution and Discipline of the Jewish Church* — in order to cast some light on the controversy concerning qualifications for the sacraments of the New Testament. New York: Hugh Gaine, 1768.

Hemmenway, Moses: *Seven Sermons*, on the obligation and encouragement of the unregenerate to labour for the meat which endureth to everlasting life. Boston: Kneeland and Adams, 1767.

Hemmenway, Moses: *A Treatise on the Nature and Subjects of Christian Baptism*, extracted from a late author. Philadelphia: Joseph Cruikshank, 1790.

Hemmenway, Moses: *A Discourse Concerning the Church*, in which the several acceptations of the word are explained and distinguished; the gospel covenant delineated. . . Boston: I Thomas and E. T. Andrews, 1792.

Hemmenway, Moses: *Remarks on the Rev. Mr. Emmons' Dissertation* on the scriptural qualifications for admission and access to the Christian sacraments; and on his strictures on a Discourse concerning the church. Boston: Printed at the Apollo Press by Belknap and Hall, 1794.

Hooker, Thomas: *The Poor Doubting Christian Drawn to Christ* (1645). Boston: Printed by Green, Bushnell, and Allen, for D. Henchman, 1743.

Hopkins, Samuel: *The Works of Samuel Hopkins D.D.* With a memoir of his life and character. (3 vol.) Boston: Doctrinal Tract and Book Society, 1854.

Hopkins, Samuel: *The System of Doctrines Contained in Divine Revelation Explained* (2 vol.) Boston, 1811.

Hopkins, Samuel: *The True State and Character of the Unregenerate*, stripped of all misrepresentation and disguise: a reply to Mr. Mills' Inquiry concerning the state of the unregenerate under the gospel: containing remarks of Mr. Hopkins' section on the use of means. New Haven: Thomas and Samuel Green, 1769.

Hopkins, Samuel: *An Inquiry into the Nature of True Holiness.* With an appendix containing an answer to the Rev. William Hart's Remarks on President Edwards' dissertation on the nature of true virtue: and brief remarks on some things the Rev. Mr. Mather has lately published. Also an answer to the Rev. Mr. Hemmenway's Vindication, &c. Newport: Solomon Southwick, 1773.

Mather Cotton: *Magnalia Christiana Americana* (2 vol.) Harford: Silas Andrus and Son, 1885.

Mather, Increase: *An Apologetical Preface to Davenport's Another Essay for the Investigation of the Truth.* Cambridge: Printed by Samuel Green and Marmaduke Johnson, 1663.

Mather, Increase: *The First Principles of New England* concerning the Subject of Baptisme and Communion of Churches, Cambridge: Samuel Green, 1675.

Mather, Increase: *The Order of the Gospel*, professed and practized by the Churches of Christ in New-England, justified by the Scripture and by the writings of many learned men, both ancient and modern divines. Boston: A. Baldwin, 1700.

Mather, Increase: *Dissertation* wherein the Strange Doctrine . . . to encourage Unsanctified Persons (while such) to approach the Holy Table of the Lord is Examined and Confuted. Boston: B. Green for Benjamin Eliot, 1708.

Mather, Moses: *The Visible Church in Covenant with God,* or an Inquiry into the Constitution of the Visible Church. New York, 1759.

Mather, Richard: *Church Government and Church Covenant Discussed,* in an answer of the elders of the several churches in New-England to two and thirty questions, sent over to them by divers ministers in England, to declare their judgment therein. London: Printed by R.O. and G.D. for B. Allen, 1643.

Mather, Richard: *An Apologie of the Churches in New England for Church Covenant.* London: Printed by T.P. and M.S. for B. Allen, 1643.

Mather, Richard: *A Defence of the Answer and Arguments of the Synod Met at Boston in the Year* 1662, a reply vs. John Davenport's treatise Another Essay for the Investigation of the Truth. Cambridge: S. Green and M. Johnson, 1664.

Mayhew, Experience: *Grace Defended,* in a modest plea for an important truth; namely, that the offer of salvation made to sinners in the gospel comprises in it the offer of grace, given in regeneration. Boston: Printed by B. Green and Co., for D. Henchman, 1744.

Norton, John: *A Discussion of That Great Point in Divinity,* the Sufferings of Christ. London: Printed by A.M. for George Calvart and Joseph Nevill, 1653.

Norton, John: *The Orthodox Evangelist,* Or a Treatise Wherein Many Great Evangelical Truths . . . Are Brieflly Discussed. London: John Macock for Henry Cripps and Lodowick Lloyd, 1654.

Norton, John: *A Brief Catechisme Containing the Doctrine of Godlines,* or of Living unto God. Cambridge: Printed by S.G. and M. J., 1660.

Ogden, David L.:*Discourses on Baptism and Close Communion.* New Haven: Hezekiah Howe and Co., 1834.

Robbins, Chandler: *A Reply to Some Essays* lately published by John Cotton, Esq.; (of Plymouth) relating to Baptism. Boston: Thos. and John Fleet, 1773.

Solomon Stoddard: *The Doctrine of the Instituted Churches,* explained and proved from the Word of God. London: Printed for R. Smith, 1700.

Thomas Shepard: *Works* (3 vol.), Boston: Doctrinal Tract and Book Society, 1853.

Published Church Records and Histories

Historical Catalogue of the First Church in Hartford. 1633-1885. Prepared
by Charles T. Welles, G. L. Walker, and Charles T. Wells. Hartford: Case,
Lockwood and Brainard Co., 1885.

Commemorative Exercises of the First Church of Christ in Hartford at its Two
Hundred and Fiftieth Anniversary, October 11 and 12, 1883. Hartford:
Case, Lockwood and Brainard Co., 1883.

Records of the First Church at Dorchester in New England 1636-1734. Boston:
Geo. H. Ellis, 1891.

History of the Second Church of Christ in Hartford. 1670-1892. By Edwin
Pond Parker. Hartford: Belknap and Warfield, 1892.

History of Hadley, including the Early History of Hatfield, South Hadley,
Amherst and Cranby, Massachusetts. By Sylvester Judd. Springfield:
H. R. Huntting and Co., 1905.

The History of the North Church in New Haven, from its Formation in May,
1742, during the Great Awakening, to the Completion of the Century in
May, 1842. In three sermons. By Samuel W. S. Dutton. New Haven:
A. H. Maltby, 1842.

Secondary Sources

Adams, Charles Francis: *Three Episodes of Massachusetts History* (2 vol.)
Boston-New York: Houghton, Mifflin and Co., 1896.

Armitage, Thomas: *History of the Baptists.* New York: Bryan, Taylor and Co.,
1887.

Bacon, Leonard Woolsey: *The Congregationalists.* New York: Baker and
Taylor Co., 1904.

Bacon, Leonard Woolsey: *History of American Christianity.* New York, 1916.

Bacon, Leonard: *Thirteen Historical Discourses* on the Completion of Two
Hundred Years, from the Beginning of the First Church in New Haven,
with an appendix. New Haven: Durrie and Peck, 1839.

Bates, Ernest Sutherland: *The American Faith*; its religious, political and
economic foundations. New York: W. W. Norton and Co., 1940.

Berkhof, Louis: *Reformed Dogmatics.* Grand Rapids: Wm. B. Eerdmans
Publishing Co., 1941.

Berkhof, Louis: *Reformed Dogmatics,* Introductory Volume. Grand Rapids:
Wm. B. Eerdmans Publishing Co., 1932.

Berkhof, Louis: *Vicarious Atonement through Christ.* Grand Rapids: Wm. B.
Eerdmans Publishing Co., 1936.

Bronkema, Ralph: *The Essence of Puritanism.* Goes (Neth.): Oosterbaan and
Le Cointre, 1929.

Buckham, John Wright: *Progressive Religious Thought in America.* Boston:
Houghton, Mifflin and Co., 1919.

Burggraaf, Winfield: *The Rise and Development of Liberal Theology in
America.* Goes (Neth.): Oosterbaan and Le Cointre, 1928.

Burrage, Champlin: *The Church Covenant Idea.* Philadelphia: American Baptist Publication Society, 1904.

Burrage, Henry Sweeter: *A History of the Baptists in New England.* Philadelphia: American Baptist Publication Society, 1894.

Burrage, Henry Sweeter: *The Anabaptists of the Sixteenth Century.* Papers of the American Society of Church History, vol. III, p. 145-164. New York and London: G. P. Putnam's Sons, 1891.

Byington, Ezra Hoyt: *The Puritan in England and New England.* Boston: Little, Brown and Co., 1900.

Calder, Elizabeth MacBeath: *Letters of John Davenport.* New Haven: Yale University Press, 1937.

Campbell, Douglas: *The Puritans in Holland, England, and America.* (2 vol.) New York, 1892.

Chitwood, Oliver Perry: *A History of Colonial America.* New York: Harper and Bros., 1931.

Christie, Francis Albert: *The Beginnings of Arminianism in New England.* Papers of the American Society of Church History. Second Series. vol. III, p. 153-169. New York and London: G. P. Putnam's Sons, 1910.

Correll, Ernst H.: *Das schweizersche Täufermennonitentum.* Tübingen: J. C. B. Mohr, 1925.

Dosker, Henry Elias: *The Dutch Anabaptists.* Philadelphia: The Judson Press, 1921.

De Jong, Ymen P.: *De Leer der Verzoening in de Amerikaansche Theologie.* Grand Rapids: Eerdmans-Sevensma Co., 1913.

Dunning, Albert Elijah: *Congregationalists in America.* New York: J. A. Hill and Co., 1894.

Ellis, George E.: *The Puritan Age and Rule in the Colony of the Massachusetts Bay,* 1629-1685. Boston: Houghton, Mifflin and Co., 1891.

Felt, Joseph Barlow: *Ecclesiastical History of New England.* (2 vol.) Boston: Congregational Library Association, 1855-1862.

Fisher, George P.: *Discussions in History and Theology.* New York, 1880.

Fleming, Sanford: *Children and Puritanism:* Children in the Life and Thought of the New England Churches 1620-1847. New Haven: Yale University Press, 1933.

Ford, Paul Leicester: *The New England Primer;* a reprint of the earliest known editions, with many facsimiles and reproductions, and a historical introduction. New York: Dodd, Mead and Co., 1899.

Foster, Frank Hugh: *A Genetic History of the New England Theology.* Chicago: University of Chicago Press, 1907.

Haroutunian, Joseph: *Piety versus Moralism* (American Religious Series IV) New York: Henry Holt and Co., 1932.

Hodge, Charles: *Systematic Theology* (3 vol.) New York: Scribner, Armstrong and Co., 1877.

Hopkins, Samuel: *The Puritans:* or the church, court, and Parliament of England during the reigns of Edward VI and Queen Elizabeth. Boston: Gould and Lincoln, 1859-1861.

Horr, George Edwin: *The Religious History of New England.* The Baptists. Cambridge: Harvard University Press, 1917.

Horr, George Edwin: *The Marian Exiles*. Papers of the American Society of Church History. Second Series. vol. II, p. 201-212. New York and London: G. P. Putnam's Sons, 1910.

Hulst, L. J.: *Kentering in de Verbondsleer*. Holland: Holland Printing Co., 1917.

Hurst, John F.: *History of Rationalism*. New York: Charles Scribner and Co., 1865.

Kramer, G.: *Het Verband van Doop en Wedergeboorte*. Breukelen: Uitgevers Maatschappij "De Vecht", 1897.

Kuyper, Abraham: *Dictaten Dogmatiek* (5 vol.) Kampen: J. H. Kok.

Kuyper, Abraham: *Uit het Woord*. Twede Serie, Tweede Bundel. "De Leer der Verbonden". Amsterdam: Hoeveker and Wormser.

Kuyper, H. H.: *Hamabdil, van de Heiligheid van het Genadeverbond*.

Longacre, Charles Smull: *Roger Williams: His Life, Work and Ideals*. Washington: Review and Herald Publishing Association, 1939.

MacGiffert, Arthur Cushman: *The Rise of Modern Religious Ideas*. New York: Macmillan and Co., 1915.

MacGiffert, Arthur Cushman: *Jonathan Edwards*. New York: Harper and Bros., 1932.

Miller, Perry: *The Half-way Covenant* in *New England Quarterly*, Vol. VI, No. 4. Dec. 1933. Portland: Southworth Press, 1933.

Miller, Perry: *The New England Mind: the Seventeenth Century*. New York: The Macmillan Co., 1939.

Platner, John Winthrop: *The Religious History of New England*. The Congregationalists. Cambridge: Harvard University Press, 1917.

Reynolds, James Bronson: *Two Centuries of Christian Activity at Yale*. New York, 1901.

Ridderbos, Jan: *De Theologie van Jonathan Edwards*. Den Haag (Neth.): Johann A. Nederbragt, 1907.

Ritschl, Otto: *Dogmengeschichte des Protestantismus*. (4 vol.) Göttingen: Vandenhoeck & Ruprecht, 1926.

Scheffer, J. De Hoop: *History of the Free Churchmen called the Brownists, Pilgrim Fathers and Baptists in the Dutch Republic 1581-1701*. Ithaca: Andrus and Church.

Scheffer, J. De Hoop: *De Brownisten te Amsterdam Gedurende den Eersten Tijd na Hunne Vestiging, in verband met het Ontstaan van de Broederschap der Baptisten*.

Schenck, Lewis Bevens: *The Presbyterian Doctrine of Children in the Covenant*. New Haven: Yale University Press, 1940.

Schneider, Herbert Wallace: *The Puritan Mind* (American Religious Series I) New York: Henry Holt and Co., 1930.

Stearns, Raymond Phineas: *Congregationalism in the Dutch Netherlands*. Chicago: American Society of Church History, 1940.

Sweet, William Warren: *The Story of Religions in America*. New York: Harper and Bros., 1930.

Tawney, Richard Henry: *Religion and the Rise of Capitalism*. A Historical Study: Harcourt, Brace and Co., 1926.

Troeltsch, Ernst: *The Social Teaching of the Christian Churches.* Transl. by Olive Wyon. New York: The Macmillan Co., 1931.

Trumbull, B.: *A Complete History of Connecticut,* Civil and Ecclesiastical, from the Emigration of its first Planters from England, in MDCXXX to MDCCXIII. (2 vol.) New Haven: Maltby, Goldsmith and Co.

Ten Eyck, William O.: *Landmarks of the Reformed Fathers.* Grand Rapids: The Reformed Press, 1922.

Uhden, H. F.: *The New England Theocracy.* A History of the Congregationalists in New England to the Revivals of 1740. Boston: Gould and Lincoln, 1858.

Vos, Gerhardus: *De Verbondsleer in de Gereformeerde Theologie.* Grand Rapids: "Democrat" Drukpers, 1891.

Walker, George Leon: *Some Aspects of the Religious Life of New England* with Special Reference to the Congregationalists. New York: Silver, Burdett and Co., 1897.

Walker, Williston: *A History of the Christian Church.* New York: Charles Scribner's Sons, 1934.

Wright, T. G.: *Literary Culture in Early New England.* New Haven: Yale University Press, 1920.

INDEX

Adam and Christ, 32, 35, 47, 53, 98, 225
Adam as Head, 137, 155f, 167, 200
Allin, John, 118
Amesius, 31, 87
Antinomianism, 92, 94, 96
Arminianism 28, 44, 91, 127, 134, 136, 143, 169, 179
Articles of Ulrich Zwingli, 33
Articles of Schlatt, 64
Assurance of faith, 96, 108, 133
Augustine, 16
Austin, Samuel, 182f

Baptism based on covenant, 55
Baptists, 97, 143, 153, 165, 172, 177
Basle Confession, 35
Believers' baptism, 64f
Bellamy, Joseph, 159, 160f
Browne, Robert, 68, 208
Bullinger, 24, 30, 37, 66
Bushnell, Horace, 151, 171, 181, 185f, 199, 207

Calvin, 18f, 30, 41, 79, 209
Cambridge Platform, 79, 104
Cambridge Synod, 102, 110, 111
Canons of Dort, 44
Chauncy, Charles, 99, 113, 116
Chauncy, Charles, 142, 158f.
Children in the church, 22, 56, 61, 111f, 114, 116, 120, 136, 141, 146, 165, 171, 172, 178, 183, 204, 218
Christ as Mediator and Surety, 25, 37f, 44, 53, 92, 108, 157, 200f
Christenliche inleitung, 34
Christian brotherhoods, 64
Church as society of experiential believers, 56, 144, 203

Church censures, 105, 115, 124, 134, 316, 220f
Church covenant, 51, 63, 68, 80, 81f, 86, 97, 116, 142, 160, 178, 207f, 215f
Civil compact, 78f, 80, 211, 214
Clark, Peter, 157
Clement of Alexandria, 16
Cloppenburg, 28
Cocceius, 29, 149
Common grace, 89, 170
Confessio belgica, 42
Confessio gallicana, 42
Confessio helvetica prior, 37
Confessio helv. posterior, 37
Confessio rhaetica, 42
Conventicles, 143
Conversion, 140, 141, 167
Converting ordinance, 132, 147, 162
Cotton, John, 87f, 97, 100f, 203
Cotton, John, 164
Covenant as communion, 51f, 62, 200f, 216
Covenant, conditional, 177, 181
Covenant, internal and external, 145, 147, 159, 164, 185
Covenant of Grace, 17, 24, 29, 45, 73, 80, 87f, 96, 116, 145, 148, 160f, 174, 178, 183, 215f
Covenant of Redemption, 29, 53, 108, 116, 174, 183, 215f
Covenant of Works, 25, 26f, 28, 31, 45, 51, 88, 96, 98
Curcellaeus, 28

Davenport, John, 105, 116
Debreczen Confession, 41
Democracy, 74, 199, 212f
Dispensations of covenant, 16, 22, 26, 39, 149, 182

261

Divine decrees, 27, 48, 53, 107, 135, 151, 216f
Double standard of membership, 93, 108, 162, 210, 222
Dutch Reformed, 31, 69, 170
Dutch refugees, 66f
Dwight, Timothy, 181

Education of children, 20, 60, 90, 101, 120, 137, 180, 184
Edwardeans, 144, 153, 167, 169, 180
Edwards, Jonathan, 99, 122, 128, 136f, 179, 197, 205f
Elders, 124
Emmons, Nathaniel, 173f
Emotionalism, 178, 185
English refugees, 68, 70
Epistle of Barnabas, 15
Erlauthaler Confession, 39
Excommunication, 60, 96, 106, 112, 113, 163
Experiential piety, 34, 39, 56, 64, 73, 90, 100, 111, 136, 151, 185, 217f
Experiential test, 106, 120, 172, 203, 209
Experiential test rejected, 129
Fall of man, 29, 52
Family religion, 127
Federal grace, 88, 203
Federal holiness, 108, 112, 114, 116, 120
Federal theology, 30, 138, 149
Fidei Ratio, 35
Forensic (legal) relation, 27, 37, 40, 42, 48, 108, 179, 188, 201
Formula consensus, 47
Franchise limited, 80, 103, 111, 213
Freedom of the will, 137

Genevan Confession, 41
Genevan theocracy, 79
Good works, 63, 96
Governmental theory, 99, 178, 202
Great Awakening, 123, 140f, 153
Green, Jacob, 163

Half-Way Covenant, 87, 107, 110f, 116, 118f, 132, 150, 160, 165, 172, 174, 195

Hart, William, 168
Heidelberg Catechism, 43
Hemmenway, Moses, 168, 173
Historical faith, 115, 123
Hofman, Melchior, 65
Holy commonwealth, 78, 80, 91, 94, 100, 115, 124, 139
Holy Spirit, 56, 96, 141, 155, 166, 176, 187, 217
Hooker, Thomas, 86, 102, 108
Hopkins, Samuel, 159, 166f
Hopkinsianism, 170
Hubmaier, Balthasar, 65
Hut, Hans, 65
Hutchinson, Anne, 92, 95f, 217

Immersion, 98
Imputation of guilt, 51, 108, 138f, 157, 159
Independentism, 64, 82
Infant Baptism, 17, 19, 24, 32, 36, 40, 46, 69, 88, 95, 143, 150, 160, 165, 171, 175, 183, 204f
Infralapsarianism, 27
Irenaeus, 16
Irish Articles, 43

Johnson, Francis, 69, 71
Junius, 26

Locher, Hans, 64
London Confession, 70
Lord's Supper, 20, 34, 43, 46, 56, 64, 65, 101, 114, 126, 128f, 144f, 161, 173f, 184
Luther, Martin, 17

Massachusetts General Court, 80, 102, 112, 114
Mather, Cotton, 104, 109, 125
Mather, Increase, 117, 119, 128, 131f, 162
Mather, Moses, 159f
Mather, Richard, 86, 101, 107, 112
Mayflower Compact, 72f, 211
Mayhew, Jonathan, 166
Means of grace, 165, 172
Melanchthon, 17

Menno Simons, 66, 67
Mennonites, 69
Mills, Jedidiah, 165, 167
Ministerial Convention, 105, 111
Mitchell, Jonathan, 113, 119
Munster tragedy, 66, 97

Natural ability, 137, 178
Natural relationship, 28, 37, 44, 139, 188
Nature and grace, 17, 58, 90, 152, 190, 191, 198, 218f
New Divinity, 153f, 161, 170, 178, 190, 205f
New Lights, 143
Next power, 169
Norton, John, 98f, 105

Olevianus, 25
Organic relationship, 38, 48, 53, 139, 143, 175, 183, 186f, 201
Original guilt, 27
Original sin, 40, 43, 45, 47, 99, 151, 154f, 166
Owning the covenant, 120, 145

Perseverance of saints, 40, 88
Philosophy of history, 61, 150
Presbyterianism, 102, 106, 111, 170, 189
Propositions of 1662, 113f, 125, 131
Pure church, 18, 21, 70, 86, 100, 102, 110, 113, 135, 143, 160, 196, 203f
Pynchon, William, 98

Qualifications for communion, 144f, 173f

Reforming synod, 126f, 128
Regenerate membership, 115, 130, 150, 174
Regeneration and covenant, 55, 58f, 86, 89, 101, 112, 130, 137, 150, 163, 165f, 169
Religious indifference, 122, 123f, 134
Renewal of covenant, 126
Responsibility of man, 135, 138, 175, 201

Revivals, 136f, 140f, 154, 165, 171, 177, 180, 195, 217
Robbins, Chandler, 164
Robinson, John, 31, 72, 81
Rollock, Robert, 30

Salvation of infants, 35, 40, 41, 44, 156, 158f
Sattler, Michael, 64
Scrooby Pilgrims, 70, 72
Scotch Confession, 42
Second Awakening, 176, 177f, 181, 185
Second Confession of London-Amsterdam Church, 70
Self-examination, 59, 96f, 146, 147, 175, 186
Self-love, 163, 168
Separatism, 31, 67, 71, 81, 94, 99, 145, 204
Seven Articles, 72
Shepard, Thomas, 107, 112
Sin, nature and extent, 50
Smyth, John, 70
Sovereignty of God, 41, 48, 92, 106, 120, 139, 176, 196, 224
State and covenant, 72
State church, 79, 81, 92, 208, 220f
Stoddard, Solomon, 128f, 211
Stoddardeanism, 145, 162, 174
Strong, Cyprian, 172
Substitutionary Atonement, 33, 44, 49, 98, 178, 200, 202
Supralapsarianism, 27
Synod of 1662, 111f, 123, 173, 210, 222

Taste psychology, 169
Ten Conclusions of Berne, 36
Thirty Nine Articles, 43
Torczal-Tordaensis Confession, 40
Total Depravity, 134, 138, 163, 164, 181, 201
Tyler, Bennet, 190

Unitarianism, 134, 177
Unity of covenants, 16, 20, 45, 161
Universalists, 177

Unregenerate and sacraments, 129f, 143
Ursinus, 25

Visible believers, 114, 175, 204
Voluntarism, 137, 151, 154, 170, 175, 195, 217f
Voluntary covenant, 64, 66, 174, 208, 211

Webster, Samuel, 156
Westminster symbols, 45, 87, 104, 149, 180, 202
Wheelwright, John, 97
Williams, Roger, 95, 98
Williams, Solomon, 147
Woods, Leonard, 179

Zwingli, Ulrich, 23, 33f, 35, 66